THE MULTILATERAL
DEVELOPMENT
BANKS

VOLUME 5
TITANS OR BEHEMOTHS?

Volume 1, The African Development Bank
    E. Philip English and Harris M. Mule

Volume 2, The Asian Development Bank
    Nihal Kappagoda

Volume 3, The Caribbean Development Bank
    Chandra Hardy

Volume 4, The Inter-American Development Bank
    Diana Tussie

Volume 5, Titans or Behemoths?
    Roy Culpeper

THE MULTILATERAL DEVELOPMENT BANKS _____

VOLUME 5
TITANS OR BEHEMOTHS?

ROY CULPEPER

LYNNE RIENNER PUBLISHERS

The North-South Institute
L'Institut Nord-Sud

Published in the United States of America in 1997 by
Lynne Rienner Publishers, Inc.
1800 30th Street, Boulder, Colorado 80301

and in the United Kingdom by
Lynne Rienner Publishers, Inc.
3 Henrietta Street, Covent Garden, London WC2E 8LU

Paperback edition published in Canada by
The North-South Institute
55 Murray Street
Ottawa, Ontario K1N 5M3 Canada

Library of Congress Cataloging-in-Publication Data
Multilateral development banks.
    p. cm.
    Includes bibliographical references and index.
    Contents: — 5. Titans or Behemoths? / by Roy Culpeper.
    ISBN 1-55587-470-3 (alk. paper : v. 5)—
    ISBN 1-55587-496-7 (pbk. : alk. paper : v. 5)
    1. Development banks.
HG1975.M848 1997
332.2—dc20   94-45003
                                                                  CIP

Canadian Cataloguing in Publication Data
Main entry under title:
Multilateral Development Banks
    Includes bibliographical references.
    Contents: v.5. Titans or Behemoths? / by Roy Culpeper.
    ISBN 0-921942-88-5 (v.5) (pbk)
    1. Development banks. I. North-South Institute (Ottawa, Ont.)
HG1975.M85 1997 332.1'52 C95-900188-3

British Cataloguing in Publication Data
A Cataloguing in Publication record for this book
is available from the British Library.

Printed and bound in the United States of America

The paper used in this publication meets the requirements
∞ of the American National Standard for Permanence of
Paper for Printed Library Materials Z39.48-1984.

5 4 3 2 1

To
Cathy, Sarah, and Emma

O! it is excellent
To have a giant's strength, but it is tyrannous
To use it like a giant.
—Shakespeare, *Measure for Measure*

&

According to Greek mythology, the Titans were the
precursors of the gods. They were eventually overthrown
by their own offspring under the leadership of Zeus and
were banished (to the British Isles), never to trouble the
world again, or, in the case of Atlas, awarded the
"exemplary punishment of holding up the sky."
—Robert Graves, *The Greek Myths*

CONTENTS

List of Tables   xi
Foreword, *John Lewis*   xiii
Preface, *Roy Culpeper*   xv
Acknowledgments   xvii
List of Acronyms   xix

1 Introduction   1
    Three Timely Reasons, *2*
    MDBs at the Crossroads, *10*
    Overview, *11*

2 History and Evolution   23
    Origins, *23*
    Institutional Characteristics, *29*
    The RDBs and the World Bank:
        Comparisons and Relationships, *37*

3 MDBs in the 1990s: Reflection and Reform   47
    Key Policy Implications of the MDB Project, *48*
    The Portfolio Reviews, *58*
    Conclusion: Relations Between the MDBs and
        Related Organizations, *67*

4 MDBs as Agents of Change: The Development Impact   71
    The First Three Decades (1945–1975): From Investment
        to Growth, *72*
    Impact of Multilateral Bank Assistance, *79*
    The Past Two Decades: From Poverty Reduction to Adjustment
        and Back, *83*
    Poverty Reduction, *85*
    Conclusion: Achievements and Prospects for Eliminating
        Poverty, *99*

5 MDBs in the Family of Development Cooperation Agencies   107

Africa, *108*
Asia, *110*
The Americas, *113*
Eastern and Central Europe and Central Asia, *115*
Systemic Principles and Structures, *118*
Harmonizing Evaluation Systems, *123*
Putting Borrowing Clients in the Driver's Seat: Harmonizing
   Country Strategies, *124*
Creating a Client Satisfaction Unit, *126*
Conclusion, *128*

6 Key Challenges for the Multilateral Banks:
   Resource Flows and Debt   133

Resources, *133*
Multilateral Debt, *138*
Nonconcessional Debt, *143*
Concessional Debt, *146*
The September 1996 Debt Deal, *147*
Summary, *149*

7 Do the Multilateral Banks Have a Future?   153

The Future of Development, *153*
Toward a Vision for the Twenty-First Century, *155*
From Vision to Reality, *156*
From Assistance to Cooperation: A Role for the MDBs, *158*
From Resource Transfers to Quality Assurance, *160*
Challenges to the MDBs: Falling Resource Flows and Debt, *161*
Titans or Behemoths? *164*
Conclusion, *166*

Appendix   171
Bibliography   177
Index   185
About the Book and Author   191

TABLES

1.1 Private Capital Flows to Developing Countries   7

2.1 MDBs: Sectoral Distribution of Cumulative Lending,
     1995   38
2.2 MDBs: Ordinary Capital and Concessional Resources,
     1995   39
2.3 Cumulative Loan Approvals from MDBs, by Region,
     Through 1995   39
2.4 MDB Loan Approvals, by Region, 1995   40
2.5 Net Transfers on Debt Owed to Multilateral Lenders,
     1987–1994   41

4.1 Resource Flows to Developing Countries, 1960–1975   77
4.2 MDBs' and Other Multilateral Development Institutions'
     Net Disbursements   78
4.3 Economic Growth in the Developing World, 1960–1982   79
4.4 Poverty Indicators, 1985 and 1990   88

6.1 Net Capital Flows to Developing Countries, 1986–1995   136
6.2 Composition of Multilateral Debt Stock by Institution,
     1985–1989, and 1994   140
6.3 Highly Indebted Poor Countries: Possibly Stressed and
     Unsustainable Debtors, 1994   141

A1   African Development Bank: Voting Power of Member
     Countries, December 31, 1995   171
A2   African Development Fund: Voting Power of State
     Participants, December 31, 1995   172
A3   Asian Development Bank: Voting Power of Member
     Countries, December 31, 1995   173
A4   Inter-American Development Bank: Voting Power of
     Member Countries, December 31, 1995   174

A5   European Bank for Reconstruction and Development:
        Voting Power of Members, December 31, 1995   175
A6   World Bank: Voting Power of Member Countries,
        December 31, 1995   176

FOREWORD

In 1991, The North-South Institute began a project to review the regional development banks (RDBs). Accordingly, studies were commissioned that have yielded the other four volumes in this series—books by Philip English and Harris Mule on the African Development Bank, Nihal Kappagoda on the Asian Development Bank, Chandra Hardy on the subregional Caribbean Development Bank, and Diana Tussie on the Inter-American Development Bank. (The European Bank for Reconstruction and Development was too new at the time to warrant a review.)

Roy Culpeper, president of The North-South Institute and director of the project, completes the set with this synthesis volume. He goes beyond the scope of the regional bank volumes in two ways. First, recognizing that RDBs are always compared with their antecedent "big brother" and quasi-model, the World Bank, Culpeper provides extensive discussion of the World Bank Group—the International Bank for Reconstruction and Development (IBRD), the International Development Association (IDA), and the International Finance Corporation (IFC). Second, he discusses at some length the evolution of development theory and development-promotion thought, in which the growth of MDB activity occurred during the last half-century, beginning in 1944.

The book is succinctly and factually informative as to the origins, lending strategies, comparative scales, interrelations, and recent self-criticisms of the four MDBs—the World Bank, the African Development Bank, the Asian Development Bank, and the Inter-American Development Bank. Culpeper is attentive to the way the issue of governance in their borrower states has evolved for the MDBs. He also dwells on the formal governance—the comparative weights—of borrower and donor countries in the MDBs themselves. On the other hand, he is circumspect about ways the de facto dominance of the United States has played out.

Some may see the history of development and development thought to be a bit stylized—having only one hinge, in the mid-1970s, between growth inputs and human-development outputs. I tend to see at least three hinges: the start of the IDA in 1960, the development community's double take on the need to couple equity with growth in 1970, and the push for market-friendly adjustment in 1980. These factors then led to the debt crisis. Furthermore, overlaying the second and third hinges was the first oil shock. This volume covers this entire time span in a spirited way.

Chapter 5 is the book's most distinctive because it looks at the MDBs systematically. The uninitiated expect the RDBs to be spokes commanded from a World Bank center, whereas in fact they have varied origins and starting stances regarding the World Bank. Culpeper spells out a recipe for competitive pluralism among the MDBs that is practical and reasonable. In Chapter 6 he makes a detailed argument for why the World Bank and the other MDBs, as well as the International Monetary Fund, can safely be less inhibited about accommodating downward adjustments in the debts that highly indebted poor countries owe the multilateral institutions.

In his final chapter, Culpeper becomes more of a preacher, but with a sermon I mostly like. He will command the attention of his readers because of the care and insight with which the preceding chapters have been assembled.

John Lewis
Woodrow Wilson School of Public and International Affairs
Princeton University

Preface

This book, the last volume in The North-South Institute's series of studies on the multilateral development banks (MDBs), brings the Institute's "MDB project" to a close. Some prefatory remarks are owed to those readers who come to the series first, or solely, through this volume.

The MDB project was conceived to fill a large gap in the literature on the regional development banks; accordingly, the other volumes in this series focus on the African, Asian, Caribbean, and Inter-American Development Banks. These institutions comprise the major regional banks and, in the case of the Caribbean Development Bank, a major subregional bank. The list does not include the European Bank for Reconstruction and Development (EBRD) because that organization had just been created at the time the MDB project was launched in 1991.

The fundamental question in each volume is: Are the institutions effective agents of development? We believe each of the volumes provides a comprehensive exposition on the development effectiveness of each of these unique and still underresearched organizations.

This final volume was conceived as a synthesis of the MDB project. But early on a decision was made not to regard this book as simply a summary of the four preceding volumes, which would have produced a generic book on the regional development banks—a possible successor to John White's pathbreaking study.[1] Although such an effort may have been worthwhile, it was decided instead (under the persuasive advice of the advisory group of scholars and sponsors of the project) to go considerably beyond the ambit of the regional banks alone in this volume and include *all* of the major multilateral banks. Such a grouping would naturally include the World Bank, the "mother of all MDBs," and it would also include the EBRD.

There were good reasons to point the final study in this direction. Perhaps the most compelling was that, ultimately, all of the studies that make up the MDB project deal more with fundamental development *issues* than with certain development *institutions,* as interesting as the institutions may be. Framed in this manner, any serious treatment of the development effectiveness of the multilateral banks must embrace the role of the World Bank, by far the largest and most important member of the group. The EBRD was included for completeness. Defining the MDB group in this manner now has some currency. For example, the Development Committee Task Force on Multilateral Development Banks, which released its report in March 1996, examined the same five organizations.

This approach also had several obvious shortcomings. First and foremost, given the inclusion of the World Bank and the EBRD, this volume could no longer be considered, strictly speaking, a synthesis of the MDB project, since these two banks were not addressed in the four companion studies in the series. Second, especially with the addition of the World Bank and given the complexity of each of the subject organizations, the scope of the study was potentially overwhelming. Indeed, the growing number of studies dedicated to the World Bank alone tends to be forbidding.[2]

Accordingly, this book aims to be selective rather than comprehensive. Consistent with the previous volumes in the MDB series, a principal focus of inquiry is *development effectiveness*. In this context, much emphasis is placed on poverty reduction as the paramount criterion of effectiveness. The study should therefore be of interest to those concerned with the rapidly evolving world of development cooperation. Another focus is on the efficacy of the MDBs as a system, or unique family of agencies. The treatment here complements rather than overlaps that of Percy Mistry,[3] whose extremely useful study concentrates on the financial structures, policies, and practices of the MDBs.

Readers seeking summaries of each of the four regional bank studies in the MDB project will find in Chapter 3 a précis of the major conclusions and recommendations in Volumes 1–4 of the series, from which I have drawn some general implications for the reform of the regional banks. Those who desire a fuller account are urged to explore those volumes.

Roy Culpeper
President
The North-South Institute

Notes

1. White, *Regional Development Banks: Asian, African and Inter-American Development Banks*.

2. A brief selection would include the encyclopedic but dated Mason and Asher, *The World Bank Since Bretton Woods;* more recently, Payer, *The World Bank;* Bretton Woods Commission, *Bretton Woods;* George and Sabelli, *Faith and Credit;* Nelson, *The World Bank and Non-Governmental Organizations;* and Lewis, Webb, and Kapur, *The World Bank*.

3. Mistry, *Multilateral Development Banks*.

ACKNOWLEDGMENTS

This volume is the final product in the MDB project, which would not have been possible without the active participation, interest, and support of many individuals and organizations. I thank them all for their contributions. The original proposal was developed with the help of Allan Barry. The project would not have been launched without the enthusiastic support of Carolyn McAskie and Bill Robinson at the Multilateral Branch of the Canadian International Development Agency. The foundation for the entire enterprise consisted of the members of the MDB project team: Philip English and Harris Mule, authors of Volume 1 on the African Development Bank; Nihal Kappagoda, author of Volume 2 on the Asian Development Bank; Chandra Hardy, author of Volume 3 on the Caribbean Development Bank; and Diana Tussie, author of Volume 4 on the Inter-American Development Bank. The project team spent many hours grappling with an apparently impossible task, but the members' good humor and dedication to what became a highly engaging project carried the day.

In addition to this core research team, a group of analysts was engaged to undertake background country studies for the project: George Reid, Andrew Katili, Moustapha Deme, Wafik Arif, Deogratias Nkurunziza, Zafar Ismail, Djamester Simarmata, Ione Marshall, Sharon Singh, Courtney Blackman, Ennio Rodríguez, and Gonzalo Chavez. The work of this backup team was of great importance to the regional bank studies.

Vital administrative, logistical, research, and editorial support was provided by the staff of The North-South Institute (NSI). Three people deserve special mention: Clyde Sanger, without whose occasional cajoling but always assiduous editorial oversight the project would not have been completed; Rowena Beamish, who shared the task of editing the various volumes; and Andrew Clark, who was part of the research team and administered contracts and organized meetings as well. In addition, I would like to thank Gail Anglin, Marta Arnaldo, Diane Guevremont, Sarah Matthews, Ted Paterson, Jennifer Rantz, and Terry Sweeney. Other NSI colleagues also provided much-needed advice and encouragement—particularly Maureen O'Neil, former NSI president, and Ann Weston.

An advisory panel participated in the project by reading drafts and commenting on the project's overall direction and content. John Lewis headed this group, which also included Catherine Gwin, the late Saburo Okita (who was succeeded by Yasutami Shimomura), Miguel Urrutia (who resigned and was succeeded by Osvaldo Sunkel), and Jonathan Frimpong-Ansah. When three roundtables were convened to discuss work in progress, the panel was augmented by representatives of the MDBs: Delphin Rwegasira and Anselm London from the African Development Bank, Ernesto Pernia from the Asian Development Bank, Jasper Scotland and Marius St. Rose from the Caribbean Development Bank, Daniel Szabo from the Inter-American Development Bank, and James Adams from the World Bank. Seamus O'Clearacain of the Ford Foundation also participated in these meetings. This group, and MDB staff members too numerous to mention, helped the project team to cross the great divide that confronts all researchers who wish to penetrate the recesses of large, bureaucratic institutions to discover their secrets.

I would also like to thank the following people for their helpful comments and suggestions as I prepared this volume: Alexander Shakow, John Lewis, Nihal Kappagoda, Catherine Gwin, Gerry Helleiner, Gerry Schmitz, Philip English, Carolyn McAskie, Bill Gunn, and Peter Mousley. Any shortcomings that remain are mine alone.

The burden of writing such a book (and of directing the MDB project), particularly when there were many other pressing duties during office hours, was shifted to spare time, weekends, and holidays. In other words, it was borne by members of my immediate family, who exercised great forbearance in tolerating the innumerable and seemingly endless incursions of the project into their time and space. It is therefore their book as much as my own.

The MDB project has been generously supported through grants from the Canadian International Development Agency, the Inter-American Development Bank, the Asian Development Bank, the African Development Bank, the Ford Foundation, the Swedish Ministry for Foreign Affairs, the Caribbean Development Bank, the Norwegian Ministry of Foreign Affairs, and the Netherlands Ministry for Development Cooperation. The views contained in this volume are mine alone and do not necessarily reflect those of the project's sponsors or funders or those of The North-South Institute, its supporters, or its board of directors.

—*Roy Culpeper*

ACRONYMS

ACP	Africa-Caribbean-Pacific
ADB	African Development Bank
ADF	African Development Fund
AsDB	Asian Development Bank
AsDF	Asian Development Fund
BHN	basic human needs
CAS	country assistance strategy
CBI	Cross-Border Initiative
CDB	Caribbean Development Bank
CEPAL	Comisión Económica para América Latina
CGs	consultative groups
CGAP	Consultative Group to Assist the Poorest
DAC	Development Assistance Committee (of the OECD)
DFC	Development Finance Company
EBRD	European Bank for Reconstruction and Development
EC	European Community
ECAFE	Economic Commission for Asia and the Far East (United Nations)
ECLAC	Economic Commission for Latin America and the Caribbean (United Nations)
ECU	European currency unit
EDF	European Development Fund
EEC	European Economic Community
EIB	European Investment Bank
ESAF	Enhanced Structural Adjustment Facility
EU	European Union
FAO	Food and Agriculture Organization
FDI	foreign direct investment
FSO	Fund for Special Operations (of the IDB)
FY	fiscal year
GCI	general capital increase
GNP	gross national product
GRI	general resource increase (of the IDB)

HD	human development
HIPCs	highly indebted poor countries
IBRD	International Bank for Reconstruction and Development
IDA	International Development Association (of the World Bank)
IDB	Inter-American Development Bank
IFC	International Finance Corporation (of the World Bank)
IMF	International Monetary Fund
LAC	Latin America and Caribbean
MDB	multilateral development bank
NAFTA	North American Free Trade Agreement
NIEs	newly industrialized economies
NGO	nongovernmental organization
OAS	Organization of American States
OCR	ordinary capital resources
ODA	official development assistance
ODF	official development finance
OECD	Organisation for Economic Co-operation and Development
OECS	Organization of Eastern Caribbean States
OED	Operations Evaluation Department (of the World Bank)
PTI	program of targeted interventions
RDB	regional development bank
RDF	regional development fund
SDA	Social Dimensions of Adjustment
SPA	special program of assistance (Africa)
TASF	Technical Assistance Special Fund (of the AsDB)
TNC	transnational corporation
UN	United Nations
UNCTAD	United Nations Conference on Trade and Development
UNDP	United Nations Development Programme
UNICEF	United Nations Children's Fund
WDR	*World Development Report*
WHO	World Health Organization

1

INTRODUCTION

This book is about a family of international organizations that has risen to prominence in the second half of the twentieth century. The world's first multilateral development bank (MDB), the International Bank for Reconstruction and Development (IBRD)—better known as the World Bank—was conceived along with the International Monetary Fund (IMF) at Bretton Woods, New Hampshire, in 1944. Subsequently, five major regional banks came into being: two in Europe (the European Investment Bank [EIB], established in 1958, and the European Bank for Reconstruction and Development [EBRD], established in 1990); one in the Americas (the Inter-American Development Bank [IDB], 1959); one in Africa (the African Development Bank [ADB], 1964); and one in Asia (the Asian Development Bank [AsDB], 1964). At least nine subregional banks were established in various locations around the world.[1] The focus of this book is on the five principal development banks: the World Bank and all of the regional banks with the exception of the European Investment Bank.[2]

The multilateral banks represent a form of international cooperation the world had not seen prior to the creation of the World Bank in 1945. The banks' institutional architecture represents an evolution from the League of Nations and UN models, in which all member countries have an equal voice and vote. Their structure is inspired by the joint-stock model of the private capitalist corporation, in which member countries are shareholders whose voting powers vary with their relative economic importance. The banks' architecture, moreover, is inspired by the innovative nature of the MDBs' fundamental mandate: to act as intermediaries between the private international capital markets, on the one hand, and governments of developing countries, on the other.

This volume has emerged from a project recently undertaken on the regional development banks. It draws together the principal

1

crosscutting themes and policy issues emerging from the regional bank studies in that project and from other work on the World Bank and the EBRD.[3]

Why are these institutions worthy of study? First and foremost, they are poorly understood not only because of the complexity of their operations but also because of their obscurantism and lack of transparency, which has only recently begun to lift. The viewpoint here is that these institutions deserve to be better known, principally because of their remarkable positive contribution to international cooperation and human welfare—and not because of the mistakes and misjudgments that have recently brought them bad press and notoriety. But beyond this basic informational objective, there are three reasons an examination of the multilateral banks is timely in the mid-1990s.

Three Timely Reasons

· The Crusade for Reform of International Organizations

The first reason a study of the MDBs is timely is the current ferment of reform that is permeating all international organizations and, indeed, all government and public agencies. Since the end of the Cold War, the entire infrastructure of international relations—of organizations both within and outside the UN system—has come under critical scrutiny from the academic community, from nongovernmental organizations, and from officialdom itself.

The timing is hardly a coincidence. International organizations have long had many, often serious shortcomings, but these problems were obscured by the froth and turbulence of superpower rivalry. International organizations either provided a field of battle for the Cold War—as in the case of the UN organizations—or were themselves combatants for one side, as in the case of the MDBs (since the Soviet Union and much of the Communist bloc were not MDB members). With the demise of the Soviet Union, the Cold War veil around the international organizations has been stripped away and their problems have openly surfaced. Further, the decreasing threat of nuclear holocaust seems to have reduced a prime incentive for the remaining superpower, the United States, to engage in multilateral cooperation.

Indeed, the 1990s have given rise to pointed questions about the efficacy of international cooperation as it has been practiced since 1945 and, therefore, about the need for the current set of international institutions. Evidence of the waste, inefficiency, and adverse impacts of some of the institutions' operations is part of the regular fare of media reports. Indications of a lack of accountability and transparency, occasional allegations of corruption or abuse of privilege, and signs of overlap, duplication, and a lack of coordination among the international organizations have all contributed to a deep and growing cynicism and declining public support. These trends on the international stage have been driven or reinforced at the domestic level by a diminishing ability and willingness of many national governments to resolve social and economic problems, even within their own jurisdictions.

In this book I aim to counteract the tide of cynicism toward and disillusionment over international cooperation and the growing appeal of isolationist foreign policy. As the world enters the twenty-first century, the framework of cooperation among the people and nations of various parts of the globe will inevitably become more important because of the steadily increasing interdependence among nation-states and among other actors on the international stage. People around the world are profoundly affected when transnational corporations invest abroad, when workers and refugees migrate across borders, when portfolio investors buy foreign stocks and bonds, when financial speculators engage in foreign exchange transactions, and when automobile owners or coal-burning electricity utilities contribute to global warming. As the world becomes more of a global community and nation-states become less able to establish and enforce the rules and norms that govern human interaction, an adequate framework of international governance will be imperative— indeed, unavoidable. Problems such as overpopulation, global warming and environmental collapse, mass poverty, and the specters of famine, civil disorder, and regional wars can only become more common in the absence of a rule-based, rule-abiding, and cooperative global community.

Such a community requires viable and effective institutions to act on behalf of the common interest. There is little doubt today, however, that most international institutions are perceived to be acting less effectively than they should be. How can we bring about reform on the scale required? Without an international cataclysm on the scale of World War II that would eliminate existing organizations and give birth to new institutions through conferences such as Bretton Woods (and Dumbarton Oaks and San Francisco), it seems doubtful that the global community can reinvent the framework of global governance. Therefore, the only feasible option is to begin with today's international institutions and improve them. For many people looking for solutions, such incrementalism may have much less political and intellectual appeal and may in some sense be less efficient than starting anew, if that were possible. This book attempts to show, however, that the incrementalist option has several practical and political advantages, including a greater likelihood of securing and implementing international agreements on a program of reform.

True, the agenda for reform of the international institutions is daunting, but the debate has already been engaged.[4] Particularly germane to the subject of this volume, in September 1994, at the annual meetings of the IMF and the World Bank held in Madrid, a task force on the multilateral development banks was launched. The June 1995 G7 economic summit held in Halifax considered an agenda of reform of the International Monetary Fund and the World Bank, among other international organizations.

Real and sustainable reform must be focused on particular institutions or, preferably, groups of institutions. The objective of this volume is to examine a group of similar international institutions, the multilateral banks. Within the present framework of international institutions, the MDBs form a group (or subculture) that is separate and distinct from the UN family.[5] In isolating the MDBs for particular scrutiny, comparisons are made as to their respective strengths and weaknesses, and their effectiveness in working together (and the issues of duplication and overlap among them) as a subsystem of development agencies can also be addressed.

Development Under Attack

A second reason for this book, closely related to the first, concerns the specific mandate of the banks to foster international development, which has also come under much criticism and even attack in recent years. The MDBs have been at the forefront of international efforts to transfer resources from rich to poor countries, to alleviate poverty, and to bring about structural transformation. Between the inception of the World Bank in 1945 and 1993, the MDBs provided around $227 billion* in net resource flows to the developing countries.[6] Most ($132 billion, or about 58 percent) of this flow of resources did *not* constitute official development assistance, or aid, in the conventional sense.[7] The remainder ($95 billion, or 42 percent) *did* constitute aid under the accepted definitions.

The legacy of the banks' lending is enormous. MDB loans have financed investments in agriculture, transport, energy, industry, and the social sectors (education, health, and nutrition). They have also provided program (as well as project) assistance, balance-of-payments support, and, on occasion, emergency assistance. More recently, loans have supported policy reform in areas as diverse as taxation,

---

*Dollar figures throughout the text and tables refer to current U.S. dollars.

public expenditures, external tariffs, and the pricing of state-owned enterprises. Hence, the banks have helped to provide the "hardware" for development—embodied in plants, equipment, and technology—as well as the "software," consisting of knowledge and sound policy advice based on technical assistance, research, and the practical experience of many years.

Such a summary does not, however, imply that the MDBs have been effective agents of development or that they have made no mistakes. As mentioned, the banks have been the subject of much comment and criticism, scholarly and otherwise, over the past two decades. Although critics come from both ends of the political spectrum, many share the view that the banks have outlived their usefulness and are an obstacle to development. Others point to a chronicle of environmental calamities associated with bank projects or to the impact of structural adjustment reforms on the poor or to the often lavish style in which the banks and their well-compensated staffs conduct their business.

Underlying these criticisms is a growing disillusionment with development in general and with the enterprise of development assistance. In the mid-1990s, well over a billion people around the world still live under conditions of absolute poverty—that is, a real income equivalent to less than $1 a day. Some critics question the ability and even the propriety of public agencies, whether national or international, to have a positive impact on investment or on the standard of living.[8] Partly in response to these criticisms and partly because of fiscal pressures, national aid programs have been pared back significantly. Even the bastions of official development assistance in the Nordic countries, the Netherlands, and Canada have not been immune.

Criticism of official aid has a long history[9] and was the subject of a special task force commissioned by the major donor countries in the mid-1980s. The task force found that most aid is effective, considered both on its own terms and in comparison with other risky international ventures, although it acknowledged that many problems deserved attention.[10] The conclusions of this study are consistent with that finding.

The Rapidly Rebounding Private Sector

A third reason for this volume is provoked by the flip side of the notion that development assistance has not worked: Development, in the view of some critics, should therefore be left to the private sector. It is appropriate to put this argument in historical context to show that the MDBs have always had a special role with regard to the private sector. The 1944 Bretton Woods Conference was preceded by a decade and a half during which international capital flows and trade had collapsed.[11] The interwar period was also marked by widespread default on international debt, particularly by developing countries in Latin America. This experience contributed strongly to the view of John Maynard Keynes[12] and others that international capital flows are unreliable or have a destabilizing effect on international economic relations. It is well known that the regime established at Bretton Woods was therefore supportive of controls on international capital movements. The Articles of Agreement of the International Monetary Fund accordingly sanctioned restrictions on capital movements to promote domestic economic stability.

At Bretton Woods, delegates from the United States and (to a lesser extent) the UK were the principal architects of the World Bank; the developing world was largely absent or ineffective in articulating its concerns.[13] Hence, among the purposes of the Bank, the objective of development was subsidiary to that of European reconstruction. Whether because of postwar reconstruction or international development, the Bretton Woods delegates felt private capital could not be expected to resume flowing internationally on the scale of the pre-Depression years. Above all, the Allied countries wanted to avoid the experiences of the era following World War I. Many of the World Bank's founders also assumed the Bank would not be involved in direct lending itself but would use its capital to guarantee loans by private investors. Thus, a close, collaborative relationship with the private sector was taken for granted from the start. But in the immediate postwar period, this assumption proved unrealistic: Private investors were simply not interested in developing countries, and during the 1950s the World Bank began to lend on its own account—a practice the regional banks soon followed.

International capital movements did, however, ultimately resume, facilitated by two factors: the spread of foreign direct investment and transnational corporations and the liberalization of financial markets—first among the Organisation for Economic Co-operation and Development (OECD) countries (from the 1960s to the 1980s) and subsequently among developing countries (from the 1980s on). The earlier part of this period consisted of large-scale unsecured lending by commercial banks, which resulted in the Third World debt crisis from 1982 until 1989. As a result, during most of the 1980s the prevailing view held that most developing countries were so risky or uncreditworthy that private capital flows could not be expected to play a large role in their development.

By the early 1990s, however, the phenomenon of emerging markets had arrived: Stock markets were thrown open to foreign investors, eager to diversify their investments and maximize global returns on their portfolios. Transborder flows of portfolio equity had hitherto been confined to the countries that were home to the world's principal stock exchanges—the United States, the UK, France, and Canada. Portfolio equity flows to developing countries were unprecedented.[14]

Almost as surprising as the birth of equity flows was the rebirth of the international bond market for developing countries, which had virtually ceased to be a source of capital following the Depression. Widespread default on developing country bonds in the 1930s, and protracted settlements with creditors that were still being negotiated in the 1950s and 1960s, made bonds issued by developing countries unattractive to the conservative investors who typically buy bonds. The same factors that led to the opening of the emerging equity markets however—global diversification and portfolio optimization strategies—led to the rebound of the debt markets (see Table 1.1).

Table 1.1   Private Capital Flows to Developing Countries

	1977–1982	1983–1989	1990–1994
Total net capital inflows	30.5	8.8	104.9
Net foreign direct investment	11.2	13.3	39.1
Net portfolio investment	−10.5	6.5	43.6
Bank lending and other debt	29.8	−11.0	22.2

Source: IMF, International Capital Markets, p. 33.
Note: These figures do not include official development assistance financing.

A key aspect of the burgeoning debt and equity markets was the fact that the funds were flowing to a rapidly growing private sector in the developing countries. Economic liberalization in many developing countries during the 1980s, often under the aegis of the IMF and the World Bank, had unshackled and in some cases created a thriving private sector eager for cash to invest in the local economy. For example, many of the bonds floated in the early 1990s were issued by power utilities that had formerly been state owned but that had been privatized during the liberalization program.

If private agents in the industrial countries can supply the required capital and private agents in the developing countries invest that capital, the claim that development should be left to the private sector has some strength. This argument, however, receives only qualified support here. Private capital can and will play a growing role in development, but it will never be a perfect substitute for public finance in a range of activities and will have limited relevance for many of the world's poorest countries for the next few decades. Such a proposition does not, moreover, rule out the possibility that some such countries will graduate from the ranks of aid recipients—some sooner than others.

A related argument is that development agencies—the MDBs in particular—should be reformed to complement, stimulate, or catalyze private sector flows rather than displace them. This suggestion is more constructive: It acknowledges that the MDBs have a role that is distinct from, although parallel to, that of private flows and that the relationship must be harmonious rather than conflictual. Originally, the World Bank was conceived as a more passive agent than it eventually became, but the assumption that it would simply guarantee private loans proved to be unrealistic. The potential for competition with (or crowding out) the private sector emerged when the Bank (and the other MDBs) became a large-scale lender in its own right but only to the extent that MDB lending actually displaced private sector lending or investment. The evidence indicates, on the contrary, that in their lending practices and priorities the MDBs have steadily evolved toward the provision of public goods. This argument is treated more sympathetically here, and its implications are the subject of particular analysis in Chapter 4.

Hard (Nonconcessional) and Soft (Concessional) Loans[1]

All MDBs except the EBRD provide financing to developing country members through two windows. The "hard window" comes closest to the functions of a bank: It provides nonconcessional loans (i.e., financing at market rates of interest) with maturities (repayment periods) up to twenty years. (Such long maturities are almost unknown among commercial banks; thus, even in this respect the MDBs differ significantly from conventional banks.) The funds for these loans are obtained through the MDBs' own borrowing on international capital markets, which is usually effected through the issuance of bonds or similar instruments.

The MDBs' bonds, which are offered in all major capital markets (and hence generate loanable funds in many different currencies), have typically attracted the highest possible credit ratings (triple A) from bond-rating agencies such as Moody's, Fitch, and Standard and Poor, thereby signifying to bond investors that they are top-quality investments and virtually risk free. Such ratings mean the banks' own cost of borrowing (or the interest paid to their bondholders) is at the lowest level possible in the market; therefore, the funds can be made available to the banks' borrowers at the lowest possible interest costs. The MDBs maintain their high credit ratings because their borrowing is 100 percent secured by capital paid in or guaranteed by the member countries. Even though loans are offered on exceptionally good terms, MDBs generally extend nonconcessional loans only to countries deemed to be creditworthy (i.e., able to repay the debt).[2]

Only a small portion of the capital subscriptions of member countries is actually paid in (less than 5 percent in recent capital replenishments). The rest is subject to call (and is therefore referred to as *callable capital*). Such calls have never been made, and all those concerned—shareholders, the banks themselves, and the capital markets—assume no call on capital will ever be made.

This convention is important for the structure and functioning of the MDBs because it enables shareholders to take large equity positions without correspondingly large cash outlays, and the large equity stake of shareholders enables the banks to secure commensurately large borrowings (with a maximum gearing ratio of 1:1, a dollar of debt for each dollar of equity) on the capital markets. Investors who purchase MDB bonds in the capital markets regard the capital structure of the MDBs as an artifice for securing their obligations against what amounts to a guarantee by shareholders to pay any amounts necessary up to the full value of bonds outstanding. In other words, the servicing—and high credit rating—of the MDBs' bonds are dependent on the implicit guarantee of the shareholders rather than on the loan repayments of the developing country borrowers that ultimately obtain the funds. The financial policies of the MDBs (which govern the repayment of loans by borrowers and the financial soundness of the MDBs) are also extremely important in maintaining the highest possible credit rating.

In contrast to the hard window, the "soft window" provides concessional loans (usually called *credits*, which carry rates of interest considerably below market levels, typically close to zero) to the poorest countries. Even though the transactions involve low-interest loans rather than grants,[3] this function is more similar to that of aid agencies than to that of banks. Indeed, the resources for soft loans come from the aid budgets of the major donor countries, which meet every three years or so to negotiate a replenishment of the soft-loan funds. These funds form a significant portion—13 percent during the period 1992–1994—of the overall flow of aid to developing countries.

Nonconcessional Loans

	IBRD(WB)	IDB	AsDB	AfDB	EBRD
Total capital	176,438	66,399	43,078	23,412	12,651
Annual lending	12,803	4,255	1,033	1,058	1,829
Total loans outstanding	123,499	26,581	17,530	13,453	2,029
Borrowing outstanding	108,405	26,384	14,598	9,197	5,941

Source: 1995 Annual Reports of WB, IDB, AsDB, AfDB, and EBRD.

Concessional Loans

	IDA (WB)	FSO	AsDF	AfDF
Total subscriptions	86,033	9,751	19,039	11,449
Credits	5,700	541	1,145	559
Total credits outstanding	72,032	6,284	12,310	6,457

Source: 1995 Annual Reports of WB, IDB, AsDB, AfDB, and EBRD.

Notes

1. The terms *hard* and *soft* refer only to the financial terms; the nonfinancial policy conditions attached are invariate between hard and soft loans.

2. An exception was the African Development Bank (see Chapter 5).

3. The grant element of such low-interest loans is usually between 80 and 90 percent; that is, the present value of the loan repayments is between 10 and 20 percent of the face value. The grant element is also high because of long grace and amortization periods on such loans. Accordingly, under the definitions of the OECD's Development Assistance Committee such transfers qualify as official development assistance (ODA), which must contain a grant element of at least 25 percent.

MDBs at the Crossroads

At the time of this writing, the multilateral development banks had reached a critical juncture in their history. Funding of the International Development Association (IDA), the World Bank's soft-loan facility, had met with serious obstacles in the U.S. Congress, which refused to honor commitments made by the administration under the Tenth Replenishment (IDA 10). U.S. intransigence in meeting its obligations provoked other donors to make special interim funding arrangements for 1996–1997 to which the United States will not contribute until it catches up with its overdue payments.[15] Negotiations for the African Development Fund (AfDF 7) led to a substantially smaller replenishment ($2.0 billion, compared to $3.42 billion in ADF 6), and parallel negotiations at the Asian Development Bank (AsDF 7) were proving equally difficult.

These difficult negotiations have thrown into doubt the future of all of the soft-loan facilities of the MDBs. The recipients of these facilities, particularly in Africa, are predominantly the poorest countries whose needs for foreign assistance are not declining. At the same time, many of the traditional Asian and Latin American borrowers from the regular (hard-loan) facilities of the MDBs are increasingly able to access private capital markets. Some, such as Thailand and Korea, have effectively graduated as borrowers from the MDBs.

The banks may be ill suited to face the challenges that confront them: They have a surfeit of nonconcessional resources for advanced developing countries that need them less and are faced with a shortfall of concessional resources for the poorest countries that need those resources more than ever. On the other hand, as the MDBs mature, their banking character assumes greater importance for the mobilization of resources. Since most MDB assistance has been provided not as grants but in the form of loans (at both market and lower rates of interest), repayments are providing a growing source for new loans. In the mid-1990s, this fact was reflected in the level of net income of the MDBs' nonconcessional operations (about $2 billion) and in the level of reflows from concessional loans (over $700 million for the World Bank and the IDB alone). Thus, the MDBs are realizing a greater degree of funding autonomy, even as their members' willingness or ability to provide them with additional funding is decreasing.[16]

Overview

Against this backdrop, the present volume is organized as follows. Chapter 2 offers a brief history of each of the MDBs—why they were created and how they have evolved since 1945. Particular attention is paid to the differences among the MDBs in their founding charters, operational activities, and political dynamics. The evidence clearly indicates that there are two kinds of MDBs: those created and controlled by the creditors (notably the World Bank, the Asian Development Bank, and the EBRD) and those created and controlled by the borrowing countries (the Inter-American Bank and the African Development Bank). Most of the differences among the banks can be attributed to this fundamental characteristic of ownership and control.

Whereas originally the MDBs were all established as banks in the sense of acting as intermediaries between the capital markets and developing country borrowers, they all—with the exception of the EBRD—eventually acquired a quasi-grant-making capacity by attracting funds from bilateral donors.[17] This capacity enabled the MDBs to become multilateral aid agencies as well as banks, thus giving them something of a dual personality (a suggestion they all stoutly deny).

The source of funds for each of the two windows matters: Capital markets are inclined to care more about the state of the MDBs' balance sheets and financial issues such as loan arrears, whereas donors are more apt to get involved with the banks' lending policies and priorities. In fact, the lending priorities of the banks differed considerably until the 1970s, when their lending allocation between sectors largely converged, with agriculture and energy at the top. The 1980s were years of divergence between the World Bank and the regional banks because of the World Bank's aggressive pursuit of adjustment-type lending. By the end of the decade, however, all of the regional banks had initiated similar lending; in some cases this lending was closely tied to that of the World Bank, whereas in others (e.g., the Asian Development Bank) it was more complementary to it. In the 1990s, negotiations between the donor and borrowing members at both the IDB and the ADB have led to parity in the voting shares in the former case and to pressures for parity in the latter.

Regarding the relative size and importance of the individual banks, the World Bank—the only global bank—is still unquestionably by far the largest and most influential. It is evident, however, that recent increases in the capital of the regional banks have given those institutions a lending capacity comparable to (and in the case of the IDB, exceeding) that of the World Bank within their respective regions. Whereas the regional banks' ability to influence the policy of borrowers still does not match that of the World Bank, it is evident that they are no longer minor actors within their regions but have become forces to be reckoned with. This fact has been even more apparent with the creation of the European Bank for Reconstruction and Development in 1990, the newest member of the MDB family. From the beginning, the EBRD has been somewhat different from its counterparts; its mandate has been driven by the fundamental objective of helping to transform the centrally planned economies of the former Soviet bloc into market-based economies. The EBRD has broken new ground with many of its financial and operating policies and has helped to stimulate change among the entire group of MDBs. Given its mandate, the EBRD has also brought into sharper focus the banks' relations with the private sector, an issue that is pursued in Chapter 4.

The focus of Chapter 3 is the pressure for reform and change in the early 1990s. Growing criticisms of the MDBs during the 1980s led to reviews of their rationale and effectiveness, including The North-South Institute's MDB project and a series of portfolio reviews undertaken at the World Bank and the Inter-American and Asian and African Development Banks.

The chapter presents a summary of the MDB project and its implications for reform in the regional banks. The project concluded that because of their regional specificity the regional banks do have strengths as project-delivery agencies. These strengths should be complemented by policy-based lending in which the regional banks specialize in sectoral niches or certain countries. There is considerable room for improvement in the core area of project delivery, however. Weaknesses in project design, supervision, and long-run sustainability often stem from lack of local ownership or poor institutional capacity. These problems should be remedied through more local participation and greater MDB presence in borrowing countries—in other words, through greater devolution to the field. Devolution can be achieved in several ways: through a greater role for MDB country offices; by "retailing" MDB funds through subregional banks such as the Caribbean Development Bank; and by working more through a range of local partners and intermediaries, including (well-functioning) development finance companies, local commercial banks, and nongovernmental organizations (NGOs).

The portfolio reviews of MDB lending undertaken for the World Bank, the IDB, the AsDB, and the ADB between 1991 and 1994 had many similar conclusions. First, they recommended that the MDBs must desist from simply meeting annual quantitative lending targets and instead must emphasize the delivery of high-quality projects as their principal objective. Second, high quality should be assured through effecting long-term and sustainable development impacts. Third, portfolio quality should be enhanced by focusing operations and performance at the country level with an eye on local constraints, opportunities, and indicators of development achievement.

Soon after these reviews were completed, the Development Committee assembled a task force to reassess the priorities, instruments, and operations of the MDBs (the World Bank and the four regional banks, including the recently created EBRD) in the light of the recent portfolio reviews and to evaluate procedures and practices for coordination among them. This task force provided a broad reaffirmation of the roles and mandates of the MDBs and made a series of recommendations that echoed those of the MDB project and the individual portfolio reviews. For example, the task force recommended that the MDBs should strive for long-term results, the strategic role of the Executive Boards should be enhanced, borrower ownership should be facilitated through public participation, and coordination among the MDBs should be intensified (a theme taken up in greater depth in Chapter 5).

Chapter 4 examines the MDBs as agents of change: What impact have the MDBs had on development? Have they succeeded in their mission? The questions are complex, since they suggest that commonly accepted definitions of development or criteria of success exist. On the contrary, the answers to these questions depend upon when they are asked because of evolving notions about the objectives of development; moreover, at any point in time no consensus can typically be found on these matters. The record of five decades indicates that the meaning of development has changed substantially. Changing notions of development led to evolving ideas about development assistance and, as a result, to changing priorities for the MDBs as development agencies.

Each step in the evolution has been, in part, a reaction to the shortcomings of the previous phase.[18] Until the 1970s, prevailing development thought and praxis regarded industrialization and economic growth as the preeminent objectives of development. Indeed, until the mid-1970s the entire process of development was viewed more as one of "the provision of scarce inputs" (particularly capital) to developing countries than as the struggle to achieve specified development outcomes.[19]

The shift in thinking toward outcomes during the 1970s led to the eruption of basic human needs and the poverty focus on the development agenda. But in the 1980s, these social dimensions of development were pushed aside by the debt crisis, structural adjustment, and economic reform. In the 1990s, poverty reduction has regained its preeminent status, along with investment in human resources, but gender equity and environmental sustainability are also typically stated as crucial objectives of development. Chapter 4 indicates that the MDBs have not only made important contributions to each of these objectives but that they have also demonstrated considerable flexibility in adapting their operations and policies to the shifting demands of the times.

Since the inauguration of the World Bank, however, one objective has stood out as fundamental to the raison d'être of the MDBs: the alleviation of poverty. Even this objective has undergone an evolution from a vaguely stated general goal in 1945 to a multidimensional set of objectives in the 1990s. The historical evidence indicates that the MDBs can claim only limited success with respect to poverty reduction. Yet, this judgment must be heavily qualified. Given the deep-rooted nature of poverty in most societies, it is naive to assume that the MDBs can single-handedly (or even in concert with each other) reduce poverty. Despite their seemingly large size, the MDBs are relatively small players, and the actions of the other players (primarily the developing countries themselves but also other external agents) are extremely important. Moreover, the linkages between the MDBs' policies and projects, on the one hand, and a sustained reduction in poverty levels, on the other, are complex, and causality between MDB actions and poverty outcomes is typically difficult to infer.

It is easier to judge the impact of the MDBs at the micro and meso levels—the levels at which, until recently, they have typically intervened through project and program lending. Here, the evidence is much more positive. The MDBs have made critical contributions to infrastructure and institutional capacity building. These endeavors have been crucial to economic growth, but evidence of the contribution of economic growth, infrastructure, and institution building to poverty reduction and private flows is of necessity circumstantial, even at the micro and meso levels. Also, the linkages between causal actions and ultimate results are bound to differ in various countries. There is widespread agreement that the development initiatives of the MDBs (along with those of other agencies) in sub-Saharan Africa have been disappointing, to say the least. But any categorical linkages between these actions and ultimate objectives must remain hypothetical.

Such an assessment must not be viewed as an abdication of a clear diagnosis of success versus failure. In any case, a diagnosis in either direction must ultimately be shared among various agents. The failure of development in Africa cannot be blamed solely on the multilateral banks or international agencies; it must be shared by bilateral donors, the world trading regime, and—perhaps above all—the African countries themselves. The MDBs, other development agencies, and the poorest countries all face considerable challenges in the next few decades in helping to bring about sustainable poverty reduction.

Chapters 5 through 7 are more forward-looking and prescriptive. Chapter 5 examines the joint effectiveness of the MDBs as a group. Even if there is a sound rationale for multilateral assistance in general, what is the comparative advantage of the multilateral banks in particular? Why does the world need so many multilateral banks doing essentially the same kinds of things—is there any scope for rationalization or a better division of labor?

The discussion indicates that there is indeed a certain amount of duplication among the banks. The MDB project suggests that the regional banks need to carve out niches in the area of policy-based lending, particularly at the sectoral level and in smaller countries, and relegate most macroeconomic initiatives to the World Bank. At the same time, no a priori rationale exists for a permanent and clear-cut division of labor among the MDBs. The principal issue is not to rationalize what the MDBs (and other development agencies) do among themselves. Rather, the main issue for *all* development agencies should be to adopt congruent country assistance strategies that would aim first at putting the developing countries in the driver's seat with respect to external assistance and second, at least insofar as the banks are concerned, at enhancing their *joint* effectiveness in reducing poverty.

On this basis, I put forward a case for competitive pluralism that accepts a certain amount of overlap to encourage friendly rivalry and thereby stimulate innovation and productivity among the banks. At the same time, greater harmonization of the reporting, evaluating, and programming of the banks would help to demonstrate *in practice* their relative strengths and the nature of their coordination and cooperation. Finally, no formal institutional mechanism currently exists with a mandate to reconcile problems of coordination and inconsistencies among various development agencies. I argue that such a body is needed and suggest alternative institutions, including the IMF–World Bank Development Committee secretariat, in which to situate that body.

To examine the comparative advantages of the MDBs, I survey each of the five major MDBs with regard to their individual opportunities and challenges. Among the regional banks, the IDB and the EBRD have the clearest agenda. Notwithstanding some serious problems of internal governance,[20] the IDB has developed its mandate, which is strongly rooted in hemispheric social and economic challenges (particularly poverty and maldistribution but also regional integration) and is strongly supported by all of its regional members. During the Eighth Replenishment, negotiations for which were completed in early 1995, the membership agreed on a new distribution of power. The IDB was thereby transformed from an organization whose borrowers exercised majority control to one in which power is equally shared by borrowers and nonborrowers. The replenishment also provided the Bank with a lending capacity in excess of the World

Bank's current lending levels to the region at a level sufficient to meet foreseeable needs. A new consensus has been forged among its membership that has also renewed the IDB's sense of mission to promote regional cooperation and to spearhead initiatives on economic and social problems common to the countries in the hemisphere. For these reasons, the IDB has become the leading MDB, and arguably the leading international institution, in the Western Hemisphere.[21]

In comparison with the IDB, other MDBs seem less well positioned to carve out a distinct role and mandate in coming years. The EBRD has developed the most distinct niche by dedicating itself largely to the transformation of the former Soviet-bloc countries from economies of central planning into well-functioning market economies. But the EBRD has specialized to a degree and in an area in which its rationale as a public institution comes into question. In operating more like a merchant bank by seeking out viable commercial partners with which to do business, and in downplaying most of the social objectives now common to multilateral institutions (except for protection of the environment), the EBRD is the most vulnerable of the MDBs to the charge that it performs few public functions and should therefore be phased out or privatized.[22]

For different reasons, the future is murkiest for the AsDB and the ADB. Ironically, the AsDB has long had the reputation of being the most efficient and well run of the MDBs.[23] But its problem begins with the fact that of the regional banks it has the least pretense of spanning a region in any geographic, economic, or cultural sense of the term—something recognized by John White in his seminal work over two decades ago.[24] Development issues on the Indian subcontinent are generally very different from those in East or Southeast Asia. Unsurprisingly, then, the AsDB has provided little intellectual leadership in examining or addressing economic or social problems common to the Asian region or in spearheading regional integration. The AsDB is also perhaps a victim of regional success: Many of its rapidly growing borrowing members in East and Southeast Asia need the services of the Bank less and less and thus are effectively graduating to private capital markets.

In contrast, the African Development Bank has somewhat more legitimacy than the AsDB in terms of its regional base—the need for an effective development institution is perhaps more evident in Africa than anywhere in the world. At the same time, the very different circumstances of North Africa from those of sub-Saharan Africa, as well as divisions among francophone, anglophone, and Arabic-speaking countries, have always been apparent. But the deeper problems of the ADB are related to its governance, which in the early 1990s resulted in financial crisis and growing differences between regional and nonregional members—frictions that led to political paralysis. These differences appear to have been reconciled with the election of a new president in 1995, but the underlying problems of the Bank still need to be resolved.

For both the AsDB and the ADB, it is suggested that the balanced power-sharing arrangement that has emerged in the IDB may offer a way forward, although with very different implications for each bank. In the Asian Bank, this arrangement implies a greater share for the regional developing countries, and for the African Bank it means the nonregionals will end their status as minority shareholders.

This brings us to the World Bank, the oldest and largest of the MDBs. This institution has been the subject of severe criticisms—some fully deserved—for well over a decade. The Bank has responded by becoming more open, accessible, and transparent. It has substantially modified its operational priorities, with much greater emphasis on human resources and social sectors as the central thrust of a renewed focus on poverty reduction and much less emphasis on large-scale infrastructural capital projects.

This transformation from a provider of foreign capital to a policy adviser on internal resource allocation issues, however, creates major questions for an external agent such as the World Bank. The Bank also faces other questions regarding its financial relationship with many of its borrowing members, particularly the poorer ones. A negative net financial transfer with respect to borrowing clients perversely makes the World Bank a destination rather than a source of capital and in some cases exacerbates borrowers' potential or actual balance-of-payments difficulties. In the past, this problem has been circumvented through continually rising lending levels. If increased levels are ruled out in the future, as seems likely, the only other solution lies in debt restructuring and relief, a remedy the multilateral organizations have hitherto eschewed.

Nevertheless, despite these problems there are good reasons for the World Bank to continue to exist over the next few decades. The Bank should continue to be the world's preeminent development agency, using its global experience to good effect in very diverse countries. Most of all, however, the Bank should help to lead the world's struggle against poverty by establishing an agenda for poverty eradication over the next half century.

The focus of Chapter 6 is on two current critical issues facing the banks: the MDBs' diminishing role as suppliers of external resources to developing countries and multilateral debt. These issues are interrelated. Several forces are pushing the MDBs away from their role as net providers of external finance. These include a change in the philosophy of lending from an emphasis on moving money to the objective of quality lending and also the consequences of decades of cumulative lending, which has generated a growing volume of repayments to the MDBs.

The conclusion reached with respect to the MDBs' role in transferring resources is that in the short term the shift to quality will significantly offset the fall in quantity. In the longer term, however, the quantum of resources transferred—albeit for higher-quality projects than in the past—may fall short, especially for the poorest. Regarding the debt problem, the multilateral institutions, particularly the MDBs, have increasingly become part of the problem rather than part of the solution. In examining the evidence on multilateral indebtedness and the arguments leveled against relief of multilateral debts by the multilateral creditors themselves, I conclude that more radical solutions—including limited write-offs—are both possible and desirable and will not compromise the solvency or the creditworthiness of the institutions.

Finally, Chapter 7 looks to the future role of the MDBs in a prescriptive manner. I suggest that over the next few decades the MDBs should participate with other development agencies and the people and governments of developing countries in a coordinated effort aimed at the sustained reduction of absolute poverty and the worst forms of social deprivation. I emphasize specific, time-bound targets such as those articulated by the OECD Development Committee in 1996.

To return briefly to the three reasons for writing this book, the MDBs are in the throes of reforming their priorities and procedures; they are reexamining their mandates and refocusing their development missions; and they are discovering new ways of working with the rebounding private sector. The overall assessment emerging is positive. The multilateral banks—some more than others—have demonstrated remarkable adaptability to a rapidly changing policy environment. They are also exemplars of international cooperation, and in the post–Cold War era agents of peaceful international cooperation are to be nurtured. This is not to say that the MDBs or any other institutions deserve to exist in perpetuity. The world's most pressing development problems, notably mass poverty, have demonstrated a stubborn persistence over the past two or three decades. To the extent that these problems are eradicated, the need for the MDBs as well as most development assistance will vanish. But history suggests that successful, sustainable development is achieved only over many decades. It is conceivable that the twenty-first century could be the one in which the eradication of mass poverty becomes a universal achievement and that most of the work could be done by mid-century. The multilateral banks should have a leading role in this momentous campaign.

Notes

1. These banks include the Andean Development Corporation, the Arab Bank for Economic Development of Africa, the Banque Ouest–Africaine de Développement, the Caribbean Development Bank, the Central African States Development Bank, the Central American Bank for Economic Integration, the East African Development Bank, the Islamic Development Bank, and the Nordic Development Bank. The distinction between *regional* and *subregional* turns on the borrowing membership: The borrowers in regional banks span entire continents, whereas the subregionals are restricted to smaller borrower groupings within the continents. Nonborrowing members may come from the borrowing region or, more typically, from outside it.

2. The EIB was created to invest predominantly within Europe, which is considered here to be a region already developed rather than developing. A similar case could be made to exempt the EBRD, since it lends to Eastern Europe and the former Soviet Union; however, the level of development in this region is more similar to that of the more developed countries of, say, Latin America or Asia than to that of the OECD countries, so the EBRD is included.

3. "Multilateral Development Banks: Toward a New Division of Labor." Background Study for the Development Committee Task Force on Multilateral Development Banks. Ottawa: The North-South Institute, August 1995.

4. See Boutros-Ghali, *Commission on Global Governance.* Nordic UN Project, 1995.

5. Only the World Bank formally belongs to the UN as a specialized agency; the regional banks have no relationship with the UN.

6. Net flows are the net of principal repayments. This may seem large in absolute terms, but it actually represented less than 10 percent of net resource flows to developing countries in the forty-eight-year period. Computed from Mistry, *Multilateral Debt,* p. 12, Table 1.

7. That is, a resource flow with a grant element of 25 percent or more.

8. See Rich, *Mortgaging the Earth,* especially chapter 8, and George and Sabelli, chapter 3.

9. See Riddell, *Foreign Aid Reconsidered,* for a good summary.

10. See Cassen and associates, *Does Aid Work?* for an update of the analysis and evidence. See also ibid.

11. See Oliver, *International Economic Co-operation and the World Bank,* chapters 2 and 3.

12. Keynes felt investments abroad were unlikely to be recouped unless additional lending or investments took place to enable debtors to make payments. This situation would be more likely under the auspices of an international, publicly funded bank (such as the World Bank) than under private investors. See Harrod, *The Life of John Maynard Keynes,* p. 671.

13. Sometimes, however, representatives from the developing world

demonstrated their perspicacity. For example, the Mexican delegation proposed that development should be the Bank's first purpose while recognizing that postwar reconstruction should preoccupy the Bank in its initial years (Mason and Asher, *The World Bank Since Bretton Woods*, pp. 22–23).

14. See Ffrench-Davis and Griffith-Jones, *Coping with Capital Surges.*

15. The United States will not be allowed procurement privileges from the $3 billion interim fund. A similar interim funding arrangement was crafted in 1984 between IDA 6 and IDA 7, since the United States had difficulties meeting its obligations under IDA 6.

16. This topic is pursued further in Chapter 6.

17. The term *quasi-grant*, rather than *grant*, is used because the principal sums made available (referred to as *credits*) are repayable over a long period (up to fifty years) at a nominal rate of interest far below market rates. The grant content of such loans is usually estimated at around 80 percent.

18. See Arndt, *Economic Development.*

19. This is undoubtedly something of a caricaturization of history. More discontinuity and less contrast exist than are found in the two-era story told here. A fuller account of the history can be found in Lewis, Webb, and Kapur, *The World Bank.*

20. Documented in Inter-American Development Bank, *Managing for Effective Development.*

21. See Tussie, *The Inter-American Development Bank.*

22. This situation appeared to be changing during 1996. The need to accommodate the social dimensions of EBRD lending was an issue raised increasingly by European member countries. A similar criticism could be leveled against the World Bank's affiliate, the IFC, which has a mandate similar to that of the EBRD around the globe.

23. See U.S. Department of the Treasury, *United States Participation in the Multilateral Development Banks in the 1980s.*

24. White, *Regional Development Banks.*

2

HISTORY AND EVOLUTION

This chapter presents a brief historical survey of the five major multilateral development banks and their interrelationships, particularly with the World Bank group.[1] The European Bank for Reconstruction and Development, the latecomer to the group (founded in 1990), naturally has a considerably briefer history on which to draw for comparisons, but it is included in the discussion for the sake of completeness.

The chapter is organized as follows. The first section reviews when, why, and how the five MDBs were born; it draws out the historical, economic, and political forces behind their creation—forces that are still basic to understanding their institutional dynamics. The following section examines key features of the MDBs' structure, policies, and operations as they have evolved over the past fifty-odd years. The next section compares the regional development banks (RDBs) and explores their relationships with the Bretton Woods organizations.

Origins

The World Bank

Much has been written about the origins of the World Bank,[2] and I will not reiterate here what is amply covered in that extensive literature. For present purposes, a few points are worth emphasizing.

First, it seemed inevitable that an institution such as the World Bank would eventually have been invented if it had not already existed by 1945. The history of the interwar period indicates that the economic and political turmoil of the time, beginning in the 1920s and lasting until World War II, led to an intensive search for a more satisfactory system of international economic cooperation that would avoid the problems associated with the Depression. Several specific proposals for new institutions were generated—many from Europeans[3]—that foreshadowed the World Bank and the International Monetary Fund; all were abandoned. Among these was a U.S. proposal for an Inter-American Bank that became moribund in 1940 but was reincarnated in the wartime discussions that climaxed in the Bretton Woods conference. (As described later, a rather different Inter-American Development Bank did come into being about nineteen years after its failed predecessor.)

Second, at a time when waning U.S. support looms like a dark cloud over the future of the World Bank, it is instructive to note that this very first multilateral development bank owed much to the United States for its creation. Harry Dexter White, a special adviser to Treasury Secretary Henry Morgenthau, was without question the key figure behind the creation of the World Bank.[4] White was greatly influenced by discussions on the stalled Inter-American Bank in the late 1930s. Under the direction of Morgenthau, in 1942 he drew up a proposal for a "United Nations Stabilization Fund and a Bank for Reconstruction and Development." In its earliest stages, this proposal was discussed only among interested agencies of the U.S. government. The proposed bank called for a capitalization of $10 billion, and its member-shareholders were to be governments whose voting power was to be determined by their shareholding.

Subsequently, President Roosevelt authorized cabinet-level discussions that, in turn, led to a U.S. proposal (drafted by a team headed by Harry White), circulated in November 1943 to other Allied governments. The proposal called for two related new institutions, which eventually became the International Monetary Fund and the International Bank for Reconstruction and Development (i.e., the World Bank). In hindsight, the two institutions, keystones in the postwar international economic order, were crafted with astonishing speed. The November 1943 draft underwent a steady evolution in the course of the international discussions, with active participation from the UK and, to a lesser extent, Canada.[5] A scant eight months later, on July 22, 1944, negotiations were completed at Bretton Woods, New Hampshire, on the Articles of Agreement of the IMF and the World Bank.

What accounted for the rapidity with which the Bretton Woods organizations were so successfully negotiated? A third point to stress is that the backdrop to Bretton Woods was the virtual collapse of the old economic order amid a worldwide Depression followed by world war. U.S. preeminence in the discussions at Bretton Woods reflected the fact that only the U.S. economy still thrived, despite the Depression, in those trying times. American support was obviously critical for any new system or institution. Other participants were depleted by the war (as in the case of the UK, France, and the Soviet Union) and stood to benefit from U.S. benevolence in the emerging postwar order or were much less powerful than the United States (as with Canada and the Latin American countries). Many other countries were not yet independent and were not at the table at Bretton Woods. In short, no other countries were in a strong bargaining position vis-à-vis the United States. The specter of intractable international negotiations did not arise. The only other country capable of resisting U.S. diplomacy—the UK—agreed substantially with the U.S. proposals and quickly conceded when it disagreed on points of detail.

The power of the United States in the wartime negotiations found tangible expression in its relative voting power as by far the largest shareholder in the World Bank. By 1947, when about forty-four countries had ratified the Bretton Woods agreements to become members of the IMF and the World Bank (membership in the IMF was a requirement for membership in the Bank), the United States had 35.07 percent of the votes. The UK was the second-largest shareholder, with 14.52 percent. Thus, the two largest shareholders had virtually a voting majority. This was the new face of international economic relations, and it marked a sharp contrast with the one-state, one-vote formula embedded in the United Nations. If the rich and powerful were to make a relatively larger financial contribution to the newly created Bretton Woods institutions, they expected to have a larger say in the affairs of those organizations.

Several features that became basic to all of the multilateral banks were established in the architecture of the World Bank. Only 20 percent of the capital subscribed by members was to be paid in,[6] and the remaining 80 percent was to serve as a guarantee fund against which the Bank could lend or borrow. The total amount of loans or guarantees of loans was limited to 100 percent of unimpaired subscribed capital, reserves, and surplus. Various conditions under which the Bank could make or guarantee loans were set out in Article III. Notably, the recipient government was to fully guarantee payments of interest and principal, the borrower must be creditworthy, and the Bank must be satisfied that money was not available for the same purpose on reasonable terms. Also central to the philosophy of the Bank was Article IV, section 10, specifying that the Bank should not interfere in the political affairs of any member and that only economic considerations should be relevant to its decisions.[7]

Other important features evolved under the aegis of the World Bank during its early years. Perhaps most important was its vocation as a bank for development rather than reconstruction. It was no accident that "reconstruction" preceded "development" in the formal title of the IBRD, since the drafters at Bretton Woods perceived the bulk of the Bank's borrowing clientele to be the war-torn countries of Europe (including the Soviet Union) rather than developing countries, many of which had not yet emerged from colonialism. In fact, the Bank provided reconstruction loans to France (a sizable $250 million), the Netherlands, Denmark, and Luxembourg during its first two years. But the United States launched the Marshall Plan in 1947 with much more financial muscle than the Bank could hope to have, so the latter withdrew from reconstruction altogether. The Bank's first loans to developing countries went to Chile (in 1948) and to Mexico and Brazil (in 1949).[8]

The World Bank's transition to *development banking*, as that term is understood today, was qualified since the Bank provided large development loans to *developed* countries—such as Japan, Australia, New Zealand, Iceland, and Finland—until the 1970s. Only the first two were large borrowers, however, and they had ceased borrowing from the Bank by 1966.

The other feature that became a cornerstone of the operational policies of the MDBs was the World Bank's decision to provide direct loans rather than guarantee the loans of other creditors. In fact, the Bank had been conceived by its founders more as a guarantor of private loans than as a lender in its own right. In other words, the Bank's guarantee was intended to act as a catalyst to revive private international lending, which had collapsed during the Depression. For example, it was imagined that the Bank would provide guarantees against bonds sold by borrowing countries to investors in industrial countries. As early as 1947, direct loans by the Bank were seen by private creditors, borrowing countries, and the Bank itself as more cost-effective and administratively manageable than being a guarantor of private loans.[9]

The World Bank's first decade was precarious. Three presidents were appointed in its first four years (Eugene Meyer, John McCloy, and Eugene Black). The Bank's primary mandate to facilitate European reconstruction was undercut by the Marshall Plan. The Bank had to convince both its shareholders and Wall Street, the only source of international capital in the early postwar years, that development was bankable. That is, it had to persuade potential investors to buy its bonds to finance development projects in countries with poor credit ratings, albeit against the guarantee of the U.S. government and perhaps one or two others.

By the mid-1950s, however, the Bank had demonstrated its potential. An affiliate, the International Finance Corporation (IFC), was established in 1956 to complement the IBRD's largely government orientation. The IFC's mandate was to lend exclusively to the private sector without government guarantees. Two years later, at the annual meetings convened in New Delhi in 1958, proposals were launched to double the capital of the Bank and to form the International Development Association (IDA), a new soft-loan affiliate of the Bank. The IDA was to provide resources to the poorer developing country borrowers (such as India and Pakistan, which were rapidly becoming among the Bank's largest borrowers) that could not be expected to service large amounts of debt on the virtually commercial terms of the IBRD.

The need for more concessional resources was readily acknowledged during the 1950s. What was debated was whether a new facility should provide its resources on grant terms or on low- or zero-interest terms. Also at issue was the institutional location of the new facility, with the principal contenders being the UN and the World Bank. The issue was swiftly decided, again largely because of U.S. strength—which, in turn, flowed from U.S. willingness to provide the bulk of the resources. The IDA came into being in 1960. The principal components of the World Bank group—the IBRD, the IFC, and the IDA—were now in place.

The Regional Banks

Two related factors, in varying proportions, were central to the creation of the RDBs. First were developing country aspirations, fed by postcolonial nationalist sentiments, toward greater regional cooperation and autonomy; the second was the U.S. geopolitical strategy during the Cold War. The latter of these factors was particularly crucial in turning U.S. resistance toward the creation of the IDB and the AsDB into active support.

It is noteworthy that the idea for the first regional development bank predated the proposal for the present World Bank by at least fifty years. Latin American countries, seeking to improve international cooperation in their region, unsuccessfully pressed the United States to create an Inter-American Bank at the First International American Conference in Washington, D.C., in 1890. Undaunted, the Latin Americans continued their quest in the following decades. In fact, a convention for the establishment of an Inter-American Bank was eventually signed by the United States in 1940 but was abandoned during World War II. The latter proposal—which had been supported and developed in part by U.S. officials, including Harry White—influenced the nature and scope of the World Bank that took form at Bretton Woods.[10]

After the war, the creation of the World Bank gave the United States a pretext to once again deflect Latin American demands for a

regional bank until the late 1950s. What tipped the balance was escalating political resentment of the United States in Latin America (epit-
omized by the hostile reception of U.S. Vice-President Richard Nixon
during his May 1958 tour) and a nascent insurgency in the region that
was manifested in the Cuban Revolution. Once U.S. support was
forthcoming, an intergovernmental committee set up in early 1959 to
consider the proposal reached agreement in three months. By
December, the Articles of Agreement were in effect, and the Inter-
American Development Bank officially began operations in October
1960.[11]

The IDB blazed a trail for the other two regional banks; in fact,
IDB officials (including Felipe Herrera, the IDB's first president)
actively supported the creation of both. But it was another six years
until the African and Asian Banks were operational. The Articles of
Agreement for the ADB came into effect in September 1964 after three
years of political negotiations, almost exclusively within the African
continent. In 1961, African countries, most of which were emerging
from colonialism, asked the UN Economic Commission for Africa to
study the possibility of a regional bank in Africa. Subsequent delib-
erations by a committee of nine states were characterized by fractious
debates, but they moved the proposal along. A conference of finance
ministers was held in August 1963 to finalize the agreement. The
ADB commenced operations in July 1966.[12]

In August of that year, the agreement establishing the AsDB
became effective. After three years of discussions under the aegis of
the UN Economic Commission for Asia and the Far East (ECAFE), the
AsDB's operations began in December 1966. As with the IDB, the
birth of the AsDB was hastened by a sudden change in U.S. foreign
policy priorities, this time as a result of the rapidly escalating
Vietnam War. Prior to 1965, the United States had been lukewarm to
the idea of an Asian bank, but in April of that year President Lyndon
Johnson called for economic development to spearhead a peace initiative in the region and shortly thereafter supported the proposal to
establish a regional bank.[13]

A quarter of a century passed until the creation of the European
Bank for Reconstruction and Development.[14] The EBRD was born in
the twilight of the Cold War and commenced operations just as the
Soviet Union ceased to exist. French President François Mitterrand
made the initial proposal to establish the bank in 1989. The French
initiative was strongly endorsed by the European Council at
Strasbourg on December 9. A meeting was convened in Paris in
January 1990 at which all twenty-four members of the OECD were
represented, along with representatives from Malta and Cyprus,
eight Central and Eastern European countries, the European

Economic Community (EEC), and the EIB.[15] Six other non-European countries subsequently joined the discussions. Negotiations were concluded in May 1990, barely four months after the initial meeting—perhaps the speediest creation of a new multilateral institution in history.[16]

The agreement that established the EBRD entered into force in March 1991. The following month, the Board of Governors met for the first time in London, where an agreement was signed that designated that city as the Bank's headquarters.

Institutional Characteristics

Organizational Dynamics

Since its founding, the World Bank has been an organization in which the industrial countries (i.e., the members of the OECD) exercise control, in the sense that the voting share of these nonborrowing countries is sufficiently large (almost 60 percent) to ensure that the Bank policies will almost always reflect their preferences. This is not to say that the Bank has always, or has even usually, been polarized between the two sets of shareholders (in World Bank parlance, the nonborrowers are referred to as "Part 1" and the borrowers as "Part 2"). The members of Part 1 and Part 2 do not typically vote en bloc. In fact, the political culture of the Bank is such that votes are rarely taken; the Executive Board has sought to make decisions on the basis of consensus. In practice, this has meant that management seeks approval only for policies or other decisions on which Part 1 support is known to be forthcoming. Furthermore, the largest shareholders within Part 1 (the members of the G7) typically launch new policy initiatives at the World Bank, the developing country members rarely do so.

At times, divisions have existed between the two blocs, as in the case of the early structural adjustment operations or when the United States exerted pressure to orient the Bank more toward the private sector. In both of these cases, some developing countries resisted the new initiatives. Although it would be misleading to say that policy issues are always decided in favor of the industrial countries, it is virtually impossible for the World Bank to flout those countries' expressed interests.[17]

The political dynamics within the World Bank, with their explicit or implicit bias toward the industrial countries, are important to understand in view of the structure of the regional banks that were formed subsequently. It is important to understand the vast differences in the political forces that led to the creation and evolution of the four RDBs because these differences contributed to contrasts in their style and performance that extend to the present.

In the case of the AsDB, the proposal for a regional bank had originated in part in a relatively developed country—Japan. (Japanese influence remains pervasive and extends to the highest levels; by tradition, the AsDB president is Japanese.) Whereas some Asian politicians were ultimately galvanized by the proposal, the initiative came predominantly from international officials—particularly U Nyun, the executive director of ECAFE. The absence of pan-Asian political movements explains the weakness of the intraregional demand for a regional bank. Perhaps the region's experience with Japanese imperialism during the war (an experience that included the Asian Co-Prosperity Sphere, formed by Japanese military conquest) undermined regional enthusiasm for a multilateral venture dominated by the Japanese. In any event, Asia is a continent that contains many "regions" with enormous cultural, linguistic, and ethnic diversity compared with Latin America or even Africa, which have more claim to being considered a single region.

In contrast to the Asian experience, the initiative for the IDB and the ADB came from politicians who were aspiring toward cooperation and integration in various regional fora such as the Organization of American States (OAS). These fora sprang from developing countries that were struggling to find their way in a postwar world order in which they were marginalized—an order typified by the Bretton Woods organizations, in which voting shares were heavily weighted in favor of the industrial countries. Accordingly, the founders of the IDB and the ADB were adamant that control over their institutions would remain in the hands of regional developing country members.

For example, the IDB Articles provide that the voting power of the developing country members cannot fall below 53.5 percent of the total. And nonregional members were not even admitted to the ADB until 1982; hence, the ADB was owned entirely by developing country members for its first eighteen years. The presidents of both of these banks have always been from borrowing member countries, unlike the president of the AsDB.

An additional factor that distinguishes the ADB is the absence of a developed country member within the region. (The possible exception is South Africa, whose membership was ruled out until 1995 because of its apartheid policies.) Thus, the conspicuous absence of any developed country members (including the United States) prior to 1982 deprived the ADB of both the financial support and the political advocacy the IDB gained from the United States and the AsDB from Japan.

Eventually, in 1973 an African Development Fund (ADF) was established to channel concessional resources from donor countries to the region (more on this later). The proposal to open Bank capital to nonregional countries was also made in the early 1970s. By that time the ADB's inadequate nonconcessional resource base was manifestly apparent, but the proposal provoked intense debate among African members. When opening the Bank's capital was finally agreed to in 1982, it was on the condition that the "African character" of the institution be safeguarded; this has been interpreted to mean preserving a clear voting majority for African members.[18] By 1992, around twenty-five nonregional countries had been admitted to membership in the ADB, but their aggregate share of voting power was only 35.5 percent compared with 64.5 percent for the regionals. The composition of the ADB's Board of Directors[19] further reflects this division: Twelve members are from Africa, and six are nonregionals.

Meanwhile, developing country members of the AsDB never sought control of the Bank through a charter-protected voting majority. Instead, the Bank's articles provide for only a 60 percent majority for regional members, including the developed country members—Japan, Australia, and New Zealand—to ensure its control by "Asian" (i.e., regional) countries. Consequently, developing country borrowers have always accounted for a minority (about 45 percent) of the overall voting shares, whereas developed country members inside and outside Asia have had majority control.[20] As a result, the sometimes acrimonious divisions between borrowers and nonborrowers in the IDB and the ADB have rarely characterized the more placid AsDB, a fact that has inspired more confidence in and support for the AsDB by developed country interests. Not coincidentally, the AsDB's inaugural meeting in November 1966 was attended by sixty commercial banks as well as representatives of chambers of commerce and other private sector organizations from across Japan, the United States, and Europe.[21]

The reason for the different outturns in the political and organizational dynamics of the three banks is straightforward. In the IDB and the ADB, developing country borrowers hold a voting majority but the developed country minority shareholders, in effect, control access to resources and can determine the size and timing of replenishments and capital increases. Thus, debates over the future direction of the bank can lead to a stalemate, as occurred in the IDB during the Seventh Replenishment in the late 1980s. In the AsDB, as with the World Bank, borrowers are in a minority and are not in a strong position to challenge the resource-providing majority shareholders on fundamental issues.[22]

In the case of the EBRD, France took the initiative to extend its influence in Central and Eastern Europe as well as in the Soviet Union. When the United States, Japan, and other non-European countries joined the discussions, the emphasis shifted to the Central and Eastern European countries that had already begun the transition away from communism to democratic, market-oriented societies. The Soviet Union, which had not yet begun the transition, was thus inhibited by the EBRD's articles from borrowing in excess of its paid-in capital contribution. Ironically, just three months after the EBRD began operations in 1991, the Soviet Union broke apart, and ultimately the cap on its borrowing was raised to 40 percent of total Bank assets.[23] In short, the EBRD belongs in the tradition of the World Bank and the AsDB: It is a donor-inspired and donor-dominated institution rather than a borrower-led one (like the IDB and the ADB).

The domination of donors was evident in the purpose of the EBRD, which was to facilitate the historic political and economic transition away from communism. Article 1 of its charter mandated the Bank to foster the transition "in countries committed to and applying the principles of multi-party democracy, pluralism, and market economics." This marked the first time a multilateral organization had wandered so far into purely political territory, and it did so to an extent that would have been unimaginable during the Cold War.

Emergence of Concessional Funds

The financial structure of all of the RDBs is similar to that of the World Bank. As mentioned earlier, each RDB, as with the World Bank, comprises a lending window (the "Bank")—which makes loans at near-market, nonconcessional rates—and a soft-loan facility (the "Fund"). The exception is the EBRD, which does not have (and probably will never have) a soft window. Resources for the Bank are obtained through borrowing on the international markets against the capital of the RDBs, a small part of which is paid in by shareholding countries with the remainder subject to call. The capital base is increased periodically through general or special capital increases that augment the borrowing and lending capacity of the Bank. Soft-loan Fund resources, on the other hand, are obtained primarily through periodic replenishments by the donor-country members.

Some notable differences in size, financial structure, and organization emerged at the inception of the RDBs. The IDB—unique among the multilateral banks—was created with a built-in soft-loan facility, the Fund for Special Operations (FSO). The World Bank's soft-loan affiliate, the IDA, was created in 1960, contemporaneously with the IDB but about fifteen years after the inception of the World Bank. The other two RDBs had to convince donor countries of the wisdom of organizing a new concessional facility that would be dedicated to the poorest countries in their regions. Moreover, the FSO was integrated into the juridical personality of the IDB and did not require a separate charter. Consequently, to this day the FSO is replenished in a set of unified negotiations (general resource increases) that also includes capital increases for the Bank. In the case of the other banks, separate negotiations are held to replenish the Fund window and increase the Bank's capital.

It is also noteworthy that at its inception the IDB was exceptionally well endowed with resources in comparison with the AsDB and especially the ADB. The IDB's ordinary capital resources amounted to $850 million (of which one-half was paid in); in addition, the FSO was initiated with resources of $146.3 million, and the United States provided an additional $394 million for a concessional "Social Progress Trust Fund" to be administered by the IDB as part of President John Kennedy's Alliance for Progress in Latin America. (The latter was folded into the FSO during the 1960s.) Subsequently, however, the FSO never reached the size of its counterparts at the Asian and African Development Banks because scarce ODA was allocated increasingly to poorer countries in other parts of the world.

Membership in the IDB was originally restricted to member-states of the OAS. In 1972, an exception was made for Canada—not then a member of the OAS—which was admitted as a regional member with a guaranteed voting share of no less than 4 percent. Beginning in 1974, the IDB opened membership to nonregionals, predominantly Japan and European countries. Since the IDB charter guarantees a 34.5 percent voting share to the United States and 53.5 percent to the regional borrowing countries, this leaves a maximum of 8 percent for the nonregionals. The Board of Executive Directors consists of eight regional developing members, two regional developed members (the United States and Canada), and two members representing nonregionals.

At its inception, the authorized capital of the ADB was $250 million, of which $218 million was subscribed by 1968. One-half ($109 million) was to be paid in, but only $52.6 million was actually paid in[24]—a fact that presaged the problem of chronic arrears in subscriptions that would afflict the ADB. The capacity of the Bank to mobilize nonconcessional resources was thus significantly impaired and was constrained to around $70–80 million per year.

The African Development Fund was launched following discussions with potential donors in both the West and the Soviet bloc during the late 1960s. Ultimately, a group of donor countries among the developed market economies agreed to participate; Canada and Japan played leading roles in the establishment of the ADF and in early replenishments. But the ADF had a slow start in 1973, with pledges of only $82.6 million. The ADF has its own governing structure designed to preserve its "African character." The Fund's Board of Directors is made up of the six nonregional directors on the Bank Board plus six of the twelve regional directors from the Board who represent the Bank (which makes a token contribution to the Fund from its net income) and the borrowers. Voting parity exists between these two groups, with each retaining 50 percent of the voting rights.

The AsDB's authorized capital was $1.1 billion at inception, half of which was to be paid in. Japan and the United States both subscribed 20.6 percent of the shares (and held 17.1 percent of the votes) and were by far the two largest shareholders. India was next at 9.6 percent of the shares (8.3 percent of the votes), with Australia, at 8.8 percent of the shares (and 7.6 percent of the votes), close behind. Initially, usable resources amounted to about $700 million. The original Board of Directors consisted of seven regional directors (including one representing Japan) and three nonregionals (including one representing the United States). Subsequently, the Board was expanded to twelve directors (eight regional and four nonregional members).

The AsDB Articles provided the Bank with a capacity to establish "Special" (i.e., concessional) Funds rather than a general-purpose soft-loan facility. In the initial years, this led to the proliferation of voluntary special-purpose funds—one on agriculture, one on technical assistance, and a Multi-purpose Special Fund—procurement for which was tied to the contributors. By 1974, Bank members agreed that these funds were jeopardizing the multilateral nature of the AsDB, and the untied, general-purpose Asian Development Fund (AsDF) was set up with contributions of $525 million.

The unit of account for the EBRD has been the ECU, a weighted average of European countries' currency in the EU's exchange rate mechanism. The EBRD's initial capitalization was ECU 10 billion (approximately U.S.$12 billion), of which 30 percent was paid in—the highest proportion of any of the MDBs.[25] The Bank's capital was doubled in 1996. The EBRD, unlike the other MDBs, has never acquired a concessional lending facility and is unlikely to do so.[26] It accepts and administers Special Funds that serve the purposes of the Bank, however, which have been used largely for technical cooperation (e.g., to identify and assist new small businesses).

Despite the fact that (as is the case in the other MDBs) the United States is the largest single shareholder, with 10.0 percent of the shares, from the beginning the EBRD has been a Western European–

dominated organization. The twelve countries of the European Union (EU), the EU itself, and the EIB collectively hold 51.0 percent of the shares and are represented by eleven of the twenty-three members of the Board of Directors. In contrast, the borrowing members of Central and Eastern Europe and the former Soviet Union hold 11.9 percent of the shares; other nonborrowing European countries and Turkey hold 10.7 percent; and non-European countries, including Australia, Canada, Egypt, Israel, Japan, Korea, Mexico, Morocco, and New Zealand, hold 14.8 percent.

Lending Strategy

The five MDBs began with somewhat different policy objectives, but with the exception of the EBRD these differences have narrowed considerably over time.

During its first twenty-five years, the World Bank concentrated its project lending heavily in the power and transportation sectors, which absorbed 69 percent of the Bank's overall lending in 1960 and an average of 55 percent during the decade 1961–1970. The productive sectors absorbed an additional 31 percent (agriculture 15 percent, industry 16 percent). The social sectors accounted for a mere 5 percent of lending (education 3 percent, water supply 2 percent).[27] This overwhelming emphasis on infrastructure and the productive sectors reflected a preoccupation by the World Bank with economic rather than political or social dimensions, an emphasis that arose from its conception of development. By the time of the McNamara administration in the 1970s, evidence showed that the Bank was changing its conception to accommodate family planning, urban development, and employment in its operations; in other words, it was recognizing that social and human development are also critical.[28]

In contrast, in the early years at the IDB a conscious emphasis was placed on *social* development, including low-income housing, water and sanitation, and education. Latin American proponents of the IDB viewed projects in these areas as vital to improving social welfare and the political stability of the region. Whereas support for these sectors has come back into vogue in the 1990s, in the 1960s social sector development was new; it was different from the World Bank's priorities (largely in the area of infrastructure) and was therefore somewhat daring. In addition, the IDB played a leading role in agriculture, including development of an active program of lending to small- and medium-scale farmers.[29] This emphasis on small-scale agriculture predated by several years the initiative launched by Robert McNamara in 1973 to refocus the World Bank's objectives on alleviating poverty. In the 1970s, driven in part by that decade's energy crises, the IDB gave greater prominence to large-scale energy and infrastructure projects and retreated from its initial emphasis on small-scale agriculture and the social sectors.

Although (as with the IDB) the stated objectives of the ADB referred to achieving "social progress," it began with a much more explicit emphasis on infrastructure: In the ADB's first five years, over 60 percent of disbursements supported projects in the transport, telecommunications, and power sectors. In sharp contrast to the IDB, there was virtually no lending to health and education from the Bank window, although these sectors were supported when the African Development Fund became operative. But the Fund skewed lending only somewhat toward the sectors in which the poor would be the principal beneficiaries. Agriculture received 33 percent of ADF disbursements from 1977 to 1982, less than the almost 39 percent allocated for transport. An explicit priority of the ADB at its creation was "multinational projects," which it was thought would pave the way to heightened cooperation and regional integration. Attempts at such projects, which involved negotiating with two or more borrowers in different countries, were invariably frustrated by disputes over the division of project benefits and costs and thus were frequently unsuccessful; as a result, these projects formed only a tiny part (less than 3 percent) of the lending portfolio of the African Bank and Fund.[30]

From the beginning the AsDB was more narrowly focused than either the IDB or the ADB. There was no mention of "social progress" in the Bank's purposes; rather, it was designed to "foster economic growth and cooperation." The emphasis on economic growth led the AsDB to support growth-inducing investment. Hence, as with the ADB and the World Bank, lending to infrastructure (energy, transportation, and communications) loomed large in the Bank's first few years. In 1974, lending to agriculture moved into the forefront ahead of energy. It was not until the 1980s that the Asian Bank abandoned its relatively conservative lending strategy and devoted more attention to the social sectors.

The EBRD's mission of fostering the transition to market-based economies in the countries of the former Soviet bloc has given it a distinct operating style. The Bank has adopted a transaction-driven orientation, or deal-making, style in implementing its mandate. In many respects, its modus operandi resembles that of the merchant banks in its London neighborhood rather than that of the other MDBs with the exception of the International Finance Corporation, the World Bank affiliate that caters exclusively to private enterprise. In focusing on particular transactions, the EBRD has been able to build capacity—especially in the private sector—by working with entrepreneurs and enterprises that promise to be strong concerns. The lack of an enterprise culture in the preceding centrally planned regimes has made the EBRD's work groundbreaking. The Bank's focus on the private sector was written into the Articles of Agreement, which restrict the proportion of its commitments to the state sector to 40 percent (Article 11, section 3[i]).

The EBRD's concentration on micro-level transactions has also mirrored much less emphasis than the other MDBs on macro-level policy issues, on which the EBRD has generally been happy to defer to the World Bank and the IMF. There are, however, two important exceptions. First, the Bank has conducted an exercise in policy dialogue on the issue of transition. Its flagship publication, the *Transition Report*, appraises each client country's progress in the transition by examining the health of the country's private sector, its climate for private investment, privatization, the role of both markets and the state, and the capacity of the financial sector to mobilize local savings for investment. Second, the EBRD has been active in environmental issues. The Bank is required by its charter (Article 2, section 7) to apply environmental diligence to all of its activities. In addition, the Bank has a major focus on nuclear safety issues and is a key player in the decommissioning and conversion of nuclear reactors in the former Soviet Union.

The RDBs and the World Bank: Comparisons and Relationships

Sectoral Allocation

By the end of the 1970s, the sectoral distribution of the lending portfolios of the three RDBs then in existence and of the World Bank had considerably converged; in other ways as well, a certain uniformity had emerged in their philosophy and behavior.

The 1980s were years of debt crisis and structural adjustment and of growing divergence between the World Bank and the RDBs. The World Bank launched its program of policy-based structural adjustment lending in 1980. But the RDBs waited several years before initiating similar lending—the ADB and the AsDB in 1987 and the IDB in 1989. The delay was in part a result of the fact that the RDBs lacked the staff capacity to prepare, negotiate, and implement policy-based loans. Related to this problem was a widespread perception, especially among developed country shareholders, that policy-based lending was best left to the Bretton Woods institutions. Moreover, the policy conditionality of adjustment lending was particularly controversial in some developing countries—notably in Latin America—

which resisted the initiation of similar programs in their own regional banks.

By the end of the 1980s, debate still occurred about the extent to which the RDBs should become involved in policy-based lending. In spite of this, there was once again a growing convergence among the RDBs and with the World Bank (see Table 2.1).

Table 2.1   MDBs: Sectoral Distribution of Cumulative Lending, 1995 (percentage)

Sector	IBRD/IDA	IDB/FSO	AsDB/AsDF	ADB/ADF	EBRD
Agriculture	20.9	15.7	22.8	27.7	2.8
Transport	15.8[a]	13.5[a]	19.9[a]	18.9	29.2
Energy	17.4	19.9	25.9	24.3[b]	10.9
Industry	15.7[c]	13.0	14.0[c]	18.4	56.1
Social[d]	13.5	16.6	15.5	10.8	1.0

Source: MDB *1995 Annual Reports.*
Notes: These categories do not add up to 100 percent and are not completely congruent among RDBs. Multisectoral (including structural adjustment) loans are omitted, but sectoral adjustment and other policy-based loans are included.
    a. Includes communications.
    b. Categorized as "public utilities."
    c. Includes Development Finance Companies and small-scale enterprises.
    d. Includes education, population, health and nutrition, and water supply/sewerage.

Resource Flows

The World Bank had a fifteen- to twenty-year head start over the RDBs. As noted, the African and Asian Banks did not have concessional lending facilities comparable to IDA and the IDB's FSO (which both began in 1960) until 1973–1974. Hence, it is not surprising that in terms of the most basic indicator of size—lending volume—the World Bank group's operations far outstrip those of the RDBs and that the IDB is second. The World Bank's cumulative approved lending, net of cancellations, of $269 billion in 1995 was almost four times greater than that of the largest RDB—the Inter-American Bank group—and was more than seven times as large as that of the smallest, the African Bank group. The larger lending capacity of the World Bank is evident in comparing the capital bases and cumulative subscriptions of the multilateral banks (see Table 2.2).

Cumulative totals, however, conceal more recent developments in the 1980s, when the World Bank group's disbursements stagnated and those of the RDBs expanded—particularly toward the end of the decade. As a result, the RDBs' share in the total net multilateral bank

Table 2.2   MDBs: Ordinary Capital and Concessional Resources, 1995

	World Bank	IDB	AsDB	ADB	EBRD
Ordinary capital ("Bank")[a]	176.438	66.398	43.077	23.417	12.650
Concessional resources ("Fund")[b]	92.891	9.751	19.989	11.434	0.000[c]

Source: 1995 Annual Reports.
Notes: a. Subscribed capital (paid-in and callable).
b. Principal "Fund" window only (IDA, FSO, AsDF, and ADF).
c. EBRD does not have a concessional window.

disbursements grew from under a quarter in 1980 to almost a third by 1990.

A more useful comparison is to gauge resource flows from the World Bank to each region in which the RDBs operate. Figures provided by the RDBs and the World Bank are not totally comparable, but they do indicate relative orders of magnitude. The data indicate that the IDB group has provided to its region about 86 percent of the net disbursements from the World Bank, the Asian Bank about 39 percent, the African Bank about 38 percent, and the EBRD about 23 percent of disbursements (see Table 2.3).

Table 2.3   Cumulative Loan Approvals from MDBs, by Region, Through 1995

MDB	Latin America/ Caribbean	Asia	Africa	Europe
IBRD/IDA	90,687	143,521[a]	78,075[b]	44,046
IDB/FSO	78,213[c]	—	—	—
AsDB/AsDF	—	56,686	—	—
ADB/ADF	—	—	29,945	—
EBRD	—	—	—	10,052[d]

Source: 1995 Annual Reports.
Notes: a. Excludes Central Asia subregion.
b. Includes Middle East subregion.
c. Includes $1.5 billion in funds administered by the IDB.
d. Includes funds directed to Central Asian republics.

Again, the cumulative data are skewed in favor of the World Bank. More recent data on loan approvals indicate a situation of near parity between the World Bank and the IDB in Latin America and the Caribbean, whereas the Asian and African Bank groups were making loan commitments at 63 and 21 percent, respectively, of World Bank levels in their regions (see Table 2.4).

Table 2.4   MDB Loan Approvals, by Region, 1995

MDB	Latin America/ Caribbean	Asia	Africa	Europe
IBRD/IDA	6,061	8,700[a]	3,263[b]	4,499
IDB/FSO	7,304	—	—	—
AsDB/AsDF	—	5,504	—	—
ADB/ADF	—	—	669[c]	—
EBRD	—	—	—	3,654[d]

Source: 1995 Annual Reports.
Notes: a. Includes East Asia and Pacific and South Asia regions.
b. Includes Africa and Middle East/North Africa regions.
c. Includes Central Asian republics.
d. This was an unrepresentative year for the ADB/ADF because of the crisis in the Bank and the failure of negotiations toward ADF VII.

At the country level, the RDBs now frequently emerge as bigger lenders than the World Bank. For example, in fiscal year (FY) 1992 the IDB approved loans of $1,050.0 million for Argentina, compared with $373.0 million from the World Bank; the figures for Brazil were $816.0 million (IDB) and $798.0 million (World Bank). The Asian Development Fund approved $410.3 million for Pakistan, compared with $324.2 million from the World Bank (IBRD and IDA combined), and $119.6 million for Sri Lanka, compared with $69.5 million from the World Bank's IDA. Similar examples for the African Bank are more difficult to find; they include Morocco, for which $332.6 million was approved from the African Bank group, compared with $325.0 million from the World Bank group, and Nigeria, for which $278.5 million (ADB group) and $263.4 million (IDA) was approved in 1992.[31]

In terms of sheer volume of lending, it seems clear that the World Bank is no longer the preeminent multilateral bank; the RDBs have been catching up and in some borrowing countries have surpassed the World Bank in the level of their loan approvals. The gap in disbursement levels will thus also tend to drop.

Another way of comparing the relative importance of the RDBs as resource providers is to examine net transfers, which take into account interest payments as well as amortization (Table 2.5). Indeed, since the beginning of 1988 (except for the year 1990), the net transfer from the World Bank group (including positive transfers from IDA) has been positive.

Regional bank group (and other multilateral) lending has clearly helped to offset the negative net transfers from the World Bank group, thereby easing the growing problem of servicing debts owed to the World Bank. By 1992, however, net transfers from the regional

Table 2.5   Net Transfers on Debt Owed to Multilateral Lenders, 1987–1994

	1987	1988	1989	1990	1991	1992	1993	1994
Concessional	4.75	4.62	4.59	5.48	5.64	5.91	5.87	7.57
IDA	3.49	3.37	3.11	3.83	3.95	4.43	4.08	5.18
RDFs[a] and others[b]	1.26	1.25	1.48	1.65	1.69	1.48	1.79	2.39
Nonconcessional	−0.89	−3.05	−2.18	−1.45	−3.77	−6.45	−4.97	−11.21
IBRD	−1.48	−4.08	−3.49	−2.07	−5.45	−7.67	−5.27	−8.32
RDBs[c] and others[b]	0.59	1.03	1.31	0.62	1.68	1.21	0.30	−2.89
World Bank group								
IDA and IBRD	2.01	−0.71	−0.38	1.76	−1.50	−3.24	−1.19	−3.15
RDB groups								
and others	1.85	2.28	2.79	2.27	3.37	2.70	2.09	−0.50

Source: World Bank Debt Tables, 1996.
Notes: a. Regional development bank concessional fund lending.
   b. Predominantly European Community and Arab multilateral lenders. Regional bank lending predominates in both concessional and nonconcessional categories.
   c. Ordinary capital resource lending.

banks and other multilateral lenders were no longer large enough to offset the negative net transfer from the World Bank. The problem of servicing debts owed to the multilaterals has become particularly acute, since these debts cannot be rescheduled or reduced in the way commercial bank debts and official bilateral debts have been restructured through, respectively, the Brady Plan and the Paris Club.[32] Hence, growing (positive) net transfers from the regional banks may be necessary simply to enable developing countries to service debts to the World Bank and to preserve the Bank's preferred creditor status. The issue of how debts owed to the RDBs will be serviced looms and is already problematic at the African Development Bank.

RDB–World Bank Relationships

The volume of lending is no longer the sole or even the most important determinant of the relative importance of multilateral agencies. With the advent of policy-based lending in the 1980s, the World Bank (along with the IMF) maintained its preeminence as a lender because of the catalytic nature of its policy dialogue with borrowing countries. The focus of this dialogue is the economic policy framework of the borrowers and that framework's conduciveness to development in the view of the IMF and the World Bank. A positive policy dialogue can unlock resource flows from the World Bank and from various other sources and can also trigger a process of debt reduction through fora such as the Paris Club. Accordingly, borrowers tend to place higher priority on their dialogue with the World Bank, even if it is no longer as large a lender as the regional banks.

The fact that all of the RDBs (except the EBRD) now also participate in policy-based lending has not altered this relationship. In 1987, the ADB became the first of the regional banks to initiate policy-based lending, and it made commitments of almost $3 billion in the five years 1987–1991 inclusive. Since 1988, between 80 and 100 percent of these operations have been cofinanced with the World Bank, and where they have not the ADB has utilized parallel financing in which the conditionality is consistent with World Bank and IMF adjustment programs. Appraisal, preparation, and supervision are undertaken jointly between the two staffs when the banks have agreed to cofinance, but it seems fair to say that the conditionality is designed by the World Bank and the ADB participates by providing additional cash.

The AsDB also initiated policy-based lending in 1987, but it has restricted its operations in this area entirely to sectoral adjustment loans. The Bank made loans totaling $2.3 billion during the period 1987–1991; in contrast to the ADB, few were cofinanced with the World Bank. Coordination does occur between the staffs of the AsDB and the World Bank, but perhaps more important the Asian Bank relies on the Bretton Woods organizations to set the macro policy framework and designs its own sector operations within and consistent with that framework.

The IDB began sectoral adjustment lending in 1990 following a rancorous debate between Latin American countries (which opposed such lending) and the United States during the Seventh Replenishment negotiations. The agreement that emerged during those negotiations was that the IDB would initially link its sector lending operations to those of the World Bank. (The requirement for formal linkage was dropped in 1993, although many adjustment operations have still been made with close collaboration between the two MDBs.) In the years 1990 and 1991, the IDB approved almost $3.4 billion in adjustment lending operations. In 1991, the IDB also made two loans (to Chile and Colombia) without parallel financing with the World Bank. Instances of such independent policy-based lending from the IDB may be increasing, but it is doubtful that an operation would be approved over the objection of the World Bank.

Again, the order of precedence between the World Bank and the regional banks seems clear. This is not surprising in view of the greater numbers and experience of the World Bank staff in dealing with policy-based lending compared with their RDB counterparts. As the RDBs build up their expertise and their portfolios in this area, however, they can be expected to challenge—at least occasionally—

World Bank leadership on the nature or scope of specific adjustment operations.

More generally, both sides describe cooperation between the World Bank and the RDBs as "close." Cofinancing is merely one facet of this cooperation, but it is an important one. The World Bank group is the most important cofinancer of IDB and ADB projects. In 1992, the IDB provided around $2.97 billion compared with the World Bank's $2.49 billion in cofinanced projects. Conversely, the IDB has recently been the largest multilateral cofinancer of World Bank projects, providing about $1.6 billion in the World Bank's FY 1995/96, although it is only one of the Bank's several external sources of funds. Much of the surge in cofinancing between these MDBs has involved the sectoral adjustment loans to Latin American borrowers. The ADB's cofinancing with the World Bank has also increased rapidly in the late 1980s and early 1990s for much the same reason as that of the IDB (cofinanced adjustment loans). The AsDB has traditionally been the least inclined of the three established RDBs to pursue cofinancing, but by FY 1995/96 it was providing $703 million for this purpose.

In addition, regular contacts occur between the staffs of each of the RDBs and their counterparts at the World Bank. These contacts occur at the annual meetings of the organizations, when senior staff meet to discuss issues of common interest, as well as during field missions and at various stages of project preparation, implementation, and supervision. The IDB, which is headquartered in Washington, D.C., has monthly meetings between its senior staff and that of the World Bank's Latin America/Caribbean region.

In spite of assertions of healthy cooperation and collaboration, occasional instances of competition and friction do occur. Evidence of such disagreements is harder to come by, which probably means conflict between the RDBs and the World Bank is exceptional. Examples include cases of "piracy" of World Bank projects by the regionals. More serious instances of disagreement include differences over the Global Environment Facility, in which the World Bank has a lead role (along with the UN Environment Programme and the UN Development Programme) and from which the RDBs have felt unfairly excluded. More generally, at times the RDBs have felt they were rubber stamps for the policies and initiatives of the World Bank.

In concluding, it can be asked, How complementary are the RDBs to the World Bank? How much duplication of effort occurs? Is there scope for greater specialization and division of labor between the World Bank, on the one hand, and the RDBs, on the other? The evidence on sectoral distribution adduced earlier suggests a broad similarity among all of the MDBs on a global basis; they generally do the same sorts of things. On a country level, an ad hoc agreement often exists between the World Bank and the RDB to specialize in certain sectors, but such agreements are fluid, are sometimes broken, and are never formalized. On this level, then, some duplication of effort and some competition are found; therefore, there may be room for greater specialization of effort—for example, between sectors or countries. One idea would be to give the RDBs greater responsibility for the smaller countries and to broaden existing arrangements such as that for the South Pacific islands, in which the Asian Bank takes a lead role.

In the realm of policy-based lending, however, a broad division of labor currently exists in which the World Bank (along with the IMF) determines the broad parameters of macro and microeconomic policy and the RDBs support economic reform programs by providing cofinancing or parallel financing with the World Bank. It is sometimes suggested that the RDBs should withdraw from policy-based lending altogether and leave the field to the Bretton Woods organizations, but this would make the RDBs primarily project delivery agencies with a very narrow mandate for tackling policy issues. Such a role is no longer possible, let alone desirable. To be credible development partners, the RDBs need to have greater capacity for policy analysis of both macro-economic and sectoral issues. Some strengthening of the RDBs' staff resources will accordingly be necessary, especially if the World Bank and the RDBs decide to divide countries or sectors in a more formal way to avoid duplication. Paradoxically, the RDBs may have to become more like the World Bank to be more different.

Notes

1. An earlier version of this chapter was prepared for the Bretton Woods Commission in Washington, D.C.

2. In addition to Mason and Asher's monumental study, *The World Bank Since Bretton Woods*, Oliver, *International Co-operation and the World Bank*, and Harrod, *The Life of John Maynard Keynes*, provide in-depth historical analyses. The literature on the World Bank has continued to grow over the past two decades.

3. See Oliver, *International Co-operation and the World Bank*.

4. White was also instrumental in the creation of the International Monetary Fund, although in this instance equal credit goes to John Maynard Keynes.

5. Mason and Asher, *The World Bank Since Bretton Woods*, chapter 2, aver that the bank "was an Anglo-Saxon creation, with the United States as the senior partner." The UK delegation made some substantive amendments to the U.S. draft proposal in the discussions at Atlantic City that led up to Bretton Woods.

6. In fact, only 2 percent of the 20 percent was actually paid in gold or U.S. dollars, and the remaining 18 percent was eventually called in.

7. Mason and Asher, *The World Bank Since Bretton Woods*, p. 27.

8. Ibid., p. 53.

9. Ibid., p. 107.

10. Ibid., pp. 14–16; White, *Regional Development Banks*, pp. 142–144; Tussie, *The Inter-American Development Bank*, pp. 17–21.

11. Dell, *The Inter-American Development Bank*, pp. 12–31.

12. Gardiner and Pickett, *The African Development Bank 1964–1984*, pp. 13–26.

13. Wilson, *A Bank for Half the World*, pp. 1–30.

14. The EBRD was not Europe's first MDB; the European Investment Bank (EIB) was. The EIB was created in 1958 under the framework of the European Economic Community, along with a concessional window, the European Development Fund (EDF). Whereas the EIB concentrates most of its investment in Europe, the EDF, which was born before the IDA, provides concessional finance primarily to the Africa-Caribbean-Pacific (ACP) states of the Lomé Convention. The EDF, which is not among the MDBs covered here, is a lender of significant proportions: By the 1980s it was making commitments of around 80 percent of the World Bank's IDA (Kapur and Webb, "The Evolution of the Multilateral Development Banks," p. 232).

15. The EEC and the EIB were designated as shareholders (each with 3 percent of the initial shares) because of their role as European institutions.

16. European Bank for Reconstruction and Development, *Basic Documents of the European Bank for Reconstruction and Development*.

17. On U.S. influence in the World Bank and other MDBs, see Jonathan E. Sanford, *U.S. Foreign Policy and Multilateral Development Banks*, and Gwin, *U.S. Relations with the World Bank, 1945–92*, pp. 54–84.

18. Gardiner and Pickett, *The African Development Bank 1964–1984*, pp. 54–57.

19. Like the World Bank, each RDB has a Board of Governors consisting of one representative (usually with ministerial rank) from each member country. The governors meet annually and do not generally intervene in the day-to-day management of the banks. Daily oversight is provided by resident Boards of Directors, consisting of twelve (in the case of the IDB, the AsDB, and the ADF) or eighteen members (ADB). Except for the largest shareholders—such as the United States, which has its own director on all Boards—most shareholders are grouped into constituencies and "share" a director.

20. Wilson, *A Bank for Half the World*, p. 9.

21. White, *Regional Development Banks*, p. 65.

22. Ibid., pp. 190–191.

23. Curran, "The European Development Banks," pp. 243–244.

24. White, *Regional Development Banks*, pp. 104–106.

25. The World Bank affiliate, the IFC, is an exception, since it has only 100 percent paid-in capital. The founding shareholders of the EBRD were clearly eager to send capital markets a strong signal of support for the new MDB, which explains why they supported such a large proportion of paid-in capital when the paid-in proportion of capital replenishments in other MDBs was typically below 5 percent.

26. Some of the EBRD's members, such as Albania and the Caucasian and Central Asian republics, are arguably among the world's poorest coun-

tries and should be eligible for concessional funds. Given the increasing scarcity of concessional funding and of ODA generally, however, it is unlikely that even if the EBRD were to establish its own concessional affiliate, such funds would become more abundant or available. These countries can and do have access to the existing concessional funds of the World Bank and the Asian Development Bank.

27. Mason and Asher, *The World Bank Since Bretton Woods*, p. 200, Table 7-3.

28. Ibid., chapter 14; also World Bank, *IDA in Retrospect*.

29. Dell, *The Inter-American Development Bank*, pp. 139–148.

30. Gardiner and Pickett, *The African Development Bank 1964–1984*, pp. 86–93.

31. MDBs, *1993 Annual Reports*.

32. Culpeper, "A Note on the Multilateral Creditors," pp. 1,239–1,244.

3

MDBs in the 1990s: Reflection and Reform

The 1980s was a sobering decade for the MDBs. Coupled with a sharp recession in the OECD countries, the debt crisis rendered the performance of many of the development initiatives of the previous decades—including those launched with the assistance of the MDBs—less effective. In part to rectify the situation and in part to ensure that their own loans were repaid, the MDBs (starting with the World Bank in 1980 and followed eventually by the three established regional banks) began structural adjustment lending to the debt-distressed countries. But there were also difficulties with the first generation of structural adjustment loans—with their design, conditionality, and political impact.

All of this meant that during the 1980s the performance of MDB loans—technically, the performance of projects financed by MDB loans—deteriorated considerably. This declining performance was registered by the MDBs' evaluations undertaken at the end of each project. (In the case of the World Bank, such evaluations are the responsibility of the Operations Evaluation Department, an independent office that reports directly to the Bank's executive directors.)

In February 1992, Lewis Preston, then president of the World Bank, announced the creation of a Portfolio Management Task Force to examine problems affecting the quality of the Bank's portfolio of loans and credits. The task force was headed by recently retired Vice-President Willi Wapenhans; consequently, the report became known as the Wapenhans Report. The report created a sensation, since it revealed the declining performance of World Bank projects and admitted that the decline was caused in part by the Bank's own weaknesses.[1]

The report was followed by similar reviews at three other MDBs—the Inter-American, African, and Asian Banks. (The EBRD, which had been established only in 1990, had barely initiated a program of lending when these reviews were undertaken; thus, there was little scope for a portfolio review.) Collectively, these four reviews of the state of the MDB portfolios constituted a major watershed in the history of the multilateral banks. They also prompted the formation of the Multilateral Development Bank Task Force under the aegis of the IMF–World Bank Development Committee[2] in 1994, on the occasion of the fiftieth anniversary of the Bretton Woods Conference.

During the same period, The North-South Institute's Multilateral Development Bank project (of which this is the final volume) conducted a series of in-depth examinations of the performance and prospects of the three established regional banks (the IDB, the ADB, and the AsDB) and of the subregional Caribbean Development Bank. These reviews were more wide-ranging than those of the portfolio task forces at each of the banks; therefore, although they reached many of the same conclusions, they raised some broader issues as well.

This chapter summarizes key findings of the MDB project along with the portfolio reviews, with a view particularly to the agenda for reform at each institution.

Key Policy Implications of the MDB Project

Inter-American Development Bank

The Eighth Replenishment, for which negotiations were completed in 1994, resulted in the IDB becoming the multilateral lender with the largest capacity to lend to the Latin American and Caribbean countries ($7 billion per annum, a level it could maintain indefinitely)—larger than the World Bank's current notional lending capacity in the region. In her book, *The Multilateral Development Banks: Volume 4, The Inter-American Development Bank,* Diana Tussie argues that the Eighth Replenishment unequivocally placed the IDB in a position of leadership in the hemisphere, at least with respect to development issues. But is the IDB prepared—indeed, is it *able*—to exercise such leadership? In her study of the IDB, Tussie maintains that the institution has firmly established its political legitimacy for such a role. The IDB has a strong relationship with its borrowing member countries. Since the turbulent Seventh Replenishment negotiations in the 1980s, its relationship with the United States—its largest shareholder and most important regional nonborrowing member—has also been positive. The IDB's leadership role in the hemisphere was reaffirmed at the 1994 Miami Summit, at which the IDB—along with UN-CEPAL (UN Comisión Económica para América Latina) and the OAS—were mandated to carry forward an ambitious agenda of intensified regional cooperation and economic integration.

Under Enrique Iglesias, its current president, the IDB has embarked on an ambitious program of social sector investment, while continuing to support the move toward both economic and political liberalization throughout Latin America. Tussie emphasizes the role the IDB must play in the fiscal policy of its borrowing members to sustain both the coherence and the momentum of this program. In other words, to support the rebuilding of health, education, and other social sector infrastructure, countries in the region must have in place expenditure plans as well as the taxation and revenue-generating capacity that will sustain recurrent and operating costs in the social sectors. Tussie argues that through policy dialogue, the IDB must assist its borrowing members in reforming fiscal policy. In this context, she also suggests that the IDB help its members in their transition from military and authoritarian rule to democracy by requiring that military expenditures be directed by civilian authorities and that their impact be incorporated into fiscal policy goals.[3]

For such an ambitious agenda to succeed, Tussie recommends a considerable degree of decentralization and delegation in the IDB's operations—from the Board level on down. Among the MDBs, the IDB has the most well-developed network of field offices, with representation in each borrowing country; however, this capacity is substantially underutilized or is wastefully allocated to overseeing the minutiae of loan execution. If field offices are to function more effectively in solving problems during project implementation and as a conduit for grassroots initiatives, the Bank needs to staff the field offices with personnel who have the skills needed for these tasks.[4] As mentioned later, this was also a principal recommendation of the Portfolio Management Task Force.

Whereas the debt problems of the region have ebbed during the 1990s (although they have been replaced by problems associated with capital surging *into* the region), the Mexican peso crisis of 1994–1995 demonstrated that the region is still vulnerable to financial panic and capital flight. Indebtedness is a two-edged threat for the MDBs: It poses economic risks to both the borrowing countries *and* the MDBs (as creditors). In the Americas, debt continues to pose a problem in the smaller, poorer borrowing countries (including Guyana, Nicaragua, Honduras, and Bolivia). To contain the problem for both the borrowers and the IDB, Tussie suggests that more concessional funding through the FSO could be made available to countries such as Peru and Jamaica and that a country risk analysis unit should be set up to anticipate debt problems in these countries, to design lending on more appropriate financial terms for borrowers, and to design debt-reduction programs for the outstanding debts of Nicaragua, Honduras, and Guyana. More controversially, Tussie suggests that such country risk analysis would allow the IDB to develop a graduation policy whereby its largest, most creditworthy borrowers (Argentina, Brazil, Mexico, and Venezuela) could phase out their active borrowing programs (on a reversible basis) to free resources for the smaller and poorer members.[5]

Tussie's most stringent recommendations relate to conditionality in the IDB's lending program. She variously refers to the Bank's loan conditions as politically insensitive[6]—arousing bitter controversy—or redundant, impeding the IDB's operational efficiency and undermining its governance. Some such conditions relate to the borrowing countries' eligibility for loans and seem to overlook country capacities and constraints; others relate to procurement and bidding procedures that keep to the letter rather than the spirit of international competitive bidding. Moreover, the Board, management, and staff have been diverted by a "culture of control" aimed at ensuring that the rules are obeyed rather than at facilitating concrete and long-term results. In general, Tussie maintains that the IDB's loan conditionality should be thoroughly streamlined and geared to building up the often weak institutional capabilities of borrowing members.[7] Again, these recommendations were subsequently echoed by the Portfolio Management Task Force.

Tussie says repeatedly that the transition away from the IDB's culture of control has important implications for the Bank's skills base. Instead of using skills to examine and enforce compliance with loan conditionality, the IDB requires a more subtle set of more pragmatic, judgmental skills to help borrowers with implementation and execution problems. Tussie relates the IDB's relatively high cost of lending to some of these problems. Whereas greater pragmatism would help to contain these costs, Tussie also suggests that for its smallest borrowing members whose loans are fairly small, the IDB is likely to remain inefficient; therefore, it should consider wholesaling its lending through subregional banks such as the Caribbean Development Bank (CDB) (discussed more fully later).[8]

The Asian Development Bank

The AsDB works with some of the most dynamic countries in the developing, and the entire, world. In some ways this has made its task easier, but in other ways its dynamic clientele puts into question its very rationale, or raison d'être. The rapidly growing countries of the region can effectively absorb the large amounts of investment capital its regional bank helps to provide. There is also ample evidence that the borrowing countries are able to access the capital markets directly, without the intermediation of the MDBs. Nonetheless, the AsDB's member countries agreed to a doubling of its capital in 1994 (the first such capital increase in eleven years), thus indicating that the Bank's shareholders—borrowers and nonborrowers alike—see a continuing and growing need for its services and resources despite the region's growing attraction for private capital.

In his survey, Nihal Kappagoda identifies several issues that face the Asian Bank over the next decade. The Bank's portfolio is heavily oriented toward projects (other MDBs are somewhat more inclined toward policy-based lending). Recent evaluation data indicate a marked decline in the ratio of successful projects in the portfolio to 39 percent during 1992, down from 62 percent in the overall period 1974–1991.[9] In all phases of the project cycle (identification, design, implementation, and supervision), the Bank could improve its procedures and thereby enhance the success of its projects. Many of the lessons learned from past projects point to the need for better project preparation, along with better assessments of the capacity of borrowing countries to implement the Bank's projects.[10] These issues are being addressed by the Bank.

Like Tussie, Kappagoda recommends technical assistance by the Bank to enhance the institutional capacity of borrowers to implement projects and maintain them over their lifetimes. He also advocates more flexibility by the Bank in making changes during the course of implementing projects (particularly complex ones) to ensure the expected net benefits actually materialize. Another vital ingredient of project success is the participation of beneficiaries in project preparation and implementation as well as operation and maintenance.[11] These recommendations are amply reflected by the Asian Bank's Task Force on Improving Project Quality.

In reviewing the governance of the Asian Bank, Kappagoda approvingly notes an increased involvement by the Bank's Executive Board in the oversight of country operational strategies; the Board has also continued to approve individual loans. Kappagoda feels helping to shape the Bank's overall lending strategy in each country is a more appropriate role for the Board than its becoming embroiled in the details of individual loans and projects.[12]

The Asian Bank presides over a region that is considerably more diverse (in terms of the historical and cultural roots of its borrowing members) than Latin America or even Africa. This diversity makes the task of Asia's regional bank considerably more complicated than that of the other RDBs. Accordingly, Kappagoda recommends a differentiated lending strategy that recognizes four distinct subregions or groups of borrowers: the newly industrialized economies (NIEs); the low-income countries of South Asia, Indochina, China, and Mongolia; the more advanced countries of Southeast Asia; and the Pacific Island countries.

In Kappagoda's view, such a strategy would call for the NIEs to cease being borrowers and become active lenders and sources of technical assistance (in concert with the AsDB) for the region. Meanwhile, the Bank should continue to support investment in a range of sectors in the low-income countries while working with the Bretton Woods institutions to improve the policy environment and to serve as a catalyst to promote foreign investment. In the advanced countries of Southeast Asia, the Bank should concentrate on physical and social infrastructure investments that represent bottlenecks to further growth. Finally, in the Pacific Island economies, some of which have no demonstrable economic viability, the Bank should coordinate aid from various donors to enhance the effectiveness of these flows as much as possible.[13] Along with other donors, the AsDB should also provide technical assistance to the limit of the region's absorptive capacity.

The African Development Bank

In their study of the African Development Bank, E. Philip English and Harris Mule refer to the lack of indigenous capacity to master the crises that continually beset the continent as the "defining feature of African underdevelopment." In their view, the African Development Bank represents a key—and, on balance, a successful—effort to build such capacity in the region.[14]

English and Mule state, however, that is not sufficient simply to create indigenous capacity; that capacity must be demonstrably effective in tackling the problems for which it was created. They argue that projects are the foundation on which the ADB was built, but its project work has been neglected over the past decade. The authors make a series of recommendations aimed at building or rebuilding the Bank's strengths in this crucial area: through its personnel policy and improved supervision missions, by establishing or reestablishing country offices that have substantive responsibilities, and through learning more systematically from past projects. They argue that macroeconomic policy reform of most African countries should be left to the Bretton Woods institutions, whereas the ADB should concentrate on the region's smallest countries and specialize in the analysis of sectoral problems. English and Mule strongly endorse the view that the quality of lending has suffered in the rush to increase the quantity of lending, and they see the hiatus caused by the 1994–1995 crisis and the change in the presidency as an opportunity to remedy the problem.[15]

At the nub of many of the Bank's problems is its current governance. English and Mule recommend a clearer division of labor between the president and the Board of Directors, with the Board focusing on policies and Bank strategy and the president implementing the Board's decisions. The authors feel a smaller Board would be more effective than the present body of eighteen directors. The president should only be appointed and (if necessary) dismissed by the Board of Governors, as at other MDBs. Most controversially, the authors advocate a radically different sharing of power between regional and nonregional members. Instead of the two-thirds majority of the regionals, as at present, English and Mule recommend parity between the two groups—thus replicating the formula emerging in the IDB following its Eighth Replenishment. A greater share for nonregional members would also reassure capital markets about the Bank's creditworthiness. Finally, the authors recommend that the Bank and its executive directors should do more outreach in order to be more visible and accountable to the citizens and taxpayers on whose behalf they work.[16]

With regard to the Bank's financial health, the authors recommend a series of measures to reverse the decline in net income, including administrative economies and direct and indirect pressures on regional borrowers to meet their repayment obligations fully and on time. The problem of lending to noncreditworthy borrowers should be remedied by a more explicit country risk policy that would render the low-income members ineligible for Bank (nonconcessional) lending; a trust fund should be established to clear up existing arrears and refinance outstanding nonconcessional loans. English and Mule recognize that these measures would deprive low-income members of Bank lending, but they argue that these members need more *concessional* lending, which can only come from donor members.[17]

In general, English and Mule argue that the African Development Bank should "get back to basics," which means core lending operations and especially projects. This does not mean abandoning policy-based lending; rather, the Bank should carve out specific niches—the authors suggest certain sectors in which the ADB has accumulated experience—and selected smaller countries. Regarding projects, the authors recommend retaining the highest priority for agriculture, the economic backbone of most African countries. They believe newer themes—such as good governance, poverty reduction, the environment, and gender—should influence sectoral and project choices; they suggest a particular focus on education, small business, and microenterprise. The authors recommend incorporating these themes into existing operations and advise against special-purpose funds or programs on women's projects, the environment, and so on. English and Mule also say that the private sector should be a high priority and that the Bank may have a special role in attracting private foreign investment to the region.[18]

English and Mule also feel the Bank should exercise more leadership in helping to resolve Africa's problems and in developing its opportunities. With regard to the former, debt continues to severely constrain growth in sub-Saharan Africa; the ADB could champion new debt-relief plans and assist members with their debt-management problems. With regard to opportunities, the Bank is the obvious standard-bearer for regional integration. The ADB should follow up on its study of integration in southern Africa and ensure that its regional initiatives, such as AFREXIMBANK, succeed. Regional leadership, however, requires vision and inspired thinking. To this end, the authors feel additional investment in research capacity is warranted, both in the Bank itself and throughout Africa. Only in this way will the ideas "in power," those that inform African development and change, originate from within Africa rather than from outside.[19]

The Caribbean Development Bank

In the view of Chandra Hardy, the Caribbean Development Bank is one of the most successful subregional development banks. The subregionals constitute a stratum of MDBs that lies below the regional banks; they generally serve a group of borrowers that share borders or geographical or other characteristics and that stand apart from their neighbors in other ways. These siblings of the major multilateral banks operate on a considerably smaller scale: An average CDB loan may be $5 million, whereas loans from the World Bank are seldom under $10 million and are often over $200 million. In aggregate, however, the CDB's loans to its borrowing countries in the 1980s averaged $40 million compared with $70 million from the World Bank.[20] Thus, in terms of its overall volume of lending, the CDB is relatively significant.

Key to the CDB's success has been a portfolio of infrastructure projects such as feeder roads, ports, airports, and power and water utilities that have shown good rates of return. Hardy maintains that the advantage of small, highly focused subregional banks such as the CDB is their ability to make loans for good projects.

These strengths of the CDB, in turn, are derived in part from its smallness. The CDB's costs of delivering projects are lower and it can be more flexible than the larger MDBs. Its staff (dominated by Caribbean nationals) has intimate knowledge of the borrowing countries—their economic problems and opportunities, institutional capacity, and project management abilities. Borrowers are actively involved in project preparation. The CDB has also proved to be an efficient vehicle for pooling bilateral aid in support of regional programs such as basic needs, training, and environmental protection.[21]

The CDB's comparative advantages have not escaped the attention of the larger MDBs, particularly the World Bank. The World Bank's relatively high costs create a situation in which it often loses money in processing the smaller (less than $10 million) loans typically negotiated with small Caribbean countries. Accordingly, in 1990 the two organizations agreed on a Memorandum of Understanding that envisages the CDB as complementing and eventually supplanting some former World Bank roles in the region. For example, the CDB is to undertake all of the investment lending in the microstates of the Organization of Eastern Caribbean States (OECS);[22] a 50:50 blend of World Bank and IDA funds are channeled to the OECS members through the CDB. The memorandum also sets out a division of labor between the two organizations on economic reporting on and adjustment lending to CDB borrowing member countries.[23] Although some inconsistent policies and procedures between the two banks remain, Hardy believes the CDB should become a greater channel of World Bank funds to the region.

Although an amendment to the IDB's charter was approved in 1974 that allowed the Bank to channel funds through the CDB to its member countries and the two institutions agreed upon a Memorandum of Understanding in 1978, little use has been made of the CDB as a "retailer" of IDB funds, in contrast to the situation with the World Bank. Like Tussie, Hardy argues that the IDB should also make more extensive use of the CDB—for example, by using it to lend to the OECS members that do not belong to the IDB. As with the World Bank, inconsistencies exist in lending policies and procedures, but these can be remedied.[24]

The MDB Project: Conclusions

Several conclusions about the regional development banks can be drawn from the MDB project. First and foremost, the studies found that the strengths of these institutions are derived to an important degree from their roots in their respective regions. The relationship of the borrowing member countries with their regional banks is based on the staffs' extensive knowledge of and experience with the problems and possibilities of development in the region. This relationship is frequently augmented by close personal relationships on both sides. These characteristics are perhaps strongest in the IDB (and the CDB), the oldest of the RDBs, in which linguistic and cultural differences among borrowing members are generally not wide. The characteristics are weaker in the Asian Development Bank because of the heterogeneity of the membership and the region, and they are the weakest in the African Development Bank, where members' arrears suggest that the feeling of ownership is often too weak to translate into financial obligations being met fully and on time. Of course, in the case of Africa one must also factor in extenuating circumstances—including the continuing debt problems in the region—that impinge upon relations with the regional bank.

All of the regional banks have built on these foundations to develop strengths as project-delivery agencies. In the case of three of the organizations surveyed (the AsDB, the ADB, and the CDB), projects still constitute the core activity. The IDB is a larger organization that is more able to act as a full-service bank by providing an array of policy-based loans as well as traditional projects. Even in the case of the IDB, however, the incursion of the RDBs into policy-based lending (or economic reform, or structural adjustment lending) received some criticism from the MDB project. Regarding the IDB, the problem has been one of controversy over loan conditionality; in the case of the ADB, the Bank has committed large sums (often through cofinancing with the World Bank) without the staff capability to provide adequate input through economic analysis or supervision. Only in the case of the AsDB[25] has a deliberate decision been made not to go beyond sectoral policy reform and to leave macroeconomic adjustment issues to the Bretton Woods institutions.

This does not mean the regional banks should have no role in policy reform; rather, it means greater selectivity is warranted. A specialization by the regional banks in sectoral policy analysis and reform (as at present in the AsDB) makes more sense than duplication of the responsibilities of the Bretton Woods organizations for macroeconomic analysis and policy design. Frequently, key points of detail in economic reform measures will require considerable expertise and analysis at the sectoral level. The World Bank cannot possibly have experts in every key sector in all of its borrowing member countries. For the regional banks to develop expertise at the sectoral level, they will need to invest in staff who have appropriate skills in research and economic analysis.

At the same time, there is also room for improvement in the domain of projects, where the regional banks continue to find their core strengths and comparative advantage. All of the MDB studies found the banks need to learn more from previous projects and incorporate these lessons into ongoing operations. Many of the weaknesses in projects arise at the borrowers' end and are manifested in inadequate human or financial capacity to implement or sustain projects during their useful life. The regional banks can exploit their local specificity by locating these weaknesses during project design and helping to build up institutional capacity in borrowing countries. The RDBs' local presence (in the form of country offices) could greatly help in this process.

Even in the case of the IDB, which has representation in each borrowing country, the regional bank's local presence represents vastly underutilized potential. In the case of the other RDBs, local representation is meager at best. A more substantive role for country offices would also have staffing implications, not just in terms of numbers of staff in the field but also in terms of their responsibility and autonomy. Rather than acting as "postboxes" in the field (a criticism leveled by Bo Jerlstrom about the ADB), the country offices have the potential to make the RDBs' interaction with local partners more dynamic, participatory, and transformative.

In other words, a measure of *devolution* would benefit the regional banks and their borrowers. In addition to a larger and more substantive role for the country offices, other aspects of devolution affect some RDBs—particularly the ADB—more than others. Perhaps most significantly, the governance of the banks requires reform—from the Executive Boards down to the local staff. The Boards are criticized for excessive attention to detail and insufficient concern with overall policy, strategy, and results. Once policies are agreed upon, it is up to management and staff to implement them and to be judged on the basis on their implementation and results.

Another facet of devolution that emerges from the MDB project refers to devolution among, rather than within, the MDBs. The study of the CDB suggests strong advantages of smallness and local presence. Particularly as MDBs' project portfolios include more social sector and microenterprise and microcredit lending, the typical project or loan will be considerably smaller than that for infrastructure-type projects. The lesson drawn from the MDB project is not necessarily that the larger MDBs should always devolve their lending to the sub-regional banks; that decision depends on the strengths and capabili-

ties of the subregional banks. Whereas the MDB project only examined one RDB (the CDB), it is fair to say that the CDB is among the
strongest of the subregionals.

An alternative channel for devolution is through national financial intermediaries based in the borrowing countries. In the past,
many of these intermediaries were public agencies (Development
Finance Companies [DFCs]), and their track record (with respect to
both performance and accountability) has been less than satisfactory.
If the DFCs cannot be reformed, other intermediaries in the private
sector (for example, commercial banks) could serve as channels for
retailing MDB loans. Alternatively or additionally, the MDBs could
retail their lending through nongovernment organizations as executing agencies for their work in the health, education, microenterprise,
and microcredit sectors.

Meanwhile, the MDBs will likely continue to play a role in large-
scale infrastructure and other projects in which the advantages of
their size (that is, their ability to arrange financing at relatively low
costs to less creditworthy borrowers) are evident and remain valid. A
continuing role for the major MDBs (the World Bank and the regional banks) in these more traditional financing activities therefore
makes much sense.

With regard to the question posed in the title of this book—Titans
or Behemoths?—the MDBs remain "titans" in their traditional fields
of project financing, and despite the increased involvement of the private sector in such financing—particularly for the more creditworthy
borrowing countries—the MDBs have a vital and continuing role in
this area. Their involvement is also critical to bring issues such as
environmental stewardship, poverty, and gender to the table,
because private sector firms are unlikely to always bring such public
policy objectives explicitly into their projects.

Regarding smaller projects and smaller-scale financing, however,
the larger MDBs may be lumbering "behemoths": They are too large,
high-cost, and distant to perform effectively and efficiently. These
projects seem destined to represent a growing share of MDB lending;
thus, it is critical for the MDBs to work with local or subregional partners that can deliver the projects with maximum long-run sustainable
benefits.

The Portfolio Reviews

The World Bank's Portfolio Management Task Force Report

Launched in February 1992, the task force reviewed a considerable
amount of documentation, including both the regular annual opera-

tions reports and specially commissioned papers. Drafts of the report were inadvertently leaked, which created considerable anticipation for the final version.

Five major conclusions emerged. First, the Bank's success should be measured by "on-the-ground" benefits or "sustainable development impact" rather than by internal measures or the volume of loan approvals. Second, successful implementation requires borrower commitment or "ownership." Third, successful project outcomes require high-quality projects and planning for results-oriented implementation from the beginning. Fourth, the proper context for evaluating the project portfolio is the "country focus" to address generic problems and opportunities. Finally, portfolio performance must be taken into account throughout the Bank if it is to remain effective.

The "performance problem" was documented by a sharp escalation in the number of projects judged to be unsatisfactory at completion, from 15 percent in 1980–1981 to 37.5 percent in 1990–1991. Projects with "major problems" increased from 11 percent to 20 percent of the portfolio over the same period. In other words, the number of projects that performed poorly essentially doubled during the 1980s.[26]

The report blamed several factors for the deterioration, including worsening global conditions (for example, the oil shock and the debt crisis) as well as country-specific factors. These factors were uncontrollable. Several factors, however, were attributable to the Bank's own policies and procedures. Most prominent among these was the "approval culture" that emphasizes timely approval of loans at the cost of assuring the quality of underlying projects. In particular, the projects' sensitivity to various risks and their implementability are not properly appraised, which leads to a bias toward overly complex design.

In addition, a series of other weaknesses in the Bank's management of project implementation were identified. Procurement was mentioned as a prominent problem area; Bank policies were often poorly understood, and country capabilities to administer the procedures (for international competitive bidding) were often weak.

Finally, the report identified shortcomings in the portfolio performance system. This system is still geared to project-by-project evaluation rather than countrywide assessment and also pays insufficient attention to actual development impact, since much of the evaluation takes place after final disbursement and, therefore, prior to the realization of most of the projects' benefits.

The report made a series of recommendations to remedy the problems identified. These included the introduction of country portfolio performance management, the provision of country portfolio restructuring to reallocate undisbursed loan balances when projects perform poorly, the improvement of the quality of projects when they enter the project pipeline, the improvement of project performance management and the internal environment to support the improvements, and the refocusing of ex post evaluation on sustainable development impact.

The report's principal organizational thrust was to make the country portfolio the unit of managerial accountability, and the ultimate objective was to achieve sustainable development benefits through more efficient implementation of a high-quality lending portfolio.[27] Its endorsement of a shift from quantity to quality lending, in the sense of measuring success in terms of sustainable development results rather than the amount of loans signed or capital invested, marked a fundamental change in the philosophy of the Bank—a change that had profound repercussions for both the Bank's own operations and its relations with borrowing member countries.

The Inter-American Development Bank's Portfolio Management Task Force Report

The World Bank's portfolio review was undertaken as an internal exercise, drawing upon the Bank's own analyses and staff. In contrast, the IDB commissioned a distinguished group of independent experts under the chairmanship of Moeen A. Qureshi, former senior vice-president (operations) of the World Bank.[28] The objective of the task force was "to advise Management on the institutional and other measures which can be taken to strengthen portfolio management, particularly in support of project implementation."[29]

The task force began its work in February 1993 and submitted its report in October the same year. The task force criticized the "control mentality" of the IDB, which discouraged innovation and risk-taking and did not reward initiatives that produced development results. Moreover, the IDB lacked the project assessment system available to the World Bank; the task force concluded bluntly that the Bank thus could not satisfactorily gauge the development impact of its lending.[30] Indeed, the IDB task force report has no counterpart to the detailed, quantified account given in the Wapenhans Report of the deteriorating World Bank portfolio.

Many of the report's recommendations were aimed at supplanting the control mentality with a culture oriented toward improving the performance of the portfolio with regard to socioeconomic development objectives. The report recommended many organizational changes to bring about such a cultural reform—changes involving the Board, management, Country Offices, and the newly unified

Evaluation Office. It also recommended new mechanisms through which the IDB's success could be properly gauged. Central to its recommendations was a proposal that each of the IDB's Country Offices[31] prepare annual country portfolio assessments, which would become integral to formulating the IDB's country assistance strategies. Parallel to the procedure in the World Bank, the report recommended that management submit to the Board an annual Portfolio Management Report (based on the country portfolio assessments) that would become the basis for assessing the quality of the portfolio and the development impact of its lending.

Many of the report's recommendations involved giving the Country Offices greater responsibility and latitude in project administration and decisionmaking. Other recommendations dealt with Board-management relations. The report suggested that the Board should concentrate on broad policy issues but should delegate to management full responsibility for day-to-day operations.

Finally, the report made some recommendations regarding the duties and responsibilities of the new Evaluation Office that were aimed at more independent assessments of the development impact of the Bank and its overall effectiveness in each borrowing country. If these recommendations were put in place, the IDB would then have the necessary tools to determine the nature and extent of its lending problems in each country.

The Asian Development Bank's Task Force Report

The Asian Development Bank Task Force was set up in April 1993 and reported in January 1994. Similar to the World Bank portfolio review, the Asian Bank's review was internally commissioned and was headed by Gunther Schultz, one of the Bank's two vice-presidents. The similarities went further, perhaps because the Asian Bank is the MDB most like the World Bank. First, the AsDB's evaluation and appraisal system was sufficiently reputable to allow the task force to base some broad judgments on its findings. For example, the task force indicated that a fifth of the projects under implementation were experiencing problems to various degrees. The report found that the overall quality of the portfolio was "reasonably satisfactory" but allowed that "it needs to be improved."[32]

The report indicated that improvements in project and portfolio quality would come from three sources: better client orientation, enhanced borrower ownership and institutional capacity, and improved accountability for quality within the Bank. The task force found that client orientation was undermined by an "approval culture" (again echoing the Wapenhans Report) that rewarded the achievement of lending targets and overlooked local needs, demands, and absorptive capacities. The report also recommended strengthening both the Bank's country focus (through better country program and project design, links with economic and sector work, and country documentation) and its internal capacity to "meet the increasing complexity of development challenges."[33]

With regard to borrower ownership and institutional capacity, the task force recommended capacity building to assist some borrowers in designing and implementing projects, as well as greater participation by borrowers in the design of projects, and through contributing financial and human resources. Finally, with regard to accountability for quality within the Bank, the report recommended changes to ensure that project administration and implementation are accorded as much importance as other aspects of project preparation. The task force also recommended greater flexibility for project staff to reallocate resources to remedy problems as they are encountered and suggested that learning from past experience be enhanced.

The two salient implications of the task force report were, first, to reassert the importance of development impact rather than loan approval as the fundamental objective of the Bank and, second, to strengthen the Bank's country focus through local capacity building and other measures.

The African Development Bank's
Task Force on Project Quality Report

The African Development Bank's Task Force on Project Quality reported in April 1994, the last of the MDB portfolio reviews to be completed. Like the IDB task force (and unlike the World Bank and AsDB committees), the members of the task force were independent experts (chaired by David Knox, a former vice-president of the World Bank),[34] and the exercise took place outside the Bank. The review was similar to the IDB's in other ways as well.

The task force identified three main sets of challenges. First, the shareholders have conflicting goals and attitudes that point the Bank in different directions. Second, significant gaps exist between the Bank's formal policies and its actual practice. Third, the "Bank is absent when it should be present" in identifying, preparing, and implementing projects and ensuring a sustainable development impact from its efforts.

The task force recommended reallocating resources to the Bank's operational departments and using those resources more efficiently. Second, the report indicated that the Bank's culture needed to change from one that emphasized the quantity of lending to one that focused on lending quality; some staff changes would be necessary to accomplish this. Finally, the task force addressed the governance of the Bank—it recommended a clarification of the duties and responsibilities of the Board and management to enable both to function more effectively.[35]

The task force report stated baldly that "the Bank does not have a comprehensive reporting system to assess the quality and the status of its portfolio" and that it was "unable to quantify precisely the Bank portfolio's contribution to development in Africa."[36] The report criticized the Bank's project evaluation system as haphazard and unrepresentative of the portfolio. As a result, the task force recommended putting in place a comprehensive reporting system to monitor projects and assess the status of the portfolio in an attempt to strengthen portfolio management and Board oversight of the Bank's policies. Many of these recommendations were directed at the Bank's evaluation procedures and policies.

The report made extensive recommendations regarding the Bank's lending procedures, which it found were generally sound but were not applied in practice. The task force attributed the Bank's lack of capacity to be an active participant in identifying and implementing high-quality projects to a shortage of staff who had relevant skills. In general, the report criticized the Bank for attempting to do too much with too little. Changes in organizational structure were recommended that would strengthen country focus, ensure project quality, delegate decisionmaking to the lowest practicable level, and ensure cost-effectiveness.

On the Bank's governance, the report advocated clarifying the roles of the Board of Directors and the president. In particular, it recommended that only the Board of Governors should have the right to dismiss or suspend the president. The Executive Board should be responsible for policy, and the president should oversee day-to-day management. The task force recommended term limits for executive directors and the sole right of the president to appoint vice-presidents, with the exception of the new post of vice-president, evaluation, which should be appointed by and report to the Executive Board.

Common Themes

Three interconnected issues emerged with almost astonishing regularity in all four task force reports:

- The need exists to end the MDBs' "approval culture," oriented toward a targeted volume of annual lending, and replace it with an emphasis on enhancing the *quality* of projects and the lending portfolio generally.

- Quality, in turn, is to be assured principally with respect to the *long-term development impact* on client countries rather than principally in terms of the MDBs' internal indicators.

- Finally, the most rational way to enhance the MDBs' portfolio quality and assure long-term impact is through *country focus*— that is, by organizing, adjusting as necessary, and assessing the portfolio at the country level with an eye on local constraints, possibilities, and indicators of development achievement.

All four reviews essentially blamed the MDBs' shortcomings on their propensity to "move money" rather than "achieve results." To achieve results (defined as sustainable development impact), however, the MDBs would have to go about their business somewhat differently. In particular, they would have to situate their efforts in the overall context of each borrowing country to seek quality projects specific to its needs and demands; to help create capacity for project identification, design, and implementation and thereby to help foster local ownership; and to better understand and appraise the performance of the overall lending portfolio and make adjustments along the way to enhance the long-term development impact.

The Development Committee MDB Task Force

The African Bank's task force reported in spring 1994 just as the Bretton Woods institutions were preparing to celebrate their fiftieth anniversary; it was a time of reflection on the achievements of these two institutions and on their future—indeed, on their relevance in a world that was very different from the one into which they had been born.[37] The fact that four MDBs had recently completed searching reviews of the effectiveness of their lending portfolios—reviews that had exposed some serious problems—had not escaped the attention of the key shareholders of the organizations. Thus, it seemed timely to review the entire family of MDBs (that is, the principal regional banks and the World Bank) together to deliberate on their future as a group of development institutions. This review was to be conducted in a formal setting and under the aegis of the shareholders.

The sponsor of this exercise was the IMF–World Bank Development Committee,[38] a forum that brought together ministerial representatives of developed and developing countries—ministers who already exercised oversight over the World Bank. The main impetus for the task force came from the United States—from Congress in particular, which was pressing to increase its oversight of the MDBs. At its meeting in April 1994, the Development Committee decided to create a Task Force on Multilateral Development Banks. Subsequently, in December of that year a committee of eighteen members was formed under the chairmanship of Abdlatif Al-Hamad, a Kuwaiti who was the director-general of the Arab Fund for Economic and Social Development. Eight members were from OECD countries, six from developing countries, two from countries in transition (Hungary and Russia), and two from major oil-exporting states.[39]

The terms of reference were approved by the Development Committee at its meeting in Madrid in October 1994. The task force was asked to assume a broad consensus on the principal objectives of the development process (for example, sustainable economic growth and poverty reduction) and to concentrate on how the MDBs would apply these objectives in practice.

In particular, the task force was asked first to "assess the implications of economic change for the development priorities, instruments, operations, and management of the five principal MDBs"; to accord "particular attention . . . to identifying 'best practice' successes in reducing poverty"; to consider "how the MDBs could best support the development process at a time when the private sector is playing a bigger role than in the past"; and, drawing on the recent portfolio reviews, to identify "where lessons learned by individual MDBs in improving portfolio performance can be replicated throughout the MDB system." Second, the task force was asked to "evaluate procedures and practices for coordination among the MDBs and other members of the development community, and consider whether it is possible to make any improvements on a regional, country or sector basis."[40]

The MDB task force brought down its report in March 1996; the following month the report was accepted by the Development Committee at its meeting in Washington, D.C. The report concluded that even though the world had changed considerably since the MDBs were created, the challenges of development remain great. Response to the needs of 1.3 billion poor in developing countries, increased population pressures, widened economic disparities, new challenges in countries in transition from centrally planned to market economies, more frequent need for reconstruction, and new environmental threats all require fresh energy, thinking, and resources.

The task force concluded that the MDBs should continue to play a vital role in all of these areas. Regarding the resurgent private sector, the report held that although private international capital flows have grown dramatically, they are focused on a relatively small number of developing countries. This situation should allow the MDBs to concentrate on activities and countries that do not readily attract stable private financing but, at the same time, to continue to contribute to infrastructure investment, policy reform, human development, capacity building, public administration modernization, and the environment.[41]

In its recommendations, the report reaffirmed the current roles of the MDBs—namely, to mobilize international savings for sustainable development, to ensure access of poorer countries to concessional resources, and to initiate policies and processes of graduation for countries that have reliable access to the international capital markets. In addition, the MDBs should act as sources of advice, experience, and research; support the transition to market systems of centrally planned economies; and support reconstruction and peace building in war-torn countries.

The report was particularly emphatic about the centrality of poverty reduction to the MDBs' work. It recommended, among other things, that the MDBs should focus their assistance on countries that demonstrate a strong commitment to reducing poverty as part of a soundly based economic and social reform program and that they should set explicit targets by country for their poverty work.[42]

The task force also concluded that the MDBs have a legitimate role in promoting effective government and a strong civil society, in making development environmentally sustainable, and in investing in infrastructure and utilities (along with private sector and local participation). Regarding private sector development, the report recommended that the MDBs should continue to provide an "enabling environment" for the private sector through a range of complementary measures, including appropriate public policies and infrastructure. The task force was somewhat more cautious about direct assistance from the MDBs for private sector activities, stating that the case for such support needs to demonstrate additionality and also a contribution to development or transition.[43]

The task force made a series of recommendations on enhancing the effectiveness of the MDBs, or "striving for results." It pointed to the need to upgrade the role of the Executive Boards and emphasized their importance in making strategic choices, particularly with respect to each MDB's country assistance strategies. The report also recommended that the MDBs foster borrower ownership, that the MDBs learn from each other's experience by harmonizing performance indicators and evaluation criteria, that the MDBs and borrowers do more to stimulate individual and collective participation in their work, and that the MDBs demonstrate heightened cost consciousness in their budgets and overall efficiency.[44] Finally, the report recommended intensifying coordination among the MDBs, at the country level, by helping borrowing members to assume responsibility for coherence between national strategies and international assistance; at the level of the MDBs, by promoting convergence of their policies, processes, and practices; and between the MDBs and others, through guiding coherent policy and fostering complementarity of programs and convergence of operational policies.[45]

Conclusion: Relations Between the MDBs and Related Organizations

The issue of coordination between, and complementarity among, the MDBs was at the heart of the mandate of the Development Committee Task Force. Similar questions could also be raised about coordination and complementarity between the MDBs and other organizations. Foremost among such organizations, perhaps, is the International Monetary Fund. There is also the host of organizations in the UN family—from the United Nations Development Programme (UNDP) to the United Nations Children's Fund (UNICEF), the Food and Agriculture Organization (FAO), the United Nations Conference on Trade and Development (UNCTAD), and so on—as well as the newly formed World Trade Organization, created during the Uruguay Round as the supreme body to oversee international trade policies and relations. There are also many subregional organizations, including, for example, the Caribbean Development Bank and the Arab Fund for Economic and Social Development. Finally, there are many bilateral agencies, most prominently national donor agencies in each of the OECD countries plus those of a few oil-exporting countries.

None of these relationships was explored by the Development Committee Task Force, since they were beyond its terms of reference. It is regrettable that those terms did not specifically include the IMF, since that body engages in work that is highly complementary to and sometimes overlaps that of the MDBs. Moreover, the IMF is constitutionally a part of the Development Committee, and the sometimes uneasy World Bank–IMF relations have occasioned several policy discussions in the Development Committee and elsewhere (for example, at the G7 Summit at Halifax in 1995). Thus, inclusion of the IMF would have been a natural extension of the terms of reference; moreover, it would have been informative to subject the relationships between the IMF and each of the regional banks to scrutiny—something that has never been done.

Notes

1. World Bank, *Effective Implementation.*
2. The Development Committee's formal title is the "Joint Ministerial Committee on the Transfer of Real Resources to the Developing Countries."
3. Tussie, *The Inter-American Development Bank,* pp. 117–119.
4. Ibid., p. 119.
5. Ibid., pp. 127, 133–134. Tussie acknowledges that the withdrawal of the larger borrowing members might weaken the overall portfolio. The logical implication of such an argument, however, would be to never graduate any borrowers; indeed, the admission of richer countries into the borrowing program could be rationalized.
6. Tussie cites as an example the policy conditions of investment sector loans aimed at the protection of intellectual property rights. She argues that such conditions cannot presently be justified either in theory or in practice. Ibid., p. 131.
7. Ibid., pp. 130–131, 134–136.
8. Ibid., pp. 136–137.
9. Kappagoda, *The Asian Development Bank,* p. 90.
10. Ibid., pp. 95–96.
11. Ibid., p. 96.
12. Ibid., p. 99.
13. Ibid., pp. 127–133.
14. English and Mule, *The African Development Bank,* p. 9.
15. Ibid., pp. 10–11.
16. Ibid., pp. 11–12.
17. Ibid., pp. 12–13. Unfortunately, the authors' plea went unheeded in the Seventh Replenishment of the African Development Fund, on which negotiations produced an agreement only for U.S.$20 billion, in comparison with $3.42 billion pledged for ADF-6 (and even the $2.8 billion hoped for earlier in the replenishment negotiations).
18. Ibid., pp. 13–14.
19. Ibid., pp. 14–15.
20. Hardy, *The Caribbean Development Bank,* p. 93.
21. Ibid., p. 5.
22. The Organization of Eastern Caribbean States is a group of seven small island nations (Antigua and Barbuda, Dominica, Grenada, Montserrat, St. Kitts-Nevis, St. Lucia, and St. Vincent and the Grenadines).
23. Hardy, *The Caribbean Development Bank,* pp. 95–97.
24. Ibid., pp. 97–98.
25. As well as the Caribbean Development Bank.
26. World Bank, *Effective Implementation,* p. ii.
27. Ibid., p. v.
28. The members of the task force were Horace Barber (Jamaica), Gerhard Boehmer (Germany), Rubens Vaz da Costa (Brazil), John Robinson (Canada), and Abelardo Valdez (United States). Yves Rovani, former director-general of the World Bank's Operations Evaluation Department, served as principal adviser.
29. Inter-American Development Bank, *Managing for Effective Development,* Annex A, p. 2.
30. Ibid., p. 31.
31. The IDB has a representative office in each borrowing country. The

task force criticized the IDB, however, for underutilizing these field offices and for according them little status and responsibility relative to the head-quarters complex in Washington. The report thus recommended a substantial devolution of responsibilities in the preparation and execution of projects to the Country Offices.

32. Asian Development Bank, *Report of the Task Force on Improving Project Quality*, p. iii. Elsewhere the report states that 60 percent of the Bank's projects are "generally successful," 30 percent "partly successful" and 10 percent "unsuccessful" (pp. 2–3).

33. Ibid., p. iii.

34. The other members were Yves Rovani (who also participated in the IDB task force), Amidou Oumar Sy, Donald Sherk, S. Ben Said, Mansour Khalid, E. Tetegan, and E. Olsen. Two of these men were former ADB executive directors, and two were former directors of the Bank.

35. African Development Bank, *The Quest for Quality*, pp. 1–2.

36. Ibid., p. 6.

37. Many NGOs, particularly in the North, believed the Bretton Woods institutions had done more harm than good and mobilized under the campaign slogan "Fifty Years Is Enough!" Danaher, *50 Years Is Enough*.

38. More formally, the Joint Ministerial Committee of the IMF and World Bank on the Transfer of Real Resources to the Developing Countries. The Development Committee was formed in parallel with the Interim Committee in 1974 in the aftermath of the breakdown of the Bretton Woods fixed-parity exchange rate system and during the growing debate on the new international economic order. Both committees have an advisory capacity rather than a policymaking role; the Interim Committee advises on IMF and international monetary matters, whereas the Development Committee advises on World Bank and development matters. The memberships of the committees reflect those of the Executive Boards of the IMF and the World Bank but at the level of governor rather than executive director; thus, the member tends to be a minister, typically a minister of finance. As in the Executive Boards, each member represents a constituency that varies in composition from one country (for the United States, Japan, Germany, France, the UK, and China) to two dozen in the case of the African constituencies. More frequently than not, the same minister represents the constituency on both the Interim and the Development Committee. The committees meet twice yearly, in April and at the time of the IMF–World Bank annual meetings in late September or early October.

39. The other members, with their nationalities, were Montek Singh Ahluwalia (India), Robert Ainscow (UK), Laszlo Akar (Hungary), Jobarah Al-Suraisry (Saudi Arabia), Alhaji Abubakar Alhaji (Nigeria), Victor Komla Alipui (Togo), Tom Bernes (Canada), Sergio Silva do Amaral (Brazil), Nicolás Flaño C. (Chile), Haruhiko Kuroda (Japan), Joop B. Hoekman (Netherlands), Neil Hyden (Australia), Zhang Junyi (China), Alexander A. Khandruev (Russia), Francis Mayer (France), Ole Lansmann Poulsen (Denmark), and Jeffrey Shafer (United States). Each of the five MDBs was formally represented by an official, and the task force was given a small secretariat, headed by Willi Wapenhans, as well as a budget with which to commission some background studies. Development Committee, *Serving a Changing World*, Annex and Attachment.

40. Ibid., Annex.

41. Ibid., p. ii.

42. Ibid., p. vii.
43. Ibid., pp. iii, ix.
44. Ibid., pp. x–xi.
45. Ibid., p. xii.

4

MDBs AS AGENTS OF CHANGE: THE DEVELOPMENT IMPACT

With the hindsight of five decades of experience, how should the performance of the multilateral development banks be judged? Such a question poses profound dilemmas, the kind historians and anthropologists must typically deal with in considering human organizations, events, and behavior of a time or place different from their own.

The multilateral development banks, which, except for the EBRD, were created between 1944 and 1965, present such dilemmas to those who wish to assess them today. But many present-day critics place an unreasonable burden on the past performance of the MDBs, forgetting that these institutions were founded in a different era with objectives that were both less clear and less rigorous than those currently demanded from them. It is necessary at the least to understand the context in which they were created to undertake a balanced assessment of their achievements. To judge the historical performance of the MDBs by the growing expectations placed upon them in the 1990s can be both unrealistic and unfair.

For present purposes, it seems appropriate to divide the historical period under review into two phases. The first phase lasted about thirty years, ending in the mid-1970s. In this period, the MDBs (along with development agencies generally) gave primacy to *resource inputs*—particularly capital for investment, since capital was relatively scarce in developing countries. It was assumed that more investment would lead to higher economic growth (technically, growth in real gross national product [GNP] per capita), which for most of the period was widely accepted as the only development outcome that mattered.[1]

The second phase began in the mid-1970s and is still in progress. In this current phase, the MDBs (again, along with most development agencies) have been more concerned with specific *development outcomes* (apart from economic growth) rather than simply with the inputs channeled to the developing countries. In this phase, a steady accretion of outcomes has been expected from development, with each occasioning some debate and not always commanding a consensus. The objectives have included poverty reduction, economic policy reform, environmental sustainability, gender equity, participation, and good governance—indeed, the list seems to keep growing.

The First Three Decades
(1945–1975): From Investment to Growth

During the period in which all of the MDBs except the EBRD were established, the world was a different place, and prevailing assumptions about "development" were unlike those of the 1990s and were more simplistic. The epoch spanned roughly three decades—from 1945, when the World Bank was founded, to 1975, by the end of which the World Bank and the Inter-American, African, and Asian Banks had all established the structures and mechanisms we see today—with soft and hard windows, affiliated agencies, periodic capital increases and replenishments, and so on.

Most theorists and practitioners of development during this period, under the influence of theories propagated by Roy Harrod[2] and Evsey Domar[3] (which became melded together in the Harrod-Domar growth model[4]), emphasized *investment* and *economic growth*. What mattered was the overall rate of growth of the economy. Who benefited from growth or how growth affected the *distribution* of wealth and poverty were questions rarely raised in the 1950s and 1960s.[5]

From the vantage point of the 1990s, it is significant that the word *poverty* did not even appear in the IBRD's Articles of Agreement.[6] It is worth citing from Article 1, which indicates that the Bank had five purposes:

1. to assist in the reconstruction and development of territories of members by facilitating the investment of capital for productive purposes
2. to promote private foreign investment by means of guarantees or participations in loans and other investments
3. to promote the long-range balanced growth of international trade and the maintenance of equilibrium in the balance of payments by encouraging international investment for the development of productive resources of members, *thereby*

assisting in raising productivity, the standard of living and conditions of labor[7] in their territories

4. to arrange the loans made or guaranteed by it in relation to international loans through other channels
5. to conduct its operations with due regard to the effect of international investment on business conditions in the territories of members[8]

By 1960, when the International Development Association (IDA)—the World Bank's concessional-lending affiliate—was established, the conceptualization of the Bank's fundamental purposes had changed little. The Articles of Agreement establishing IDA state that

> The purposes of the Association are to promote economic development, increase productivity and thus raise standards of living in the less-developed areas of the world . . . by providing finance to meet their important development requirements on terms which are more flexible and bear less heavily on the balance of payments than those of conventional loans.[9]

The centrality of *investment, loans,* and *the balance of payments* in the basic purposes of the World Bank reflects the notion that until the 1960s, capital was regarded as the "engine" of development. Developing countries were seen as facing capital scarcity; industrial countries, in contrast, were capital abundant. The chain of causation in the development process envisaged capital, invested prudently, as increasing productivity and thereby raising living standards.

The first question prompted by this view was, Why were the MDBs needed to stimulate flows of capital to the developing countries? If markets functioned properly, capital would flow naturally from industrial to developing countries—that is, from capital-abundant economies, where returns are low, to capital-scarce economies where they are relatively high. The financial turmoil of the 1930s, however, with widespread default on debt by developing country borrowers, suggested to the architects of Bretton Woods that the capital markets were unlikely to be reliable agents of development in the postwar era.[10]

Thus, the purpose of the MDBs was to overcome capital market failure: They were seen as agents to facilitate the transfer of private capital from North to South, which would otherwise take place only at a much lower level. This prompted a second question: How would the MDBs discharge this function of financial intermediation? As the World Bank's Articles of Agreement make clear, the Bank was originally envisaged as a catalyst, guaranteeing private flows (for example, bonds sold to investors in the principal markets by developing countries) rather than lending on its own account. This role was not fulfilled for several reasons. The World Bank discovered early in its history that it could borrow more cheaply than its client members in the New York market. Intermediation by the Bank thus became preferred to guarantees by all three parties: the bond underwriters, who felt more comfortable dealing with the World Bank than with a series of disparate and relatively unknown borrowing countries; the borrowing countries, which could obtain lower costs through the Bank than by borrowing directly; and the Bank itself, since lending on its own account gave it more control (through loan conditionality) over investment of the proceeds than it would have had as a more passive guarantor of the borrowers' own bonds.

Moreover, if the Bank had opted for guarantees instead of loans, that situation would probably have led to differential costs among borrowers—with large, well-known borrowers paying less than smaller, less-known borrowers. In addition to the horizontal inequities such a situation would have introduced among borrowers, a shadow might also have been cast on the Bank's creditworthiness if some of the bonds it guaranteed were quoted at a low rate. Finally, since the Bank's Articles constrained the sum of its guarantees and lending to a maximum equal to its capital and reserves, guarantees and loans competed with each other for the Bank's limited intermediation capacity. It was inevitable that cheaper loans would crowd out more expensive guarantees.[11]

Thus, the World Bank established itself primarily as a lender on its own account to its developing member countries. The Bank sought to become an intermediary by raising its own funds in the northern capital markets and on-lending these to its developing country members at a spread over its costs to cover administrative and other expenses. To do this, it had to demonstrate its creditworthiness as an issuer of bonds in the U.S. market by winning the confidence and support of the investment community and of government supervisors at the federal and state levels. Much of the work of the Bank's first three presidents and their administrations (Eugene Meyer, John McCloy, and Eugene Black, spanning the period 1946–1963) was devoted to this task, with highly successful results. Once solidly established as a borrower in the U.S. market, the Bank began to diversify its sources of borrowing to other markets in Canada and Europe.[12]

The evolution of the World Bank into a direct lender rather than a guarantor of other creditors' loans was a significant departure from its original conception as a passive catalyst of private capital that would tend to flow spontaneously to developing countries. Instead, the Bank became a proactive (as opposed to a passive) lender, seeking out investment opportunities—typically in infrastructure projects. This position strengthened the assumption that without the Bank's intervention, capital would not flow at the levels required by the developing countries. To seek out opportunities proficiently required a staff competent to assess not only the financial merits but also the technical merits of the projects for which the Bank was considering support, since the skilled personnel required to propose and design sound projects were typically scarce in developing countries. In other words, the Bank had to equip itself with the engineering, agronomic, and other kinds of expertise necessary to satisfy itself that the projects it financed were indeed sound and would make their intended contribution to the local economy.

The putative failure of private capital markets to lend sufficiently to many poorer countries also made the MDBs cautious. From the viewpoint of commercial banks, it seemed risky to provide loans to borrowers whose creditworthiness (that is, ability to service debt) in many cases (e.g., newly independent countries) had never been put to the test. Although the MDBs were development banks rather than commercial banks, they nevertheless had to ensure that they were not putting their own capital (in practical terms, the capital subscriptions of the richer member countries) at risk. For this reason, the World Bank's Articles included a provision to the effect that in making or guaranteeing a loan, "the Bank shall pay due regard to the prospects that the borrower . . . will be in a position to meet its obligations under the loan."[13] That same Article also contains a provision under which the repayment of principal and payment of interest and other loan charges must be fully guaranteed by the government of the borrowing member country, its central bank, or some other agency acceptable to the Bank.[14]

These two provisions, which were reproduced by other MDBs,[15] had important ramifications during their evolution. First and foremost, the guarantee by the borrower government meant in practice that a very large portion of MDB loans went to government agencies rather than to private borrowers. This issue developed ideological overtones during the Cold War, when assistance to state-owned enterprises was seen by some critics—particularly those in the United States—of the new multilateral institutions as tantamount to support of socialism and Soviet-style central planning. Consequently, very early in its life (1956) the World Bank established an affiliate—the International Finance Corporation (IFC)—whose mandate was to lend to or invest directly in private sector enterprises in developing countries *without* the cover of a guarantee from the borrowing member government.

But in many developing countries the private sector was small and opportunities to invest in private entities were limited; thus, for the first three decades of its existence, the IFC was a marginal lender compared with the main part of the World Bank group. This situation fueled an ongoing debate by the same conservative critics, some of whom continued to see the World Bank and other multilateral agencies as stalking horses for Soviet communism—even though the Soviet Union never joined any of the MDBs. Even in the 1990s, after the demise of the Soviet Union and of central planning throughout most of the world, the role of the MDBs in supporting the private sector has remained a prominent issue among members.

Even if the MDBs' loans were guaranteed by borrowing member governments, however, this did not assure repayment of principal and interest charges. It is important to note, first, that MDBs make loans in usable (i.e., convertible) currencies, which during this period were overwhelmingly U.S. dollars but that gradually included other currencies as well (European and Japanese); second, MDB loans must be repaid in such a way that the banks are not exposed to any losses from appreciation of exchange rates.[16] By the end of the 1950s, it was evident that most poorer countries' needs for foreign exchange were likely to exceed the amounts available to them from export earnings and other sources, a situation that undermined their ability to service debt even on the excellent terms available through the MDBs.

The other major ramification for the evolution of the MDBs was that the poorer borrowers—including India, Pakistan, and Indonesia in the 1950s—were both unwilling and unable to absorb large amounts of debt on commercial terms. Accordingly, during the 1950s several developing countries began a campaign at the United Nations to institute a multilateral development fund based on grants rather than loans. The story of the diplomatic maneuvering that took place is told elsewhere,[17] but the upshot was the creation in 1960 of a new facility—based on soft, interest-free loans rather than grants—at the World Bank. The new entity, the International Development Association, had been presaged the previous year by the Inter-American Development Bank, which had been created with a full-blown soft-loan window, the Fund for Special Operations.

Once the soft-loan facilities had been established at the IDB and the World Bank (by 1973 they were also established at the Asian and African Banks), the notion of the MDBs as capital-transfer mechanisms became entrenched in the official policy of aid donor countries.[18] The growing indebtedness of the MDBs' poorer borrowers was no longer a constraint on their absorptive capacity for soft loans. Periodic and mounting replenishments of the MDBs' soft windows became routine in the rapidly growing international aid bureaucracy.

Thus, World Bank President George Woods articulated the conventional wisdom of the time (1966) when he said that "developing countries could put to constructive use, over the next five years, some $3 to $4 billion more than is currently being made available to them."[19]

The ethos of transferring capital soon spread from the concessional ("Fund") facilities to the conventional ("Bank") portion of the MDBs, which led to a dramatic expansion of the capacity of both windows under Robert McNamara's presidency of the World Bank (1968–1981). A thirteen-fold increase in lending by the Bank and the IDA (considered together) raised commitment levels from $953 million in 1968 to $12.4 billion in 1981.[20] This increase occurred at the same time McNamara was redirecting the focus of the World Bank toward poverty reduction. Old habits die hard, however, and the practice of transferring large amounts of capital had considerable inertia. But the rationale of large-scale capital transfer through the Bank was quickly and seamlessly transformed. Previously, the stimulation of economic growth was an end in itself; now it was seen as a means toward the alleviation of mass poverty.

Cynics have come to caricature the transformation of the MDBs from promoters of long-term development into agencies that "move money." It is wise, however, to put the MDBs' money-moving efforts into perspective. To begin with, although the total amount of MDB disbursements (concessional and nonconcessional) did increase significantly, from $1.74 billion in 1960 to $9.47 billion in 1975, and the share in total flows to developing countries more than doubled, this represented only 11.2 percent of total flows at the end of the period—indicating that the MDBs still accounted for only a small portion of overall capital flows (see Table 4.1).

Table 4.1   Resource Flows to Developing Countries, 1960–1975

	1960–1961	1970	1975
Bilateral official development assistance	18.60	19.38	25.88
Multilateral official development assistance	0.94	2.80	5.71
Multilateral loans	0.80	1.86	3.76
Subtotal, multilateral flows	1.74	4.66	9.47
Export credits	4.83	7.01	8.35
Private flows	8.72	18.30	35.35
Total resource flows	34.83	53.09	84.59
Multilateral flows as percent of total	5.00	8.80	11.20
Private flows as percent of total	25.00	34.50	41.80

Source: OECD, Twenty-Five Years of Development Co-operation: A Review.

Among multilateral development institutions, however, the MDBs accounted for a rapidly growing share of total multilateral flows. The other main source of multilateral financing—the UN family—matched the MDBs in terms of concessional financing, but in contrast to the MDB group the United Nations did not (and still does not) provide nonconcessional financing, which generated 50 percent more financing than the MDBs' concessional windows (see Table 4.2).

Table 4.2   MDBs' and Other Multilateral Development Institutions' Net Disbursements (at 1983 prices and exchange rates)

	1965–1966	1970–1971	1975–1976
Concessional flows			
MDBs	696.0	1,127.0	2,326.0
UN agencies	666.0	1,330.0	1,984.0
Nonconcessional flows			
MDBs	939.0	1,978.0	3,649.0

Source: OECD, *Twenty-Five Years of Development Co-operation: A Review,* p. 143.

The historical evidence indicates that whereas there was unquestionably a rapid buildup in the MDBs' lending during their first three decades, their relative share of total flows remained small—under 12 percent. Financing from other sources, official and private, also expanded rapidly during the same period.

It is interesting to note that the share of private financial flows (made up primarily of foreign direct investment, bank lending, and bond lending) to the developing countries also increased rapidly, from 25 percent of the total in 1960 to almost 42 percent in 1975 (Table 4.1). The share of private flows reached highs of 44.2 percent in 1973, 44.1 percent in 1978, and 44.0 percent in 1981, boosted by petrodollar recycling in those years.[21] Moreover, private flows have been subject to much more volatility than official (including multilateral) flows: Year-to-year swings of 20 percent are common, and yearly swings have occasionally been as high as 50 percent. In contrast, official and multilateral flows have been almost placid in terms of their low year-to-year variability. The greater regularity of official (including multilateral) flows gives them the significant advantage of more certainty and predictability than private flows for long-term development purposes.

Impact of Multilateral Bank Assistance

What about the MDBs' impact on development—putting aside the fact that at the time, inputs received more attention than outcomes? Since *economic growth* was regarded as the key indicator of success, the evidence suggests modest and perhaps diminishing results (see Table 4.3). It should be emphasized at the outset that it is extremely difficult to disentangle the impact of MDB assistance from that of other donors.[22] Typically, MDB assistance has been accompanied by bilateral aid as well as private foreign investment. Moreover, the role of the recipient country in determining the outcome of aid-funded initiatives is crucial and often makes the difference between success and failure. In a few countries and at particular points in time, MDB assistance (usually from the World Bank) has loomed particularly large, but this has been the exception rather than the rule.

Table 4.3   Economic Growth in the Developing World, 1960–1982

Region	GNP Annual Growth Rate		Per Capita GNP Growth Rate	
	1960–1970	1970–1982	1960–1970	1970–1982
Asia	6.2	5.7	3.8	3.7
Sub-Saharan Africa	4.7	3.0	2.2	0.1
The Americas	5.6	4.7	2.8	2.2
All developing countries	6.2	5.0	3.8	2.8

Source: OECD, *Twenty-Five Years of Development Co-operation*, pp. 264–265.
Note: Data for North Africa, the Middle East, European developing countries, and Oceania are not shown but are included in the average for all developing countries; growth rates in these areas were *higher* than average.

The averages for "all developing countries" are clearly skewed by the Asian data, since they are population weighted and Asia is the most populous region. Several conclusions can be drawn from the data. First and foremost, per capita growth was exceedingly modest throughout the period; such rates of growth are unlikely to have a perceptible impact on living standards of the poor, assuming growth is evenly distributed. Second, a slowdown in growth evidently occurred from the 1960s to the 1970s despite an acceleration in the volume of aid (and other flows). Third, the slowdown was most acute in sub-Saharan Africa, where the per capita growth rate was already lower than that in other regions. No causality can be inferred, however. The slowdown in growth rates may have been caused by many factors, including the savings and investment efforts of the developing countries, sluggish export markets, and so forth. We can only conclude that growth slowed down *despite* an increase in aid and other official (including multilateral) flows. In many countries, an argument can be made that growth was higher than it would have been in the absence of aid. The relationship between aid and economic growth is different in each country, and in each country the situation is slightly different.[23]

A better place to seek evidence of the MDBs' work in their first quarter century is at the project level, since most of their energies and efforts were directed toward seeking investment in specific capital projects designed to add to the infrastructure and other capacities of recipient countries. Here the evidence is much more tangible, and it has been the subject of exhaustive analysis elsewhere.[24] But even at the project level, it is not always easy to distinguish the role of MDBs from that of other aid donors or sources of external financing or the role of the government or other agents in the recipient country. In India, contributions of aid (including agricultural research and technical assistance) were essential to the green revolution, which in turn has transformed India from a food-deficit into a food-surplus country. In Malawi, aid paid for most public investment through the 1970s and contributed to successful institution building. In Bangladesh, aid was vital for the reconstruction effort following that country's war of independence in 1971 and, subsequently, for the prevention of famine and food insecurity.

In terms of specific contributions from the MDBs, the role of the World Bank in some of its major borrowers during its first quarter century was carefully assessed in the monumental study by Edward Mason and Robert Asher.[25] In Colombia, the Bank helped to meet the huge investment needs in the power and transport sectors associated with rapid urbanization and industrialization. The Bank provided financing for highways among Colombia's three major cities and installed about half of its power-generating capacity. The Bank made important contributions to policy and institution building in the power sector (for example, by helping to establish a public utilities commission to regulate tariffs). The Bank's experience in the railway sector was less successful, if the criterion of economic rate of return is used as the indicator.

In Brazil, the Bank had such major problems with macroeconomic and other facets of domestic policy that it stopped its lending between 1954 and 1965; its overall impact on Brazil during its first twenty-five years must be considered minimal. In Pakistan, during the 1950s the Bank assisted in building a pipeline to exploit reserves of natural gas; subsequently, using feedstock from this natural gas field, it assisted in doubling the power-generating capacity in Karachi. In the 1960s, the Bank's proclivity toward megaprojects continued, as it supported construction of large dams on the Indus watershed. The Bank's first major agricultural loan (a 1962 credit from the IDA) assisted mostly larger farmers in increasing their exports of cotton and rice.

In India, the Bank assisted in modernizing railways and expanding electric power, iron and steel production, and port capacity during the 1950s. By the 1960s, India was by far the World Bank group's largest borrower, but fundamental economic problems (exchange rate policy, administrative controls over imports, and the neglect of agriculture) put the Bank at odds with India. This led in 1966 to the mobilization of $900 million (of which the Bank contributed $215 million) in program assistance (for balance-of-payments purposes) in return for liberalization by India of its import-control program—an early forerunner of the structural adjustment lending that became more fully developed in the 1980s. The Bank expedited, but cannot claim the credit for, the green revolution of the 1960s. There are also many stories of failure, including the Bank's support of the Indian railway system, which absorbed a quarter of all lending to India from the 1950s until 1971.[26]

Among the regional development banks, by 1975 only the Inter-American Bank had experienced more than a decade of lending. By that time the Asian and African Banks were only beginning to consolidate their soft-lending windows; hence, they are not considered in this part of the summary assessment.

In its first decade, the IDB allocated 40 percent of its lending resources to the productive sectors (agriculture, industry, and mining); 30 percent to infrastructure (electric power, transport, and communications); and 25 percent to social sectors (water and sewerage, urban development and housing, and education). Moreover, the IDB was the source of two-thirds of all external investments in potable water during the 1960s and 1970s. As Chapter 2 pointed out, the IDB's lending in the social sectors and in agriculture (small- and medium-scale farmers were the primary focus) set it apart from— some might say ahead of—the World Bank, which allocated 90 percent of its loans in Latin America to infrastructure alone.[27]

In summarizing the efforts of the MDBs during their first thirty years, a project focus is entirely appropriate, given that the institutions emphasized assistance through real capital formation—that is, through concrete, bankable projects. In the most general terms, the legacy of these projects was considerable, and many of the capital works constructed continue to stand and provide a flow of benefits to people in the form of goods and services.

Two other legacies of the first thirty years were less positive. The first was the notion that development was in some way an increasing function of the volume of resource transfer. Not until the 1990s, when the MDBs commissioned task forces to examine the quality of lending, was this doctrine seriously questioned (more on this later). Since the MDBs were uniquely equipped to become efficient capital-transfer mechanisms, this notion was a recipe for explosive growth of the MDBs.

The second unfortunate legacy was the limited extent to which larger development objectives were met through a lending program that consisted of discrete projects. Did a succession of projects succeed, in the words of the World Bank's Articles, in "raising the standard of living and the conditions of labor?"

Such questions led the MDBs, perhaps ahead of other development agencies, to evaluate their efforts using economic cost-benefit analysis—an alternative methodology that became fashionable in the early 1970s.[28] Such analysis inevitably led to the rate of return becoming the principal criterion of project success or failure. On first blush, cost-benefit methodologies seemed to provide a crisp calculus with which to both appraise (ex ante) and evaluate (ex post) specific projects. But precisely because cost-benefit analysis that was restricted to the confines of the projects themselves could not capture the larger issues of development impact, the methodology was continually broadened to include factors such as indirect, social, and other non-market costs and benefits.

Moreover, the broader the analysis became, the more difficult it was to render crisp and objective judgments of success or failure, and the more prone it became to manipulation.[29] For example, project managers are able to alter assumptions at either the appraisal or the evaluation stage to obtain the "desired" minimum economic rate of return (generally 10 percent) or a result below the threshold figure if a negative assessment is desired. This is less a matter of illicit or unethical behavior than a reflection of the fact that sophisticated cost-benefit methodology is, in many respects, ultimately subjective.

In any event, by the early 1970s it was becoming evident that despite the positive (if decelerating) economic growth rates at the macroeconomic level and the positive rates of return generated by projects at the microeconomic level, the overall incidence of poverty in many countries was, in fact, increasing. This simple observation led to the conclusion that development programs and agencies were not succeeding in their fundamental aims. In other words, neither the indicators of success utilized over the past three decades nor the programs and instruments of development agents were adequate to meet these larger challenges. The shift in perception occurred abruptly in 1973. The shift in policy and program design has been more turbulent and sometimes inconsistent during the two decades since.

The Past Two Decades:
From Poverty Reduction to Adjustment and Back

It was not until 1973 that the World Bank equated development with the objective of poverty reduction. As Robert Ayres[30] puts it, the benchmark event was Robert McNamara's celebrated speech at the Bank's September 1973 annual meetings in Nairobi, in which he focused on the dimensions of world poverty—particularly rural poverty—and on how little had been done (by the World Bank along with other development agencies) to alleviate the poverty of those who depended on subsistence agriculture.

The old regime's momentum, however, was difficult to halt. Loans for large-scale infrastructural investment thus continued to be the mainstay of activity for all of the MDBs throughout the 1970s, a tendency reinforced by that decade's energy crisis. The 1980s were consumed by the debt crisis. Its handmaiden at the MDBs was structural adjustment, which, with its emphasis on fiscal balance, in practice often represented a retreat from the poverty focus. The regional banks essentially followed the World Bank's lead in adjustment, or policy-based, lending during the 1980s. Only in 1990 did the World Bank rearticulate its poverty strategy, shortly after which its president, Lewis Preston, announced that "poverty reduction is the Bank's overarching objective."

In the 1990s, however, the MDBs were not simply going to turn the clock back two decades to renew their focus on poverty, having taken a long detour toward structural adjustment. For one thing, although structural adjustment programs received well-deserved criticism, the underlying rationale of such programs—to bring about the internal and external sustainability of borrowers' economic policies—was alive and well. Or as the authors of perhaps the most celebrated critique of adjustment policies put it, it was less a question of *whether* adjustment policies were needed and more a question of *how* they should be designed to make their human impact as beneficial as possible.[31]

For example, on the issue of fiscal policy reform, through most of the 1980s the MDBs were concerned more with overall targets for expenditure reduction than with particular details. In the 1990s, the focus has become much more discriminating—*against* unproductive expenditures such as defense and armaments and *in favor of* strengthening education, health, and the social safety net. Thus, adjustment policies and programs have become internalized—in other words, part of the policy dialogue with borrowing countries—rather than irrelevant. Indeed, adhering to a program of economic policy reform (as agreed to and monitored by the IMF and the World Bank) has remained very much a part of the conditionality associated with debt relief from the Paris Club in the 1990s.

Moreover, new objectives were put on the table. For example, during the 1980s the environmental impact of the MDBs' infrastructural lending was surfacing for the first time, thanks to an active international environmental movement and greater awareness—especially among northern publics—of the importance of this hitherto neglected aspect of development programs and projects. At about the same time, other critics were beginning to point to yet another neglected aspect of development programs—their impact on women (or in more current parlance, their "gender dimension").

A few years later—soon after the Berlin Wall fell and a democratic wave swept across Africa and Latin America—the interrelated issues of good governance and human rights erupted onto development agenda. Coincidentally, the newest member of the MDB club, the European Bank for Reconstruction and Development, was founded in 1991 with a charter that explicitly endorsed its borrowing members' transition to multiparty democracy.[32] This set of issues has been particularly contentious for the MDBs, since until the advent of the EBRD their charters had prohibited political considerations from having any bearing on their operational decisions. The charters also eschewed any hint of explicit political bias, although sufficient evidence can be found to support the claim that the MDBs were never politically neutral.

In other words, their situations have become considerably more complicated for the MDBs—and all development agencies—as the consensus notion of development has moved from providing resource inputs to ensuring certain stipulated outcomes. John P. Lewis (1993) refers to this tendency as "target proliferation." It is not surprising that as development targets have proliferated, the perception that the MDBs have fallen short has grown. This perception is often based on media reports or on advocacy work of NGOs that dwells on particular outcomes of the MDBs' activities—for example, environmental impact or the inequitable treatment of women and girls.

In principle, there is no reason the various desirable outcomes expected from development activities should be at loggerheads with each other, although some argue that tradeoffs or compromises must be made. In practice, operational programming to achieve multidimensional targets has proven to be challenging. In the remainder of this chapter, I briefly survey the policies and achievements of the MDBs in the fundamental area of poverty reduction.

Poverty Reduction

The World Bank

It took a quarter century for the agencies involved in development assistance to distinguish between assisting poor *countries* and poor *people*. The notion that stronger economic growth for recipient countries would lead directly to poverty reduction—a "trickle-down" view of development—was not challenged. Thus, we should not be surprised that most of the instruments established to alleviate poverty (for example, the IDA and the soft-loan windows at the regional banks) were directed toward the performance of the poorest developing countries rather than toward the conditions of their poorest inhabitants. As mentioned earlier, this view began to break down in the 1960s when an increasing body of evidence indicated that the condition of the poor was not improving despite rapid economic (i.e., GNP) growth at the country level. By the early 1970s, there was a pressing need to find ways to direct the benefits of economic growth to the poorest people within the poorest countries.

The World Bank's first conceptual framework for poverty alleviation was articulated by Hollis Chenery and associates in 1974 in *Redistribution with Growth,* a work that embodies the theoretical rationale of McNamara's initiative at Nairobi. Four avenues to improve the welfare of the poorest are suggested: maximizing GNP growth and redirecting investment, redistributing income, and transferring assets to poverty groups. *Redistribution with Growth* favors the second option because each of the other three, it argues, would encounter severe economic or political obstacles. In other words, the essence of the strategy is to increase the productivity and hence the output and incomes of the poor by investing in their productive capacity.[33]

Who were "the poor" the Bank tried to reach? The group constituted the *absolute* rather than the *relatively* poor—those below some minimally acceptable threshold standard of living rather than simply those who happen to be at the bottom of the income spectrum.[34] The choice of absolute rather than relative poverty as the Bank's target was both deliberate and revealing. The notion of absolute poverty seems to lend itself to crisper, more focused, and more quantitative measures (e.g., in terms of caloric intake levels). Relative poverty, on the other hand, characterizes every society as having unequal income distribution; thus, any attack on relative poverty could involve far-reaching measures that could affect the welfare of the rich as well as the poor.

In practice, such a strategy meant allocating investment at the margin to the poor. Accordingly, many of the World Bank's poverty-focused initiatives over the next decade were directed toward providing impoverished farmers in the countryside with high-yielding inputs (examples include irrigation, fertilizers, and agricultural extension services). In urban areas, the strategy was aimed at creating employment in the informal and modern sectors and at providing better access to utilities, social services, and housing.[35]

In hindsight, fundamental conceptual flaws underlay this approach to poverty alleviation. First and foremost, it was not based on any stated theory or analysis of the generation or causes of poverty. Without such an understanding—and the causes of poverty could differ among countries or regions, which implies the need for different remedies—how could any strategy succeed? Second, even though its political framework was minimalist, the approach was nonetheless naive: It assumed that redistribution at the margin (through incremental investment allocated in favor of the poor) could take place despite possible resistance from ruling elites or even through their voluntary assent.[36]

In 1980, the World Bank recapitulated its first-generation poverty reduction strategy in its then-novel flagship publication, the *World Development Report* (WDR). It is interesting that the report suggested that whereas economic growth was necessary, it was insufficient to ensure poverty reduction. Such reduction would depend on the pattern or the quality as much as on the rate of growth. The report also mentioned that other measures—such as land reform, employment creation, access to education, health and nutrition, scientific and technological advances aimed at the poor, and migration—could all contribute to the reduction of poverty. (As I note later, this list of measures presages the second-generation strategy introduced ten years later in a subsequent *World Development Report*.)

The World Bank's first-generation strategy of poverty reduction is, as Robert Ayres puts it, best seen as a relatively slight modification of the institution's mission and operational philosophy. The strategy did not come close to addressing the more fundamental issues raised by an alternative school of thought under the rubric of basic human needs (BHN). Whereas the Bank aimed at providing the poor with the means (through increased productivity and higher incomes) to rise above poverty, there was no guarantee they would succeed in doing so, even with increased productivity and incomes. The BHN approach went considerably further in postulating targets (for food, shelter, and so on) for the poor to be met through development programs—whether through the market (the Bank's strategy) or through nonmarket channels, principally the state.

It is not surprising that the BHN approach never came to fruition within the Bank or elsewhere. There was far too much scope for differences both at the conceptual level (how *does* one define basic human needs) and at the level of policy (what are the appropriate roles of markets, states, and other actors). By the 1980s, the World Bank's focus on poverty was in retreat, in part because of a critique leveled by its largest shareholder (the United States) against the Bank specifically and foreign aid generally. The incoming Reagan administration took a decidedly more conservative view of U.S. geopolitical objectives and foreign aid. The poverty-focus initiative under McNamara was seen at best as a wasteful welfare program and at worst as a demonstration of the Bank's tendencies toward socialist policies and its support of countries that were unfriendly to the United States.

Moreover, the 1980s also experienced the developing country debt crisis, which resulted in many borrowers running acute balance-of-payments deficits as their debt-service payments escalated and their receipts from exports slumped. The World Bank's lending was radically reoriented (in parallel with the IMF, which played a leading role in the crisis) to provide balance-of-payments support through structural adjustment programs that provided general financing for imports in exchange for economic policy reforms, or macroeconomic conditionality.

The poverty focus was not abandoned in the 1980s; there was continued lending on poverty-focus projects. But the rapidly growing proportion allocated to adjustment and policy-based lending (about a quarter of total lending by the end of the decade) represented a considerable diversion of funding that could have been allocated to poverty reduction projects. A more serious issue, however, was the criticism of loan conditionality in adjustment programs.[37] For example, policies to reduce government spending on social and other services, along with higher interest rates and currency devaluation, sometimes made life more difficult for the poor in borrowing countries. The immediate impact of many adjustment programs was to reduce state-financed investment and economic growth; other casualties of expenditure reduction were state education and health programs, of which the poor were meant to be the prime beneficiaries.

Such criticisms increased during the 1980s, as did evidence from much of Africa and Latin America that the period was becoming a "lost decade" as far as development was concerned. In some cases per capita incomes had fallen back to the levels of the 1960s and 1970s. Enrollment in public schools was in decline, and some diseases were on the increase. After having declined for two decades, in the 1980s the incidence of poverty was on the rise, particularly in Africa and Latin America (see Table 4.4). The situation called for an urgent response from development agencies—particularly the MDBs, which (along with the IMF) were largely responsible for the adjustment policies. As a result, the World Bank launched a "new" poverty initiative in 1990.

Table 4.4   Poverty Indicators, 1985 and 1990

Region	Number of Poor (millions)		Headcount Index (percentage)	
	1985	1990	1985	1990
Eighty-six developing countries	1,051	1,133	30.5	29.7
Latin America/Caribbean	87	108	22.4	25.2
Middle East/North Africa	60	73	30.6	33.1
Sub-Saharan Africa	184	216	47.6	47.8

Source: World Bank, *Implementing the World Bank's Strategy to Reduce Poverty,* p. 5, Table 1.

Note: The poverty line is $31.23 per month at 1985 prices and purchasing power parity exchange rates. Headcount index measures the percentage of the poor among the overall population.

The Regional Banks

Turning to the policies of the regional development banks, the three longer-established RDBs adopted poverty alleviation as a strategic objective well after the McNamara initiative at the World Bank—in some cases only very recently. The IDB was perhaps the exception, since it began its life in the 1960s with a markedly different focus from that of the World Bank. The IDB provided loans to farmers and for social overhead projects (e.g., water and sanitation, urban development and housing) as well as infrastructure, industry, and mining.[38] There were political motivations behind the creation of the IDB and its early ventures into the social sectors: In particular, the United States was eager to avoid repetitions of the Cuban Revolution elsewhere in Latin America. Despite such early indications of a bias toward social development, however, there was little coherent effort toward poverty reduction by the IDB until the late 1970s.

During the IDB's Fifth Replenishment negotiations, which concluded in 1978, a "low-income goal" was adopted by the Bank's
membership. The United States, along with Canada and other nonregional members that had recently joined, seemed to provide the
impetus for this proposal. At least 50 percent of the overall lending
program would be oriented directly to benefit low-income people,
primarily through employment creation.[39] Over the next decade, the
low-income goal became the IDB's policy framework with respect to
poverty alleviation.

The implementation of the low-income goal encountered several
pitfalls—methodological, operational, and political. Methodologi-
cally, the decision of where to draw the low-income line was left up
to the borrowing countries: In Mexico, it was $1,245, whereas in Peru
it was $646. Widely varying benchmarks meant the nature of the low-
income population differed substantially throughout the region.
Operationally, about a third of all loans were excluded because it was
impossible to measure their distributional impact. Finally, borrowing
member governments were frequently unwilling to allow the low-
income goal to interfere with their own priorities for which they
sought IDB financing. They found the low-income guidelines sufficiently malleable, however, to allow them to put forward their project
preferences and still meet the target.

Despite the loopholes surrounding the low-income goal, the IDB
still fell short of consistently achieving the 50 percent objective. That
target was not met until 1982; thereafter, the proportion of overall
benefits of IDB loans flowing to low-income beneficiaries sank to 35
percent before rebounding to 44 percent by the end of the 1980s.
Clearly, the debt-distressed environment made the low-income objective even more difficult to achieve, as available financing was reallo-
cated to help fill widening balance-of-payments deficits.[40]

The ADB and the AsDB crystallized antipoverty strategies relatively recently—in the late 1980s. The former had begun in the 1960s
with a mission clearly stipulated in its articles of "achieving social
progress." Nevertheless, during its first two decades the ADB allocated its resources on a pattern that more closely resembled that of
the World Bank, with priority given to infrastructure projects. It was
not until 1992 that the ADB articulated an explicit strategy to measure
its performance with regard to the alleviation of poverty or to target
the needs of the continent's poorest citizens.[41]

From the very beginning, the emphasis of the Asian Bank was on
"economic growth and cooperation" rather than "social progress," so
it is less surprising that the AsDB's lending priorities resembled those
of the World Bank.[42] By the late 1980s, however, the Asian Bank
seemed to have become more conscious of its relative neglect of social

equity and poverty objectives. In 1989, a high-level panel of experts appointed to advise the Bank on policies over the next decade recommended that priority be attached to social infrastructure (health and education projects) and poverty alleviation, thus presaging the World Bank's "rediscovery" of the poverty issue the following year.[43]

The poverty strategies launched by the African and Asian Banks essentially coincided with the rebirth of the poverty focus at the World Bank in 1990 described in the next section. The EBRD was created in 1991, but it has never really had a poverty focus. Indeed, from the beginning its raison d'être has been not to foster development but to facilitate the transition from centrally planned to market-oriented economies. That is not to say that the EBRD has disregarded *all* noneconomic issues. The EBRD is enjoined by its charter to oversee the *political* transition to democracy as well, although in practice this objective has played second fiddle to the economic transition. Another noneconomic objective—improving environmental stewardship—has been accorded great priority in the EBRD's programming and project design. But *social* objectives, including issues of income distribution and gender equity, have been conspicuously absent.

Rebirth of the Poverty Focus

Apart from some internal analysis of the issue in the late 1980s,[44] the World Bank's focus on poverty reduction became dormant in the 1980s, overshadowed by the debt and adjustment crises in Africa, Latin America, and some parts of Asia. The Bank broached the issue in the 1990 edition of its *World Development Report,* which unveiled an analysis of the problem as well as a prescriptive strategy. The latter was summarized in a subsequent policy paper[45] and was operationalized in a handbook.[46]

The Bank's prescriptive strategy has two parts. First, developing countries should adopt economic policies that encourage broadly based growth by making extensive use of the most abundant resource of the poor: labor. Second, developing countries should provide social services—particularly primary education, basic health care, family planning, and nutrition—to improve both the living conditions and the capacity of the poor to respond to income-earning opportunities that arise from economic growth.[47] In addition, a social safety net should be in place for the particularly vulnerable.

How does this strategy compare with that of the 1970s? In general, the strategy of the 1990s is consistent with and complements its antecedent; indeed, its main elements had been anticipated in the 1980 *World Development Report.* Emphasis is placed on economic growth as a fundamental underpinning—a sine qua non—of poverty reduction. Another common element is the idea of investing in the poor to increase their productivity and income-earning potential.

What is different about the recent version is, first, its greater specificity about the *kinds* of growth-oriented policies, or incentive structures, that are conducive to poverty reduction—namely, policies that encourage labor-intensive activities in agriculture and manufacturing. For example, competitive exchange rates and other policies encourage labor-intensive agricultural exports while discouraging imports of artificially cheap capital goods for use in capital-intensive manufacturing.

Second, whereas the earlier strategy emphasized physical and infrastructural investments (for example, irrigation and other inputs to increase agricultural yields), the 1990s strategy focuses on social investment and human resources development. Physical infrastructure and support services (such as agricultural extension services) are still acknowledged as important, but it is recognized that their delivery should not be biased against the poor.[48] It is also recognized that even with access to social and other services, some of the poor may still be unable to lift themselves out of poverty. For this reason, the Bank's 1990s strategy also argues for social safety nets for the vulnerable.

As with the earlier version, however, the World Bank's more recent strategy does not depart from a theory of the causes of poverty; rather, it simply jumps into general remedies and prescriptive policies. This is the case because, again like its antecedent, the focus of the Bank's efforts is absolute poverty, based on notions of a threshold poverty line (approximately U.S.$1 per person per day) that is typically used to distinguish the absolute poor. With absolute poverty as a target, the politically delicate issues of income distribution entailed by a focus on *relative* poverty do not have to be addressed.

Some critics have pointed out that in some respects the recent strategy represents a setback. In practice, more emphasis is placed on the objective of economic growth per se than on the necessity of a labor-intensive pattern of economic growth. The current strategy also stresses research on poverty (perhaps revealing its inadequate theoretical underpinnings) rather than detailed implementation or operational issues. The criticism that the Bank has emphasized theoretical rather than practical aspects is reinforced by the fact that lending for agriculture and urban employment creation—sectors that offer high potential for poverty reduction—was falling in the early 1990s.[49]

Other critics doubt that it is even possible for the World Bank to combine a market-oriented philosophy with an objective of poverty reduction, since the two may be mutually exclusive.[50] Still others claim a bias toward large-scale lending is inconsistent with a strategy of poverty reduction, since such lending inevitably benefits the better-off rather than the poorest.[51]

In 1994, the World Bank adopted a classification system whereby each of its projects is classified according to whether it is poverty focused or is part of the so-called program of targeted interventions (PTI). Projects are included in the PTI if they incorporate a specific mechanism for reaching the poor or if the participation of the poor significantly exceeds the proportion of the population as a whole. The PTI classification is then used to calculate the relative importance of poverty-focused projects in the Bank's overall portfolio. In FY 1994, the share of all Bank lending classified as PTI was 21 percent (the PTI share of all IDA lending was slightly higher, at 28 percent).[52]

As with the World Bank, the regional development banks "rediscovered" the poverty issue toward the end of the 1980s. In the case of the Asian Bank, an internal task force recommended a policy on poverty reduction in 1988; the policy was strengthened in 1990 during the Sixth Replenishment negotiations of the AsDF. The policy recommended direct action to generate employment and income-earning activities for the poor; implementation of more general development policies leading to investment and employment creation; and improved access to health, family planning, and related services. This initiative was embedded in a wider policy that emphasized social dimensions other than poverty: These included enhancing the role of women in development, developing human resources, and protecting or mitigating the adverse impacts of other policies on the vulnerable.[53]

The IDB had established a low-income target during the late 1970s; as already indicated, it was highly subject to manipulation, and its actual impact on the poor—or even on the behavior of the borrowing member countries—was questionable. In the 1980s, the IDB and its largest borrowing members became embroiled in the debt crisis and in debates about appropriate economic policy responses to the crisis. Specifically, the protracted negotiations on the Seventh Replenishment involved bitter disputes between the regional members (particularly Argentina, Brazil, Mexico, and Venezuela) and the nonregionals (particularly the United States). These disputes were centered on the necessity and efficacy of structural adjustment policies parallel to those supported by the IMF and the World Bank.

In general, poverty reduction and social policies were neglected in this debate—in fact, increased poverty and social deprivation were a legacy of the 1980s,[54] problems the IDB turned back to during the 1990s. During the Eighth Replenishment negotiations, which concluded in 1994, a "second generation of socio-economic reforms" was born that combined social equity with sustainable long-term growth. These reforms focused on creating employment for the poor and on stimulating investment in human resources (through education and health programs in particular) and in the urban environment.[55] In general terms, the IDB's strategy is similar to that launched by the World Bank in 1990.

The ADB was the last of the MDBs to develop a poverty reduction strategy; its plan materialized in 1992. This may be the case because poverty is more ubiquitous in Africa than in other parts of the Third World such as Latin America, where disparities are wide and poverty coexists with conspicuous wealth. Poverty reduction was seen as a subtext of everything the ADB did rather than as a special challenge.[56] Nonetheless, it is somewhat curious that an issue so prominent to the Bank's existence was not the subject of explicit policies until fairly recently. The ADB joined a multidonor initiative led by the World Bank in 1988 on the Social Dimensions of Adjustment (SDA), which may have influenced the ADB to change its policy.

Donors found the SDA program to be inadequate to tackle the challenge of poverty, so the African Bank devised a Poverty Alleviation Strategy and Action Program in 1992. The strategy called for an integrated approach that involved many elements—from the macroeconomic environment to participation of beneficiaries, particularly women. Despite the breadth of its approach, by 1995 the Bank had only one social policy specialist working on poverty alleviation and was severely constrained by its financial situation from allocating additional staff or other resources to this area.[57]

In surveying the changes in the operational strategies of the MDBs that bear on the reduction of poverty, it is important to distinguish rhetoric from reality and to discern what has actually changed in practice. As a result of pressures from donor shareholders to demonstrate results in this area, the MDBs emphasize indicators such as the PTI as signs of progress toward the objective.

But much more significant than the display of such statistical measures (which are always subject to a degree of arbitrariness and manipulation) has been the growing role of *participation* in the design and implementation of MDB projects. If participation by beneficiaries is substantive rather than token (again, this may be a big "if"), it connotes a major shift in the MDBs' operational practices. In a real sense, this is new territory for the MDBs and all agencies involved in development. Ensuring that participation is satisfactory and meaningful for both the beneficiaries and the agencies is a challenge that will face the development community for some time. Such a situation will not necessarily always make development activities easier or more successful, but participation has definitely become the sine qua non of both ownership and sustainability.

More than anything else, then, the MDBs' recognition of participation represents the essential new element of their antipoverty strategies in the 1990s. This represents more than a shift in process, since lessons learned from participatory processes will undoubtedly help to shape subsequent MDB initiatives.

The reaffirmation of the MDBs' poverty focus in the late 1980s and early 1990s was in part a result of intense donor pressures mounted during replenishment negotiations—particularly by donors such as the Nordic countries, the Netherlands, and Canada, with support from the UK and France. There was a shared recognition by donor officials from these countries that the policies of the 1980s had made progress against long-term poverty reduction difficult and in some cases had caused setbacks. These pressures also occasioned sharp debates among the donor community.

Developments in Theory

By the mid-1990s, there was widespread agreement that the necessary elements of a strategy aimed at poverty reduction included the two elements set out in WDR 1990: broad-based, labor-intensive or participatory economic growth and access for the poor to social services that would enhance productive, income-enhancing opportunities. Continuing debate has focused on the weights of these factors, on what additional elements are sufficient to assure poverty reduction, and on the time horizon involved.

Conventional economic theory holds that for the poor, employment and income are derived from the utilization of their major asset—labor power.[58] Much of the economic reform and structural adjustment policy designed and supported by the MDBs during the 1980s and 1990s has been aimed at rectifying economic distortions that have a negative impact on employment and on labor income. For example, policies that maintain an artificially high exchange rate make imported goods, including capital goods, relatively less expensive. The import of relatively cheap capital goods favors capital-intensive production and is biased against labor-intensive products, in which developing countries typically have a comparative advantage. Conversely, maintaining the actual effective exchange rate at an appropriate level encourages the production and export of labor-intensive goods in the agricultural and manufacturing sectors.

Other policies that often accompany an overvalued currency include selective protectionism through import tariffs and other measures. The intent of such policies is usually to foster the growth of certain domestic industries, but the resultant employment is often created at high cost and favors relatively few workers—particularly when local markets are small.

More generally, the conventional economic reform programs supported by the World Bank and other MDBs (dubbed the "Washington consensus" by John Williamson) are premised on growth-enhancing, market-friendly, noninterventionist policies that encourage productive investment by firms and households. Investment by households includes most notably the development of human resources through education and skill training.

The problem with the conventional economic approach is that whereas it may provide a menu of policies necessary to enhance employment and labor incomes, these may be insufficient to ensure outcomes that are considered fair or socially equitable. The best illustration, one more germane to the developed than the developing countries, is the failure of such policies to ensure full employment. Until 1980, interventionist Keynesian policies were the conventional response to the failure of markets to ensure full employment (or unemployment at acceptably low levels). Subsequently, Keynesian interventionism has fallen from favor and been supplanted successively with monetarist and rational expectations doctrines, both of which are inclined toward a much smaller role for and share of the government in the economy. Unemployment in the developed countries, however, has continued to be a major problem these recent economic policies have failed to remedy—and, arguably have even made worse.

Moreover, there has been increasing debate about whether all of the policies included in the Washington consensus are necessary and whether certain interventionist policies can indeed serve the causes of both growth and equity. One vortex around which debate has swirled has been the interpretation of the so-called East Asian miracle—the high-growth experiences of Japan and the newly industrialized countries of the Asian Pacific Rim.[59] Indeed the debate was sparked by Japan, which took issue with the World Bank's orthodox structural adjustment approach. Moreover, the Japanese contended that their own experience and those of the neighboring "tigers" (particularly Korea and Taiwan) suggested that carefully crafted interventionist industrial policies can play an important development role and result in higher and more equal growth.

At the same time, a broader conception of development has gained widespread support, particularly among those who view income per capita as a very narrow—indeed, mechanistic—measure of economic or social "progress." This line of thinking, which owes much to Amartya Sen,[60] questions much of the conventional wisdom on both the objectives, or ends, of development and the means to those ends. Instead of measuring progress by income per capita (the conventional approach), which regards ever-increasing production and consumption as unambiguous improvements in welfare, the alternative approach regards such material indicators as important (even necessary) but not exclusive criteria of development. Rather, the alternative conception is one of people-centered, or human, development, which views the well-being of people—measured by their ability to enjoy a long, healthy, and fulfilling life—as the objective of development. In this view, social indicators, such as the level of literacy and longevity, are as important as the material standard of living in capturing the well-being of people.[61]

The alternative school of human development seems essentially to converge with the school embodied in the World Bank's poverty strategy (as articulated in WDR 1990). For example, the latter emphasizes access by the poor to social services such as health and education, services that are central to human development. The two approaches may diverge considerably, however, when it comes to practical policy implications.[62] In particular, the human development school tends to emphasize the importance of the role of the state and the public sector, since social services are public goods that must essentially be provided by the state. In contrast, the World Bank stresses the fundamental importance of achieving at least a minimal level of economic growth as well as the necessity of market-oriented economic reforms (or economic liberalization) as a means to increase the level of economic growth. Such reforms have generally meant a *reduction* in the role and size of the state, often prompted by chronic fiscal deficits and unsustainable debts.

The fundamental question facing the MDBs, and all institutions and programs involved in development, is, Are these two main policy thrusts—of poverty reduction and support for private markets—consistent and complementary, or are they at war with each other?[63] To tackle this question, the MDBs have drifted into a rather ad hoc assortment of policies and programs that make up the notion of the World Bank's program of targeted interventions and support for microcredit; although these policies may contribute to the objective of poverty reduction, they seem to lack comprehensiveness and appear to be working at the periphery of the issue. As Louis Emmerij[64] put it, economic growth plus education does not add up to a poverty reduction strategy, for which one needs a much more cogent attack on inadequate employment and incomes.

The issue, however, need not be presented as a dichotomy—either more economic growth through liberalization and a smaller state or more human development and a larger state. Advocates of human development accept the need for economic liberalization but emphasize the need to go well beyond market-oriented reforms to enhance people's capabilities through greater literacy, better public health, social security, gender equality, land rights, and a measure of democracy.[65] A lack of such capabilities prevents widespread participation in economic growth and therefore inhibits the reduction of poverty. Regarding the size of the state, advocates of human development do not necessarily press for a larger state per se but for a more effective state—one capable of discharging its social responsibilities to all its people. This could be accomplished without enlarging the state by reducing the state's role in productive sectors (for example, by divesting loss-making parastatals and reducing the size of the bureaucracy) and expanding its role in social sectors. In other words, a strategy of human development may well be rather consistent with a strategy of economic liberalization.[66]

The implications for policy of this evolution in thinking about poverty remain unclear. Among other things, this evolution has led to increasing attention to public expenditure, particularly in the social sectors; more generally, it has brought into the limelight the entire spectrum of budgetary expenditures. The examination of expenditure priorities has gone beyond the simple matter of bureaucratic involvement in productive sectors (for example, in manufacturing or distribution) to state involvement in any nonproductive activities—often a euphemism for military expenditures. Such an examination has been seen by many developing country members as an unwarranted intrusion on their sovereignty.

At any rate, the nature and extent of poverty are undoubtedly much better understood today. This understanding has contributed to a greater sophistication in the policies and specific poverty-focused interventions of the MDBs and other development agencies. Moreover, the post–Cold War environment has been conducive to confronting certain issues (such as military expenditures, political structures and governance, and corruption) that had previously been overlooked.

Programming and Projects

In practice, the poverty strategies adopted by the MDBs in the 1990s have not articulated concrete, productive initiatives that would translate economic growth and access to social services into employment- or income-creating opportunities for the poor. Part of the reason for this failure is that the strategy of market-oriented economic reform advocated by the MDBs holds that governments are explicitly advised not to be dirigiste; thus, income-creating opportunities are meant to be created spontaneously by market forces once an "enabling environment" for the private sector has been put in place.

The problem with such an essentially passive approach to employment- and income-creation is that although such opportunities may be created by private markets, there is no guarantee that they will necessarily exert demand for the only resource the poor have in abundance: unskilled or low-skilled labor. Private investment is more likely to flow into activities that satisfy owners' demand of capital for adequate returns—which, depending on the labor-intensity of the investment, may or may not lead to demand for the labor services of the poor.

Here lies the critical weakness of the poverty strategy of the 1990s: the haphazard nature of its demand for the labor of the poor and hence the uncertainty of the strategy's eventual impact on the material well-being of the poor and its ability to lift the poor out of poverty. The challenge was to find ways of channeling investment capital directly to the poor to create income or employment. The World Bank attempted to respond to this challenge in part through its program of targeted interventions, but this seemed more like ex post rationalization of projects the Bank intended to finance in any case; additionally, the estimation of the beneficiary population (i.e., the calculation of the number of beneficiaries defined as poor) was subject to the usual statistical pitfalls.

Moreover, even if the poor were beneficiaries of PTI-designated projects, did this constitute "sustainable human development" for the poor? In some cases, short-term employment was created for the poor; in others, policy changes or public works created better income or employment opportunities. But there was no guarantee that such opportunities would materialize or be sustained over a significant period. Ultimately, the PTI was an indirect way of reaching the poor. What was needed was a much more directive approach whereby the MDBs could channel resources primarily to those who were poor. A partial programmatic response has materialized in the form of *microcredit* and *microenterprise.*

Although the birth of microcredit is widely associated with the Grameen Bank created in Bangladesh in the late 1970s,[67] it is worth noting that the IDB played a particularly innovative role through its microenterprise program, which began in 1978. Individual projects were restricted to loans of no more than $500,000 and were intended to involve the poor in productive activities. These loans were typically retailed through private nonprofit organizations, and loans to ultimate borrowers were often less than $100. Typically, loans were used for material or fixed assets, or as working capital.

The innovative feature of microcredit is that it eliminates the need for conventional collateral. Lack of adequate collateral was the critical obstacle that prevented conventional lenders (i.e., the formal banking system rather than traditional moneylenders) from making credit available to poor borrowers. Loans carry market rates of interest. Most of the ultimate borrowers are female, and the default rate is very low. (These characteristics are shared by the Grameen Bank's lending program and a growing number of microcredit agencies throughout the world.) Through its program, the IDB also helped to create Banco Sol (in Bolivia), the first NGO in the world that successfully converted itself into a commercial bank.[68]

By the early 1990s, microcredit had come of age; in the absence of obvious alternatives, it became the leading means of channeling investment to the poor. At a World Bank conference on global hunger in late 1993, an initiative was launched to explore ways to systematically increase the resources available to the very poor. This initiative led to the creation in 1995 of a Consultative Group to Assist the Poorest (CGAP)—a microfinance program. Nine founding donor organizations, including the World Bank, collectively pledged $200 million toward CGAP. The principal objective of CGAP was to support microfinance institutions that deliver credit and savings services to the very poor on a financially sustainable basis. In addition, the initiative sought to strengthen the institutional framework of microfinance by learning from the practices of existing lenders, strengthening donor coordination, and helping to establish new, viable microfinance institutions.

The advent of microcredit and microenterprise projects represents a significant departure for the MDBs for two reasons. First, in contrast to traditional poverty-oriented projects, which were targeted to projects, activities, or sectors in which the poor were well represented, these projects initiate direct lending to the poor for projects of their own volition or invention. Second, the relatively small scale of the ultimate lending operations (loans of $100 to final borrowers) stands in stark contrast with both conventional MDB lending operations (the average World Bank loan is well in excess of $100 million) and development finance operations that are similarly retailed through intermediary lending institutions to ultimate borrowers in the industrial sector.

Conclusion: Achievements and Prospects for Eliminating Poverty

It is tempting to conclude with a simple summary that pronounces the success or failure of the MDBs as agents of change. Unfortunately and unsurprisingly, the evidence does not permit such a simple conclusion. There is also a tendency, however, to be too myopic in judging the efforts of the MDBs and, for that matter, of the entire development enterprise in the postwar era by looking for the evidence solely in contemporaneous data.

Put differently, if sustainable improvements in the human condition can be confirmed only by observing long-term trends in the available data over several decades, it makes more sense to compare the performance of the postwar development era with the eras that preceded it. Such a comparison leads quickly to the conclusion that the progress engendered in developing countries since 1945 considerably supersedes that in preceding eras (which in large parts of the developing world were characterized more by stagnation than by progress). It is perfectly plausible to conclude that the gains made in the postwar era, whether measured in terms of economic indicators (measured by per capita income and its proxies) or social indicators (such as longevity, health, availability of clean water, or various educational indicators), owe a considerable debt to the development programs of the period—which in many cases were made possible through development assistance.

The particular legacy of the MDBs, through the financing of infrastructure and projects in the agricultural and industrial sectors, played a significant part in this story. In the absence of the MDBs, much of the infrastructure of roads, ports, power generation, and telecommunications would not exist today; much of the improvement in agricultural productivity and food production would also not have occurred.

Furthermore, there have been dramatic reductions in poverty in certain countries—notably those on the Asian Pacific Rim—and this improvement has occurred even during the relatively short period since World War II. The record of South Korea, Taiwan, and, more recently, China, as well as Indonesia, Malaysia, and Thailand is extraordinary in comparison with that of any country—developed or developing. These examples are cited as a reminder that dramatic reductions in poverty are feasible within very short periods of time. The secrets of these countries' success are still the subject of considerable debate. Although external agents (including the MDBs) may have had a role in these success stories, the policy regimes in these countries (which generally favor exports), their heavy investment in human capital, and other factors such as land reform likely played a much more crucial role.[69]

Seen in this more long-term and comparative perspective, all development agencies, including the MDBs, have clearly only begun to address the challenge of eliminating poverty in a comprehensive and strategic manner. A quarter of the world's population, now concentrated heavily in South Asia and sub-Saharan Africa but with pockets throughout the rest of the world, still subsists under the bondage of absolute poverty. Whereas poverty-targeted interventions and microfinance represent important initiatives toward the objective of eliminating poverty, it is doubtful that by themselves such programs will succeed in achieving this objective. Indeed, there is a danger that microfinance will become something of a panacea for the reduction of poverty. Infrastructure-type projects, which MDBs are well placed to support and on which they have a strong record (except for the important environmental impact issue), can also contribute significantly to reducing poverty by providing the poor with greater access to markets (through transportation networks) and helping them to be more productive (through energy and telecommunications).

Perhaps even more important than the specific lending directed toward the poor is the policy dialogue conducted by the MDBs with developing country governments, which increasingly places the onus on the governments to adopt "pro-poor" policies to be eligible for MDB lending. The major donor countries (for example, those at the 1995 G7 Summit in Halifax[70]) have placed great emphasis on such conditionality, in part as a way of rationing aid budgets that are under severe fiscal pressure and are being significantly cut. But this, too, leads to a dilemma—if recipient governments are unwilling or unable to accept pro-poor poverty conditionality and thus become ineligible for MDB assistance, donors are then forced to make a choice between simply forgetting about the poor in such countries or finding ways around local governments to reach the poor. Neither choice may be easy or desirable. Moreover, major questions exist about the consistency between the economic policy environment required for the elimination of poverty and the economic reforms currently advocated by the MDBs and the G7 countries.

Effective pro-poor (or antipoverty) interventions will necessarily be based on an understanding of the nature and causes of poverty—including its relationship to economic growth, social progress, and governance. In this respect, our understanding of the dynamics of poverty and the reasons for its intractability is relatively recent. Many current hypotheses—such as the importance of good governance—are hotly debated, and it is by no means clear that certain precepts (for example, that the poor fare better under more democratic regimes) are universally valid. The MDBs can help to shed light on such issues through their research as well as their practices. Their advantage is that as organizations in which membership is shared by donor and borrowing countries, they help not only to facilitate understanding of the problem but also to innovate solutions that command the support of donors and borrowers alike.

Notes

1. See, for example, one of the earliest treatises on development by W. Arthur Lewis, *The Theory of Economic Growth*. Also, Mason and Asher, *The World Bank Since Bretton Woods*, chapter 14 ("The [World] Bank's Conception of Development"), perceived two phases prior to McNamara—the first, ending in the mid-1950s, in which the World Bank was very narrowly focused on assisting the most creditworthy countries by meeting some of their foreign exchange costs in development projects (the "bank" phase); the second, in which the Bank expanded its support to include local costs and also sectors such as agriculture that do not necessarily or directly generate foreign exchange with which to service the Bank's loan (the "development" phase). Throughout the period up to the 1970s, however, there was an implicit assumption that *development* meant principally increasing GNP per capita. This philosophy changed under McNamara, when it came to include a broader array of social improvements not necessarily reflected in or requiring rising GNP.

2. Harrod, "An Essay in Dynamic Theory."

3. Domar, "Capital Expansion, Rate of Growth, and Employment."

4. The model posits an algebraic relationship among g, the rate of economic growth, s, total savings or investment as a proportion of total income, and C, the incremental capital-output ratio: $g = s/C$. In the earliest, most naive versions of the model, C was assumed to be fixed by technology and invariate among different economies; thus, the rate of economic growth was singularly dependent on the savings or investment ratio. It should be added, however, that in its first decade the World Bank saw itself as a project financing organization whose projects must be based on sound engineering, just as its loans must be based on sound banking principles. It was not until the 1960s that the ideas of economists (including their theories on growth) were taken seriously, which led to the early departure from the Bank of the eminent economist Paul Rosenstein-Rodan in 1948. Oliver, *International Economic Co-operation and the World Bank*, pp. 272–273.

5. As Drèze and Sen point out, however, classical economists from Adam Smith to John Stuart Mill took a much broader view of economic growth, a view that encompassed the enhanced quality of life that potentially accompanies growth, rather than adhering to the much narrower preoccupation of their successors—the neoclassical economists—with growth in income alone. Drèze and Sen, *India*, pp. 9–10.

6. *Articles of Agreement of the International Bank for Reconstruction and Development* (as amended effective December 17, 1965) (IBRD: Washington, D.C., n.d.), Article 1.

7. Emphasis added.

8. *Articles of Agreement of the International Bank for Reconstruction and Development* (as amended effective December 17, 1965). (IBRD: Washington, D.C., n.d.), Article 1.

9. International Development Association, *Articles of Agreement and*

Accompanying Report of the Executive Directors of the International Bank for Reconstruction and Development (Washington, D.C., April 1977), p. 1.

10. Keynes's lack of enthusiasm for foreign investment led him to advocate policies that would have given priority to domestic over foreign investments. See Oliver, *International Economic Co-operation and the World Bank*, pp. 64–66. An interesting question is whether the behavior of foreign investors indicates "market failure." If one assumes, for example, that returns on foreign investment when adjusted for risk are no higher than less risky domestic investment, markets could be performing rationally, with little need for correction or intervention by the MDBs. Why would the MDBs, in other words, know better than the markets where to invest? One argument, advanced by Dani Rodrik, is that multilateral lenders play a vital role in policy reform and information monitoring, which reduces the risk to both their own investments (loans) and those of foreign investors. Rodrik, "Why Is There Multilateral Lending?"

11. Mason and Asher, *The World Bank Since Bretton Woods*, pp. 106–107; Richardson and Haralz, *Moving to the Market*, p. 31.

12. Mason and Asher, *The World Bank Since Bretton Woods*, pp. 124–142.

13. World Bank, *Articles of Agreement*, Article III, section 4 (v).

14. Article III, section 4 (i).

15. It should be noted that both the IDB and the AsDB were allowed by their charters to lend directly to the private sector, but traditionally they have not used this capability. And the World Bank's IFC, as with the EBRD, was established principally to lend to (or invest in) the private sector.

16. The problem of bank losses through appreciation of exchange rates arose because of fluctuations in exchange rates among the various currencies disbursed by the MDBs. Thus, even though loans were denominated in U.S. dollars, a significant portion was disbursed in yen and deutsche marks, which appreciated against the dollar. The outstanding amount of the loan (in U.S. dollars) would thus be adjusted upward as the non-U.S. currencies appreciated. This policy implies that the exchange risk—the risk of having to pay more in terms of dollars than originally contracted in the loan—is borne by the borrowing member. See Mistry, *Multilateral Development Banks*, p. 18 and chapter 6.

17. Mason and Asher, *The World Bank Since Bretton Woods*, pp. 380–389. The developed countries generally opposed locating the new facility in the UN. They preferred the World Bank, in which they had a voting majority, as its home.

18. It should be noted that only the soft-loan portion of the MDBs' overall lending qualifies as official development assistance (ODA), or foreign aid, as defined by the OECD Development Assistance Committee (DAC). According to the DAC definition, the grant equivalent (the difference between the actual flow and the discounted present value [using an arbitrary discount rate of 10 percent] of principal and interest payments) of financial assistance must be at least 25 percent of the overall flow. Since the interest charges on soft loans tend to be close to zero and principal payments stretch out to fifty years, the present value of future payments is considerably lower—around 15 percent of the actual flow, indicating a grant equivalent of 85 percent. The MDBs' hard loans, however, typically carry a grant equivalent of less than 25 percent, so under this definition they do not constitute ODA.

19. Woods, "The Development Decade in the Balance," p. 214.

20. Ayres, *Banking on the Poor, p. 4*.

21. OECD, *Twenty-Five Years of Development Co-operation*, p. 165.

22. If resources are fungible, as they often are in development projects financed with a variety of foreign and domestic sources, it will always be difficult to identify the impact of any particular flow. The implication of this line of thought is that what is most important is the total size of resource flow to each country, the effectiveness with which that flow is used by each country, and the distribution of scarce foreign resources among countries.

23. Cassen and associates, *Does Aid Work?* pp. 29–31.

24. For example, on the World Bank, see Mason and Asher, *The World Bank Since Bretton Woods*, especially chapters 19 and 20; on the IDB, see Dell, *The Inter-American Development Bank;* on the AsDB, see Wilson, *A Bank for Half the World;* and on the ADB, see Gardiner and Pickett, *The African Development Bank 1964–1984*. Also see earlier volumes in the current series on MDBs by Kappagoda, *The Asian Development Bank;* Tussie, *The Inter-American Development Bank;* and English and Mule, *The African Development Bank*. Also ibid.

25. Mason and Asher, *The World Bank Since Bretton Woods*, chapter 19.

26. Ibid., p. 680.

27. Tussie, *The Inter-American Development Bank*, p. 46.

28. Little and Mirrlees, *Project Appraisal and Planning for Developing Countries;* UNIDO, *Guidelines for Project Evaluation;* and Squire and van der Tak, *Economic Analysis of Projects*.

29. See Carlsson, Köhlin, and Ekbom, *The Political Economy of Evaluation*, for a critique of cost-benefit analysis in development programs. As soon as nonobservable parameters or data are required for the analysis (as with "shadow prices" that diverge from market prices), the scope for subjective or arbitrary assumptions increases.

30. Ayres, *Banking on the Poor*, p. 4.

31. Cornia, Jolly, and Stewart, *Adjustment with a Human Face*.

32. *Agreement Establishing the European Bank for Reconstruction and Development*, Article 1, "Purpose."

33. Ayres, *Banking on the Poor*, p. 79.

34. It should be pointed out, however, that the McNamara initiative became associated with assistance to the lowest deciles (the "bottom 40 percent"). This did not signify a bias toward alleviating relative poverty as much as it signified a proposition that the proportion of humanity living below an absolute poverty line amounted to 40 percent.

35. Ayres, *Banking on the Poor*.

36. Ibid., pp. 79–80.

37. Leveled by Cornia, Jolly, and Stewart, *Adjustment with a Human Face*.

38. Tussie, *The Inter-American Development Bank*, pp. 46–51.

39. Ibid., p. 81.

40. Ibid., pp. 80–83.

41. English and Mule, *The African Development Bank*, pp. 162–163.

42. Culpeper, "Regional Development Banks," p. 464.

43. Kappagoda, *The Asian Development Bank*, p. 42.

44. "Report of the Task Force on Poverty Alleviation," document R88-183, 1988, and "The World Bank's Support for Poverty Alleviation," Strategic Planning and Review Department, June 1988 (cited in World Bank 1993b).

45. World Bank, *Assistance Strategies to Reduce Poverty*.

46. World Bank, *Poverty Reduction Handbook and Operational Directive*.

47. World Bank, *Assistance Strategies to Reduce Poverty*, p. 11.

48. Ibid.

49. Emmerij, "A Critical Review."

50. George and Sabelli, *Faith and Credit*, p. 147.

51. Rich, *Mortgaging the Earth*, pp. 86–89.

52. World Bank, *1994 Annual Report*, pp. 34–35.

53. Kappagoda, *The Asian Development Bank*, pp. 144–145.

54. Between 1960 and 1980, Brazil's headcount index fell from 50 to 21 percent; from 1981 to 1987, it rose from 19 to 24 percent. World Bank, *World Development Report 1990*, pp. 41, 43. See Stewart, for an analysis of the impact of adjustment programs on poverty.

55. Tussie, *The Inter-American Development Bank*, p. 11.

56. English and Mule, *The African Development Bank*, p. 163.

57. Ibid., p. 165.

58. See World Bank, *World Development Report 1995*, for a recent statement of such views.

59. World Bank, *The East Asian Miracle*; Fishlow et al., *Miracle or Design?*

60. Sen, "Development"; Sen et al., *The Standard of Living*; and Sen, *Inequality Reexamined*. See also Drèze and Sen, *Hunger and Public Action*, and Anand and Ravallion, "Human Development in Poor Countries." In 1990, the United Nations Development Programme (*Human Development Report 1990*) initiated a new index, the human development index, based on the new precepts.

61. UNDP, *Human Development Report 1990*. The human development (HD) school may have a superficial resemblance to the basic human needs (BHN) school described earlier. As Anand and Ravallion "Human Development in Poor Countries" point out, however, BHN has more in common with the mainstream (economic growth) school in that both emphasize commodity outputs as indicators of progress. To be sure, the outputs stressed by BHN are food, drinking water, and shelter rather than output in general. BHN is still philosophically different from HD, however, which stresses people rather than commodity outputs as the objective of development.

62. Anand and Ravallion, "Human Development in Poor Countries."

63. The "possible incompatibility, in the short term, between the objectives of promoting private-sector–led economic growth and reducing poverty" was noted by Mitsuo Sato, president of the Asian Development Bank, in a response to the Development Committee's MDB Task Force Report. He went on to say, "The rapid shift to a market-based private-sector–led economy . . . often does not benefit people evenly. How to reconcile private-sector–led growth and poverty reduction at the macro-policy level is, accordingly, a major question that the governments of developing countries and MDBs must address." (Development Committee, "Comments of the Multilateral Development Banks.")

64. Emmerij, "A Critical Review." It is true that Emmerij's description of the World Bank strategy amounts to a caricature. Its value lies in provoking us to reflect on what constitutes the essence of the Bank's strategy and whether it amounts to anything new.

65. Drèze and Sen, *India*, p. 181.

66. Drèze and Sen (ibid., pp. 197–200) point out that some "success stories" in human development, such as the Indian state of Kerala, are also relative failures in terms of economic growth and could benefit considerably from liberalization.

67. See Counts, *Give Us Credit,* and Otero and Ryne, *The New World of Microenterprise Finance.*

68. Moseley in Griffith-Jones et al., *Assessment of the IDB Lending Programme,* p. 29.

69. See Fishlow et al., *Miracle or Design?* as well as Drèze and Sen, *India,* pp. 32–42.

70. G7 Halifax Summit, *Communiqué,* June 1995.

5

MDBs in the Family of Development Cooperation Agencies

By the early 1990s, at least two multilateral development banks were operating in each region of the world—the World Bank, with operations in every region, along with one of the four regional development banks. In addition, a larger number of subregional development banks, such as the Caribbean Development Bank,[1] were operating within each region. Since all of these banks do essentially the same sorts of things in the same countries, the question arises as to whether unnecessary duplication, overlap, or redundancy occurs in their activities or responsibilities. Indeed, the issue of coordination and consistency among the MDBs was central to the work of a task force set up in 1994 by the IMF–World Bank Development Committee.[2]

This chapter examines interrelationships among the five major multilateral development banks, including issues such as competition, coordination, and complementarity. It asks whether the five MDBs, as a family of similar development agencies, work together as effectively or efficiently as they might and considers ways to enhance their joint, systemic development impact. Between 1992 and 1994, all of the MDBs examined in this study (with the exception of the EBRD) undertook performance reviews of their lending portfolios. These reviews, as noted in Chapter 3, emphasized the need to reorient the corporate culture of the MDBs away from lending volume and toward quality lending in the sense of producing long-term sustainable human development. The reviews also emphasized borrower ownership and participation—putting developing countries back in the driver's seat—as particularly critical to successful and sustainable development.

The key issue examined in this chapter is whether a different division of labor, one based on clear principles (for example, comparative advantage), might enhance the MDBs' development effectiveness both individually and collectively. It is worth observing that the issues of MDB coordination and cooperation typically refer to a *pair* of MDBs in each region: the World Bank and the regional development bank.

This chapter first sets out some observations on how the MDBs collaborate or coordinate their activities in each of the four main continental regions. The typical situation in each region involves the World Bank and the regional bank, so attention is focused on the relationships between the two MDBs. Based on these observations, some medium-term arrangements are suggested, with a focus on the capabilities of the two institutions and the needs of the region.

The chapter then advances some propositions about the functioning of the overall system of MDBs. It suggests a principle on which the division of labor might be based—competitive pluralism—and recommends some procedural innovations that would enhance the systemic effectiveness of competitive pluralism among this family of development agencies over the long term.

Africa

With regard to coordination between the African Development Bank and the World Bank (which covers all of continental Africa), the present division of labor is such that the ADB group is focused more on agriculture and infrastructure and the World Bank on urban and social sectors. In recent years, the World Bank's emphasis on education, health, and population has increased, and the share of agriculture sector lending has fallen to 9 percent. The most striking contrast with the ADB, however, is the much greater scale of operations through the World Bank's IDA compared with the African Bank's concessional window, the African Development Fund. Whereas the ADF approved loans of about $3.2 billion during the period 1991–1993, IDA credits approved for Africa during the same period amounted to $8.6 billion. In the same period, the ADB approved nonconcessional loans amounting to $5.8 billion, whereas IBRD nonconcessional loans fell sharply and amounted to $1.4 billion.[3]

The much harder blend of resources (in terms of their overall nonconcessionality) flowing to African borrowers through the regional bank has been a controversial issue between regional and nonregional shareholders. The controversy obstructed negotiations on the replenishment of the ADF, which drove its soft-loan commitment authority virtually to zero during 1994. Even though the dispute was essentially resolved at the May 1995 ADB annual meetings, it appears the ADF's donors will reduce their contributions to a level even lower than that of the previous replenishment. The same fate is befalling the IDA: The Eleventh Replenishment, agreed in March 1996, resulted in new donor contributions of $11 billion, compared to $16 billion for IDA 10.

The basic point, however, is that concessional resources for sub-Saharan Africa are in desperately short supply. Given that most of the region's borrowers are not creditworthy for nonconcessional loans, active participation and intimate collaboration of both MDBs and other donors (which are particularly significant in sub-Saharan Africa) is needed in the next few years.

Donor coordination in sub-Saharan Africa has recently taken a promising turn with the advent of integrated sector investment programs. These programs are sectorwide in scope, are prepared by local stakeholders, comprise all donors active in the sector, and involve common implementation arrangements and minimal resort to long-term foreign technical assistance. Perhaps most important, these programs seek to effect local ownership by putting the recipient country government in the driver's seat rather than subject to the beckoning of donors both individually and collectively. As major donors in the region, both the ADB and the World Bank will need to be significant players to ensure such programs succeed.

Regarding specialization, the ADB's current strengths lie in its lending to traditional project sectors. Given the importance of agriculture to most African economies, the ADB group's history of support to this sector, and the apparent withdrawal of the World Bank and other donors, it seems crucial that the ADB maintain its support and perhaps increase its expertise in this area. The same can be said regarding the other traditional project sectors—principally infrastructure. The World Bank, along with the IMF, can be expected to continue to lead in the area of macroeconomic policy dialogue and the policy-based lending associated with such dialogue. There may be exceptions, such as the smallest borrowers in the region,[4] where the ADB is a larger lender than the World Bank and could take the lead in macroeconomic policy dialogue and policy-based lending.

The social sectors (education, health, and population) are likely to be areas of shared interest, given the increasing emphasis by all donor agencies on human resource development. Another area of shared interest is regional integration. Normally, the lead role in this area should fall to the regional bank. Given the magnitude of investment requirements associated with integration all over the continent, however, the involvement of the World Bank and other donors will be imperative.[5]

Better coordination is needed with the World Bank (and the IMF) in regard to regional countries' arrears to the ADB on nonconcessional loans. Given the seriousness of mounting arrears and the interest of the World Bank and the IMF in ensuring that the ADB remains financially sound, the three institutions could adopt a common policy to facilitate the payment of overdue obligations or, more positively, a common policy on burden sharing and the orderly reduction of such multilateral debts. The Bretton Woods institutions could exercise their leverage by withholding approval of new balance-of-payments loans, or at the least disbursements on such loans, from countries with overdue obligations to the ADB. As Philip English and Harris Mule put it, the Bretton Woods institutions have an important interest in a healthy regional development bank.[6]

Finally, a case exists for the need for more research by the ADB on African development problems. Currently, this area of research is dominated by the World Bank. Given the severity of the problems faced by member countries and the disappointing results of many of the initiatives by the donor community to date, there is scope for a greater competition of ideas about African development. This need not involve increased total expenditures on research; it can be accomplished by the World Bank subcontracting some of its research to the ADB, through joint research projects, and through consciously helping to build research capacity in the ADB and in African countries generally with support from the World Bank's research budget.[7]

Over the next few years the membership of the two MDBs should work to ensure that the African Bank's capacities to act effectively are restored following the period of uncertainty and turmoil that has marked the early 1990s. The World Bank could do more to assist its regional counterpart in this process of capacity building. The actions suggested here represent a medium-term investment in the collective strength of all MDBs as well as in the economic and social progress of Africa.

Asia

Similar to the case in Africa, the resources that flow to the Asian region from the World Bank far exceed those of the Asian Development Bank. In the Asian case, however, the lending volumes through both the World Bank's primary windows (nonconcessional and concessional) far exceed those of the regional bank's. The differential may decrease somewhat with regard to the hard window following the AsDB's general capital increase that was approved in 1994. The replenishment of the Asian Development Fund is still under negotiation, however, and may be delayed. Meanwhile, there are new claimants for concessional resources in Vietnam, Mongolia, and Central Asia. The continuing paucity of concessional resources means the active collaboration of both MDBs will be required in the poorest countries.

A high degree of complementarity exists between the two MDBs in the areas of policy dialogue and policy-based lending; for some time the AsDB has deferred to the World Bank and the IMF on matters of macroeconomic management. The AsDB has restricted its policy-based lending activities to issues of sectoral policy and investment.

The AsDB's strengths lie in its delivery of well-designed and well-executed projects, particularly its projects in the infrastructure and power utilities sectors, to which historically the Bank has allocated a significantly greater proportion of its lending resources (54 percent) than has the World Bank (28 percent). The World Bank, in contrast, has allocated considerably more to program and adjustment lending (24 percent) than has the Asian Bank (3 percent).[8] These data on allocation do not necessarily mean the AsDB has a comparative advantage over the World Bank in projects, although the AsDB's evaluation reports suggest this is an area of relative strength.[9]

In 1991, the AsDB adopted five strategic development objectives: improving the economy, reducing poverty, supporting human development and population planning, improving the status of women, and protecting the environment. These objectives are very similar to those of the World Bank and the other regional banks (with the possible exception of the EBRD); thus, over the next few years the lending allocations of the two banks in Asia may not diverge nearly as much as they have in the past.

Both MDBs will need to cooperate intensively on poverty reduction in the region. The area is still home to most of the world's absolute poor; therefore, reducing poverty remains the main development challenge facing borrowing member countries. As with the African Bank, much more scope exists for collaborative effort, especially on the research front. For example, the World Bank's poverty assessments in the Asian region should be undertaken jointly and could become the basis of joint poverty reduction strategies for regional borrowers.

More generally, the degree of collaboration on research by the two MDBs is astonishingly low. For example, AsDB staff gave virtually no input to the World Bank's East Asian miracle study,[10] which has raised as many questions as it has settled. With AsDB collaboration, this work may have reached more satisfactory conclusions, particularly from the viewpoint of the Asian countries (both developed and developing).

No formal cooperation agreement exists between the World Bank and the AsDB, but relations at the operational level are said to be very positive. Complementarity between the two MDBs is the rule; thus, within the same country they might operate in different regions (which is usually the case in the power sector) or in different subsectors (for example, the World Bank tends to concentrate on primary education, and the AsDB focuses on secondary and technical education).

The issue of coordination in the Asian region also involves the EBRD, which is active in the Central Asian republics. The AsDB and the EBRD *have* reached a formal cooperation agreement that is not aimed at exclusivity but gives the EBRD the lead role in private and financial sector development and the AsDB the lead in the social sectors. The need for coordination among these newest members of the MDBs is particularly acute, since they are unique among borrowing countries in belonging to two regional banks as well as to the World Bank.

The model of integrated sector investment programs, discussed earlier in the context of the African Development Bank, has been practiced in the South Asian subregion for many years; examples include the Bangladesh health sector and the Pakistan Social Action Program. Both MDBs are active in the latter program, which focuses on primary education and health, population, water, and sanitation. Such approaches to donor coordination appear promising because of their emphasis on capacity building, local ownership, and sustainability. The AsDB and the EBRD share an interest in ensuring that these programs work well.

One of the notable and long-standing strengths of the AsDB is its capacity to support technical assistance with grant funding. The Bank has used this capacity to its advantage, and other agencies including the World Bank, the IMF, and the UNDP have often relied on the Asian Bank's Technical Assistance Special Fund (TASF). Unlike the World Bank and other MDBs—which have recently allowed a profusion of consultant trust funds to be established by individual bilateral donors, with sourcing usually tied to the donor countries—the AsDB's facility is untied and thus remains faithful to the multilateral principle of competitive bidding. At the same time, the TASF is frequently used to develop borrowing country capacity by hiring local consultants.

Regional cooperation has recently been the focus of much AsDB activity because of heightened political interest by member countries. This is an issue on which the Bank should take the lead role. Regional members have looked to the AsDB as an honest broker in the Greater Mekong subregion to facilitate projects in the power and transport sectors that have cross-boundary externalities (both positive, as with the sale of surplus power, and negative, as with pollution).

As with the other regional banks, the Asian Bank has a more intimate and continuous relationship with its smaller borrowing members, including (among others) the Pacific Island microstates. The World Bank has difficulty justifying a continuous lending program in these countries, since their scale of operations is vastly smaller than the World Bank's average loan of around $100 million. Here, the Asian Bank's lower costs give it a natural advantage, in addition to other advantages such as its closeness (geographically and culturally) to the borrowers.

In summary, the Asian Bank does not need to intensify its specialization or differentiation from those of the World Bank. In many ways, it is one of the most successful of the MDBs and is often cited as a model of efficiency.[11] Cooperation between the two MDBs at the working level appears to be fully satisfactory.[12] What could perhaps bear improvement is the degree of collaboration between the two MDBs in regard to the research they undertake, in their economic and sector work, and on issues in which the Asian experience (with the newly industrialized economies and, more recently, economies in transition in Indochina and Mongolia) may be significantly different from that in other parts of the world.

The Americas

Since the completion of negotiations for the Inter-American Development Bank's Eighth Replenishment (general resource increase [GRI] 8) in 1994, the sustainable level of lending for the IDB group has been $7 billion per annum. Even during the Seventh Replenishment period (1990–1994), the IDB group's lending capacity had risen to parity with the World Bank's annual commitments to the Latin America/Caribbean (LAC) region—that is, to between $5 billion and $6 billion. Hence, the IDB is unique among the regional development banks in having a greater lending capacity in its region than the notional lending capacity of the World Bank, which makes its relationship with the World Bank significantly different from the relationships of the other regional banks. Moreover, not only does the IDB's *gross* lending capacity exceed that of the World Bank in LAC, in terms of *net flows* and *net transfers*, the World Bank—by virtue of its heavy lending during the 1970s and 1980s—will be a growing recipient rather than a provider of financial flows to the region, whereas the IDB will continue to be a net source through the end of the 1990s.

The IDB has almost, but not completely, captured the leadership role in the region as a result not only of the Eighth Replenishment but also because of the dramatic economic and political liberalization that has swept the borrowing member countries during the past decade. When the protracted negotiations for the Seventh Replenishment were finally resolved in 1989, the IDB quickly positioned itself to become an active partner with the World Bank and the IMF in the economic reform programs that were in advanced stages of implementation. The democratic transformation of the region and the end of the ideological tensions associated with the Cold War have also allowed the IDB to pursue an agenda of social justice and equity without the overtones doing so might have carried in the 1970s and 1980s. Finally, with the advent of the North American Free Trade Agreement (NAFTA), Mercosur, and other regional trade agreements, the IDB has become active—indeed central, especially since the Miami Summit of December 1994—in the movement toward trade liberalization throughout the hemisphere.

The growing regional preeminence of the IDB was set back—perhaps temporarily—by the Mexican peso crisis in early 1995, which catapulted the IMF and, to a lesser extent, the World Bank back into prominence as the key multilateral agencies in the region. This is not surprising, given the global dimensions of the peso crisis.

In some critical areas a high degree of complementarity has existed between the IDB and the World Bank since 1989. With regard to policy-based lending, the IDB (as with the Asian Bank) has carved out a role at the sectoral level, leaving macroeconomic issues to the Bretton Woods organizations. But with regard to projects, the operations of the two MDBs are similar in their sectoral scope. A more evident difference is seen, however, in country coverage: As with the Asian and African Banks, the IDB is a more significant lender to the smallest borrowing countries in the region.

In other areas, considerable overlap is found. As with the World Bank, the IDB is planning to broaden and deepen its support for social sector and poverty reduction programs. These programs were given special emphasis in GRI 8, with a target of 40 percent of total lending and 50 percent of the number of operations. This dramatic shift in lending priorities has been made necessary by sharply deteriorating living standards in the 1980s.

The congruence between the planned lending programs of the two MDBs reflects current realities and needs in the region. The issue is not whether the two MDBs should both be so deeply committed to the social sectors or whether a greater division of labor is needed between them but, rather, how their coexistence can serve to benefit the borrowers. In fact, a higher degree of collaboration characterizes the operations of the two institutions than is found between the World Bank and the other regional banks. A great number of operations are cofinanced, and in these cases joint missions and appraisal reports are common. There appears to be much more evidence of positive cooperation than of waste and duplication.

Such cooperation is unquestionably facilitated by the location of both headquarters in Washington, D.C., but it has also come about because of the extremely close working relationships that have developed between the two MDBs at all professional levels. Indeed, to expedite coordination reorganization at the IDB has purposely resulted in country groupings and structures similar to those at the World Bank. This relationship now extends to issues such as portfolio performance indicators, which have been developed by the World Bank and adopted in three sectors by the IDB.

At the same time, at least occasional predatory competition appears to exist in the smaller borrowing countries. This may occur because the scope for the MDBs to initiate projects is greater among the smaller borrowers; the larger borrowers are more likely to put forward their own project proposals.

In summary, the IDB is cutting a distinct swath from that of the World Bank through its central role in regional economic integration (a role it shares with the Organization of American States and the UN Economic Commission for Latin America and the Caribbean [ECLAC]). In addition, the IDB has launched a creative dialogue on the governance issue—which is politically sensitive in the region—by concentrating on the development of civil society and issues such as judicial reform. With these exceptions, the bulk of the IDB's activities and operations are likely to be indistinguishable from those of the World Bank. Notwithstanding intense cooperation and collaboration between the two MDBs at the working level, they overlap considerably in the scope of their activities and capabilities—more so than is seen in the corresponding relationships between the World Bank and the RDBs in other regions. Therefore, this region of the developing world has the greatest need for more transparency in the plans and programs of the two leading development institutions to ensure that their joint endeavors represent the best possible allocation of resources.

Eastern and Central Europe and Central Asia

Six years after its creation in 1991, the European Bank for Reconstruction and Development is clearly different from the other MDBs in its constitution, its modus operandi, even its approach to development. Indeed, the concept of *development* is conspicuously scarce in EBRD documents and discussions. The Bank's raison d'être is more to foster the transition to market-based economies in the former Soviet bloc rather than to facilitate development in the manner of other MDBs, multilateral organizations, and bilateral donors.

The EBRD has encountered numerous pitfalls and diversions on the path it has taken to achieve its distinctive niche. By mid-1995, however, the Bank seemed confident that it had chosen the right direction and that its mission was, in fact, unique among the MDBs.

As with its counterparts in the private sector, the Bank is largely a deal-driven organization that is constantly seeking opportunities or going concerns in which to invest. The Bank is mandated to allocate at least 60 percent of its resources to private sector enterprises, a target it could not reach during its first three years because the state sector was still predominant in its countries of operations; thus, opportunities for private sector investment were relatively few. This situation had changed substantially by 1994, when around 73 percent of projects signed were in the private sector; this brought the EBRD's cumulative total allocated to the private sector since 1992 to above 60 percent.

Total project approvals did not gather momentum until 1993; by 1994, they amounted to about $2.95 billion. In FY 1994, the World Bank (mostly the IBRD, with a small amount from the IDA) committed $3.73 billion in lending to Europe and Central Asia. In addition, the World Bank's International Finance Corporation approved $443 million for projects in Europe and $51.2 million for projects in Central Asia. The World Bank group thus committed about $4.22 billion to the EBRD's region of operations. Although this amount is significantly larger than the EBRD's commitments, the EBRD is clearly becoming an MDB that has comparable investing capacity in the region.[13]

As a transaction-driven organization, the EBRD is in many ways unlike the World Bank (IBRD/IDA) and the OCR (ordinary capital resources) or Fund operations of the regional banks, but it is rather similar to the World Bank's IFC and the small, private sector windows of the other regional banks. For example, the EBRD conducts a very different kind of policy dialogue with its borrowing members (normally referred to as "countries of operations"). The Bank does not engage in quick-disbursing balance-of-payments assistance, which—along with issues of macroeconomic policy reform—is left to the Bretton Woods institutions. The EBRD is not unwilling, however, to broach matters of macroeconomic policy informally when occasions arise or at the highest levels of government if necessary.

The basis of the EBRD's relations with its countries of operations is its investment portfolio. The Bank's investments can be made in the public or the private sector. In either case, each investment provides opportunities to engage in policy dialogue—typically at the sectoral level—on issues such as pricing, taxation, regulation, infrastructure, government services, and so on. The difference in the EBRD's approach to policy dialogue (from the approach of the other MDBs) is that it usually connects policy issues to the viability of its investments and those of its investing partners and to concrete matters of whether firms will thrive or perish rather than to issues of high principle or economic correctness. The incentive of government authorities to listen is high, because the EBRD can help to deliver major foreign direct investments to their countries depending on the outcome of the dialogue.

The EBRD's structure enables it to foster transition more easily than the World Bank group. The Bank can lend to and invest in a public sector enterprise—helping to restructure its balance sheet and helping the enterprise to become a commercially competitive entity—as part of a longer-term program of privatization. Following privatization, the EBRD can continue to be an investor—without the backing of a government guarantee—to ensure that the transition is smooth and that the private firm continues to be viable. Ultimately, the EBRD may sell its equity or participation to local or other private sector investors. In contrast, the World Bank must terminate its support of a firm when it is privatized unless the firm's local government can guarantee the loan, which would often defeat one of the objectives of privatization. The IFC has the opposite problem: It cannot become engaged with a firm until it has become a private entity.

A higher degree of complementarity is clearly found between the EBRD and the World Bank core (the IBRD and the IDA) than between the World Bank and any other regional bank. In addition to adjustment and policy-based lending, the World Bank undertakes lending to the social sectors,[14] which are not among the EBRD's sectors of investment. Agriculture is an important sector of activity for the World Bank but not for the EBRD (although the latter supports agribusiness and agricultural marketing). In contrast, finance and business investments are by far the largest of EBRD's sectors of activity (39 percent of total approvals in 1994, compared with 7.5 percent at the World Bank).

When activity overlaps with the World Bank core (in the transport and energy sectors), coordination and collaboration are said to be satisfactory. The most explicit competition is provided by the IFC, which shares with the EBRD a mission to support private sector investment. In this case, as the figures given earlier demonstrate, the IFC is a smaller player than the EBRD in Europe and Central Asia.

Competition is acknowledged on both sides and is regarded as positive (and, in fact, as unavoidable) in transaction-oriented business. Collaboration between the IFC and the EBRD does occur in the form of technical assistance activities and some joint ventures and cofinancing.

The challenge likely to face both the EBRD and the IFC over the longer term is to demonstrate that as international public agencies they provide additionality and social benefits that would not otherwise come about through spontaneous private sector investment. For example, both organizations have emphasized the need for responsible stewardship over the environment, which is a particularly acute social concern in Eastern Europe and the former Soviet Union.[15] But in emulating the private sector by constantly looking for and investing in going concerns, in many ways the EBRD and the IFC may also displace or duplicate private investment.

With the increasing emphasis of some industrial country shareholders on the fact that the MDBs should facilitate private sector growth, it seems particularly important for these two members of the MDB family—which are exemplars of support for private sector development—to demonstrate the larger benefits their efforts, backed by taxpayer funding, can help to bring about. If the EBRD and the IFC were to participate fully in the harmonized systems and procedures suggested in this report (evaluations, country strategies, and a client satisfaction unit), these benefits would become more transparent.

Systemic Principles and Structures

Should there be a permanent division of labor among the MDBs in general, based on their comparative advantage or otherwise? A division of labor based on comparative advantage presumes that each bank has relative strengths that are immutable and that no changes in relative efficiency or capabilities will occur over time to alter the base-case measures on which a division of responsibilities is first made. As well, the most crucial development tasks will change over time, with changing circumstances (positive or negative) altering the priorities that need to be addressed. Moreover, *any* division of labor—the notion that the operational functions of each MDB should be formally separate and distinct from others so no overlap occurs between two or more MDBs operating in the same geographical or thematic area—is questionable unless it is embedded in the MDBs' respective mandates as articulated in the founding charters.[16] This suggests, implausibly, that bestowing a permanent monopoly on a particular MDB is in the best interests of the borrowing members, the MDBs' clients. This is not to deny that each of the banks does have comparative advantages in the sense of relative strengths in certain functional areas on which a division of labor may bring about efficiencies in the medium term; it only questions making such arrangements formal or permanent.

For the past decade—particularly since 1990—the MDBs and many of their nonborrowing members have promoted competitive markets by supporting economic reform and liberalization policies throughout the world. The same principles that underlie such policies suggest that there is merit in encouraging competition among the MDBs. The existence of competition is an important antidote to complacency and insularity as well as a stimulus to efficiency gains and to learning from the experiences of rival MDBs. Perhaps most important, competition is most likely to generate new ideas and innovations, which is vital if the development agencies are to rise to the challenges they face in the fight to eradicate poverty and achieve sustainable human development.

Given the context of increasingly constrained resource availability, particularly through their soft windows, it seems important that the MDBs be given as much incentive as possible to innovate and to enhance their overall effectiveness in facilitating long-term sustainable development. Thus, competitive pluralism among the MDBs, which will involve some overlap in coverage and services, is likely to result in a more dynamic and innovative system than are mutually exclusive, monopolistic arrangements. For example, competitive pressures are responsible for the innovation and spread of single-currency loans.[17] Indeed, scope should exist for competitive bidding among MDBs, as is found in the MDBs' procurement procedures—with the proviso mentioned in the following paragraph.

The model of a perfectly competitive market in which a large number of firms face a large number of consumers may not be apt for the context in which the MDBs operate. First, MDBs are public entities, and they should not behave exactly like profit-maximizing private firms. Furthermore, the market structure in which MDBs operate is clearly imperfect. Virtually all borrowing members borrow from the MDBs unless a graduation policy renders them ineligible.[18] As a result, it is common for both the World Bank and the regional development bank to have lending operations in the same sectors and even in the same geographical regions of a large number of borrowing countries. Because of the sovereign guarantee, the ultimate client in each case is the same—that is, the borrowing country government.

This situation can more accurately be characterized as a monopsony (the government, as sole client) facing a duopoly (the two MDBs as lenders) rather than as a perfectly competitive market. In such circumstances, (nonprice) competition may in fact lead to a lowering of project quality (in the sense of the sustainability of development benefits)—for example, if one of the MDBs relaxes conditionality or the enforcement of loan covenants to appear to be the more attractive lender. Conversely, competition can lead to collusion among the MDBs and to the "ganging-up" problem associated with cross-conditionality. Thus, from the standpoint of development effectiveness, the important question is to what degree inter-MDB competition serves either to improve project quality or, alternatively, to intensify conditionality.

Moreover, a system in which each MDB provides a large range of lending and other services to all of its borrowers is unlikely to be the most efficient one. Thus, the question of whether the MDBs' scarce operational and administrative resources are collectively allocated to achieve the optimum development impact in every developing member country is also legitimate. The greater the services provided by each MDB, the higher the overall administrative costs are likely to be. Administrative overheads at the MDBs amounted to over $2 billion in 1994.[19]

In an oligopolistic market, private firms have an incentive to maximize profits and recover the costs of their typically high administrative overheads through monopolistic (discriminatory) pricing or nonprice competition and to prevent rival firms from benefiting from externalities (for example, by keeping their research secret). In contrast, public entities such as the MDBs, which were created to maximize social benefits rather than their own profits, *should* have an incentive to maintain lower overheads and service costs to their clients—for example, by engaging in price and product competition with each other (as with the example of single-currency loans mentioned earlier); by sharing rather than duplicating their public goods functions, such as research; and by encouraging other development agencies and developing countries themselves to benefit from their work. Resources allocated to the World Bank's research complex could be allocated instead to research capacity building in developing countries. Thus, a rationale exists for sharing such functions or the resources that support them.

In the same vein, even though openness to competition should be the norm, MDBs should also be allowed to develop niches of expertise and service delivery. For example, where the market for MDBs' services is particularly small—that is, in the smallest borrowing countries—the scope for a high degree of specialization among MDBs by sector or geographical region is more limited. It may be inefficient (i.e., it may increase aggregate administrative costs) for more than one MDB to provide a continuous lending program to such borrowers. This is a case for specialization among MDBs, with the lower-cost MDBs (typically the regional banks) providing most, if not all, lending and other services to these borrowers. Where the market is larger—that is, in larger borrowing countries—there is room for more than one MDB to be operationally and continuously active and for each to develop specialized niches. Obviously, the nature of specialization will also differ according to the relative strengths and capabilities of the MDBs.

As argued earlier, however, such arrangements should not be formal or permanent; some borrowing countries might object to market sharing by the MDBs and to their loss of access to one of the MDBs. As shareholders of both the regional bank and the World Bank, their objections cannot be lightly overruled. They will need to be reassured that the regional bank will provide whatever services the World Bank provided and at the same level of quality.[20] Furthermore, specialization among MDBs is not guaranteed to enhance the development impact in all developing countries even if it achieves administrative efficiencies. In some cases, the increased division of labor will serve borrowers well; in others, a good match may not exist between what the MDBs offer individually and collectively and the full range of a borrower's requirements—financial, technical, and advisory.

The adequacy of what MDBs (and other donors) offer will depend on each borrower's circumstances and needs and on overall resource availability. (For example, it may be some time before the ADF has sufficient resources for all its borrowers that require concessional resources; therefore, the continuing involvement of the World Bank, through the IDA, will probably be necessary even in the smaller countries.) Some suggestions for greater specialization and coordination are offered later on a bank-specific basis.

Accordingly, it seems imperative to reinforce *complementarity* and *coordination* among the MDBs (as well as with other multilateral and bilateral donors) to enhance their individual and joint effectiveness, to try to fill any gaps in assistance, and to eliminate wasteful overlap and duplication. Little evidence is offered by the MDBs of overlap, duplication, or poor coordination among themselves. Most of the evidence suggests strong complementarity and very positive interactions, at least among the MDBs. This is not surprising, since it is unlikely that the MDBs would willingly proffer contrary evidence. Anecdotal evidence suggests, however, that coordination, overlap, and duplication *are* significant and perennial problems—even *within* particular MDBs, such as the World Bank group (i.e., between the IBRD/IDA and the IFC). Moreover, problems of coordination among donors, bilateral and multilateral, extend far beyond the MDBs and are generally more severe than issues of inter-MDB coordination. On these issues, some systematic input from the borrowing countries— *unfiltered by donor-led agencies*—would be particularly useful.

The optimum division of labor among MDBs suggested here is similar to that which prevails within the modern transnational corporation (TNC), in which a certain degree of rivalry among affiliates is typically encouraged; at the same time, an important degree of sharing also occurs among affiliates (of technology, for example), and they share a common goal of maximizing global profits. The analogy is not far-fetched, since even though the various MDBs are not affiliates of the same corporate structure (as are the members of the World Bank group), the shareholders are essentially the same. The important difference, however, lies in the overarching objective: Rather than maximizing global profits, as in the case of the TNC, the common goal of the MDBs is reducing poverty and providing sustainable human development in the borrowing member countries. Hence, shareholders should be in a position to know and to compare how rival MDBs perform, both individually and collectively, in terms of this basic objective.

In a dynamic TNC, the roles and activities of its affiliates are constantly changing in response to the changing environment and their performance as profit centers. Applying this model to the governance of the MDB system, with its more diffuse objectives, is less straightforward than comparing the profitability of TNC affiliates. If competitive pluralism is to be the fundamental rule that informs the changing relationships among MDBs, they need better tools to ensure that the system and each of its parts is performing at its maximum potential. To make comparisons of individual MDBs' performance, to judge the adequacy of their present and planned cooperation and coordination in member countries, and to garner systematic input from the borrowing countries, one must conclude that the systems and procedures within and among the MDBs at the time of this writing (mid-1996) are inadequate. To compare the current performance of the MDBs' operations, ex post operations evaluations should be consistent and comparable across MDBs. To judge the adequacy of planned coordination among MDBs, country focus strategies for each MDB borrowing member should be harmonized. Finally, to garner systematic input on these matters from the borrowing countries, a new client satisfaction unit is suggested that would act on behalf of borrowing countries by undertaking selective examinations of coordination at the country level. These systemic recommendations are discussed in turn.

Harmonizing Evaluation Systems

The ex post evaluations systems of the MDBs have similar objectives and deploy similar instruments, but the details of their methods and end results differ significantly, making comparability difficult. For example, in its Post-Evaluation Reports the Asian Development Bank has three categories of outcomes for its operations—generally successful, partially successful, and unsuccessful—whereas the World Bank has two categories, satisfactory and unsatisfactory. The Inter-American Development Bank recently merged its two evaluation offices into a single entity that reports to the Board of Executive Directors, much like the World Bank's Operations Evaluation Department (OED). Much of the emphasis of the new office, however, is directed at building up the evaluation capacity of the regional borrowing members. The World Bank has the most comprehensive evaluation coverage of all of the MDBs; unlike the others, it also has an active program of evaluation of the long-term development impact of its operations and of the effectiveness of its nonlending services. Underlying such differences are important issues concerning the specific role of evaluation in the governance of each MDB and in each MDB's relations with its borrowing and other shareholders.

It is important for each evaluation office to discharge its principal responsibilities to its Board and its member countries by distilling the lessons learned from past and ongoing operations and feeding them back into the process of identifying, designing, and implementing new projects. The ultimate objective of each evaluation office must be to enhance the overall development effectiveness of its own institution. For this reason, it would be counterproductive to completely externalize the evaluation function by, for example, merging the evaluation units into a new evaluation agency, independent of the MDBs, that would undertake identical functions in each bank. There is considerable merit, however, in *harmonizing* the methodologies and the scope of work undertaken by the separate units to facilitate comparisons among them and also to expedite the lessons learned by the MDBs.

In the wake of the portfolio performance reviews undertaken by the MDBs since 1992, the scope for harmonization extends beyond the activities of the evaluation offices. The World Bank is developing new indicators that go beyond the traditional evaluation benchmarks of economic and financial performance at the project and sectoral levels and focus on the intended development results of operations, the equity and sustainability of benefits, and the participation of beneficiaries. Such tools are vital to facilitate the transition from quantity to quality lending. Such portfolio assessments will be highly useful if they are undertaken by all of the MDBs using comparable methods.

There have been ongoing discussions among the evaluation offices about making their methods more consistent. These discussions have suggested that all of the MDBs should work toward a harmonized system of evaluation that would make the results of their ex post operations evaluations directly comparable. In addition, the regional banks should follow the lead of the World Bank in developing a system of portfolio assessments that would be comparable across all of the MDBs. Finally, the IMF needs to be brought into such a system of harmonized evaluations to ensure consistency between the IMF and the MDBs in interpreting the outcomes of adjustment operations.[21]

The option of a unified evaluation office, external to and independent of the MDBs, is a logical extension of the idea of harmonized evaluation. It is less likely, however, that an external unit would be effective in reinforcing lessons learned within each MDB. Moreover, the client satisfaction unit elaborated later provides some of the advantages of independence and quality assurance an external evaluation unit might provide.

Putting Borrowing Clients in the Driver's Seat: Harmonizing Country Strategies

Since 1990, all of the MDBs have converged on a similar mode of organizing their lending programs within each of their borrowing clients; these are referred to generically as "country strategies."[22] In the case of the World Bank, the organizing framework is called the Country Assistance Strategy (CAS). The CAS provides a context within which new operations proposed for the Bank's country-specific assistance programs are identified. Since the release of the Portfolio Management Task Force Report, the CAS has also provided the context within which the Bank's portfolio performance is evaluated. Although each CAS is slightly different, the strategy presents an assessment of development priorities in the particular country, its economic performance, and the impact of the external environment. The Bank situates its lending strategy (level and composition of lending) within this context, presents a risk analysis based on alternative scenarios, and discusses any relevant analyses it may have undertaken—such as a poverty assessment or an assessment of economic and sector work—and the role of aid coordination.

Similarly, the Asian Bank prepares Country Operation Strategy Studies, the African Bank develops Economic Prospects and Country

Programming Papers, and the Inter-American Development Bank prepares Country Papers for each borrowing member. Drafting these papers serves a similar strategic purpose in all of the MDBs: They are vehicles for planning each MDB's future operations in a medium-term framework as well as for judging the performance of the bank's portfolio within the country.

Essentially, each country strategy, and the document that presents the strategy to the MDB Board for discussion, consists of two parts: a front end, which is an analysis of the borrowing country's development priorities and the external environment it faces, and a back end, which contains a review of the performance of the bank's portfolio and a proposed pipeline of operations in the light of its own performance and that of the borrowing country. Although there is provision for discussion of aid coordination, this tends to be pro forma and does not aim at presenting comprehensively the activities or intentions of other MDBs or donors.

The country strategy exercises of the MDBs thus serve objectives that are largely *internal* to each bank by presenting its past and future operations in the context of the needs, opportunities, and challenges of the borrowing country. What the exercises fail to do is to "put the borrower in the driver's seat"; they also miss an important opportunity for more transparency and accountability to shareholders with regard to aid coordination. It should be possible to resolve both shortcomings by making the process of preparing and discussing country strategies one that is largely common to all MDBs (and, ideally, to all donors).

The front end of the document, which is currently drafted by MDB staff at each institution, should be drafted by the borrowing country authorities in collaboration with MDB staff, if needed. If local ownership of the country strategy is a key ingredient of its coherence and its success, preparation of the strategy should be the central responsibility of the developing countries. Further, the process should preferably be open to public input and debate rather than the prerogative of governments and bureaucracies. The back end of the document would have to be compiled in sections by MDB staffs, each preparing a review of its past interventions and current portfolio presenting its proposed lending program for the next two to five years. The document would be in two distinct sections. The first would contain the portfolio review and planned program for the subject MDB, prepared by its own staff. This section would be discussed by the Executive Board, and discussion would focus on whether that MDB was performing to its potential. The second section would contain the portfolio review and planned program for the other MDB and perhaps reviews and programs of other multilateral and bilateral donors as well. This section would be appended "for information only" for the Executive Board of the subject MDB. The details would display much more fully than current country strategies the extent of collaboration, cooperation, and overlap between organizations operating in the same client country. If prepared in this way, the country strategy document would still serve the functions for which it was originally designed—to provide for oversight and due diligence by the Executive Board over the performance and plans of its institution.

Problems with timing and datedness would probably occur if such a harmonized procedure were adopted, since different Executive Boards would inevitably be considering a particular country strategy at different points in time; such logistical problems are surmountable, however. The main benefit of this suggested procedure would be that the performance and planned programs of both MDBs would be more transparent. Although the planned operations of nonsubject MDBs would not be open to discussion, the degree of collaboration, coordination, and duplication among agencies—the interface between proposed programs—would be.

Issues of coordination and collaboration among donors are central to the many consultative groups (CGs) and aid consortia that are organized for individual developing countries. Such fora can also play a vital role in reconciling inconsistencies in the country assistance strategies among the donors or between the country strategy of the borrower and the assistance strategies of members of the donor consortium. Ultimately, the purpose of the CGs should be to enhance the capacity of the developing country rather than to serve the convenience of the donor countries (for example, providing them with a bully pulpit from which to lecture the developing countries or to sort out coordination problems that arise as a result of donor countries' policies and practices). The CGs should also be used as fora to provide public input to enhance public participation in the planning process.[23]

Creating a Client Satisfaction Unit

Finally, the present study recommends the institution of a client satisfaction unit. The rationale for such a unit is that the development cooperation system, as presently structured, lacks a monitoring and evaluation unit that undertakes its work *on behalf of the aid recipient countries*. All bilateral and multilateral aid agencies have their own internal evaluation units, and for three decades the DAC of the OECD donors has acted as the formal monitoring institution with the goal of enhancing both the quantity and quality of aid flows. Consultative groups and roundtables bring together the various donors of a particular recipient country; these are usually chaired by the World Bank (or the UNDP in the case of roundtables). The recent portfolio reviews at four of the MDBs were also undertaken with a view to obtaining better, more sustainable development results from their individual organizations.[24]

Given the number of such evaluation units and reviews, the need for another should be questioned. The unit proposed here, however, would not replicate any existing evaluation or coordination mechanism, and it should first be required to prove itself on a very modest experimental basis before becoming a permanent fixture. The problem with the existing monitoring and evaluation mechanisms is that their purpose is generally to enhance the individual effectiveness of the donor agencies.[25] Even if all donor agencies heeded the lessons learned from, and the moral suasion of, these various exercises—and there is abundant evidence that they do not—what is still missing is the recipients' view regarding the strengths and problems, at the country level, of the individual and collective efforts of donors. (By its nature, the consultative group mechanism makes it difficult for the recipient country to be constructively critical of the efforts of its donors or to make suggestions for improvement.)

The purpose of the unit would be similar to that of organizations that carry out consumer satisfaction surveys, which are important sources of market intelligence. If they are undertaken at arm's length and in the public domain, such surveys can provide important objective feedback to producers and consumers alike. Producers benefit by finding out what consumers actually think of their products; accordingly, they may take remedial action or capitalize on unanticipated opportunities. Prospective consumers benefit by reviewing other consumers' responses to the products before making their own purchase decisions.

Similarly, the client satisfaction unit would survey borrowing clients on a range of questions regarding the efficacy of various programs and agencies—including, but not necessarily restricted to, the MDBs. The unit would, in general terms, survey clients on the basic issues underlying this study—the relationship between the MDBs and other donors (including the IMF), the relative strengths and weaknesses of different donors in functional areas, and whether they feel well served by the current or planned division of labor. As much as possible, the unit would focus on specific technical issues—for example, the procurement practices of various donors, consultant selection practices under technical assistance programs, and so forth. Among other things, the unit could examine the efficacy of the integrated sector investment program approach to coordination from the viewpoint of recipient countries. In general, the unit would function as an external quality assurance mechanism for all donors, including the MDBs.

The work of the unit would be facilitated if the two systemic recommendations made earlier—for harmonized evaluation systems and harmonized country strategies—were also adopted. Surveys of the unit would provide an extra test of the consistency of evaluation systems and the comprehensiveness of country strategies.

It is suggested that if such a unit were created, it would be important to have it funded in part by the developing countries. The unit should have sufficient resources to enable it to carry out its duties,[26] and it should be housed outside the MDBs. There are several potential hosts for the unit: It could be part of a reformed Development Committee secretariat;[27] it could be part of a new G-24 secretariat,[28] established as part of the institutional apparatus of the Interim and Development Committees; it could be part of a reformed UNCTAD secretariat; or it could be part of the relatively new South Commission. Some initial financial and logistical support could come from the World Bank, the IMF, and the regional banks, since the unit would represent an investment in quality assurance. The unit would be useful to the MDBs by providing a reality check on the effectiveness of their operations. The perceived independence of the unit would be compromised, however, if it were heavily or chronically subsidized by the international financial institutions or the donors. In other words, financial support from the developing countries would be necessary to demonstrate some ownership of and commitment to such a unit.

Conclusion

Even though they undertake very similar sets of activities, since their creation the five multilateral development banks have become partially differentiated. As they have matured, they have adopted, in varying degrees, complementary specializations. This chapter has addressed several fundamental questions: Are these specializations based on an underlying logic of comparative advantages, and does the current division of labor constitute a sufficiently rational division among the MDBs—that is, one that allocates scarce resources with the optimum development impact on the borrowing countries? Is there scope for further differentiation and specialization?

It is impossible to answer these questions definitively. There is no way to estimate the outcomes of plausible counterfactuals (i.e., different divisions of labor among the MDBs). Moreover, development theory and practice are in a constant state of flux, as is the often difficult environment in which borrowing countries and development agencies must operate. As is the case in the real world of international trading relationships, comparative advantages among MDBs and development agencies are dynamic and will shift continuously. Accordingly, a premium must be placed on development policies, interventions, and institutions that are flexible and innovative and that can constantly incorporate the lessons of experience. The model of competitive pluralism recommended in this report lends itself to flexibility, innovation, and learning within and among the MDBs and seems to offer the greatest advantages to the borrowing countries. A harmonized system of operations evaluations would more easily allow comparisons to be made among the MDBs and would facilitate the learning of lessons from one another.

Furthermore, in practice, the fundamental questions underlying this study necessitate a pairwise comparison between the World Bank and the regional development bank in each of the four regions—the Americas, Africa, Asia, and Eastern Europe and the former Soviet Union. In each region, the World Bank has taken the lead role (usually along with the International Monetary Fund) in macroeconomic policy dialogue and, where applicable, in lending aimed at macroeconomic policy reform. This role has required a considerable investment by the World Bank in research and country economic and sector work. The regional banks draw substantially upon this research and have little incentive to replicate it.

The regional banks also participate, to a greater or lesser degree, in policy dialogue with their borrowing clients, but they limit their efforts at most to sectoral policy issues and sectoral adjustment operations. Indeed, the EBRD does not undertake policy-based operations in the sense of nonproject-based balance-of-payments assistance; its policy dialogue with borrowing countries is much more informal.

At this level, the division of labor seems rational. If the MDBs were all to provide overlapping policy-based lending, this could lead to conflicting or inconsistent advice. If there is scope for improvement, it is with respect to the complementarity of sector-based operations, in which both the World Bank and the regional bank are sometimes active and the rationale for the division of labor between them is not always clear. There is also scope for the regional banks to take a leading role in the smallest borrowing countries. A harmonized system of country assistance strategies for all of the MDBs, as suggested here, would force them to make the rationale for the de facto division of labor explicit and defensible.

The current division of labor is cloudiest in the sphere of project lending, which still accounts for the bulk of the MDBs' operations.

The regional banks—particularly those in Asia and Africa—enjoy relative cost advantages over the World Bank. It would be easy but wrong to conclude that those regional banks should specialize in project lending if this implies that the World Bank should phase out of project lending. First, the needs of borrowing countries are typically greater than the resources available to both MDBs. Moreover, relative cost advantages tell us nothing about *benefits*—that is, the relative development effectiveness of the MDBs. Harmonized operations evaluations would enable the project effectiveness of competing MDBs to be compared to effect the optimum deployment of the resources of both the World Bank and the regional bank within the regions and sectors of each borrowing country. A unified country assistance strategy should indicate to the borrowing country and to the shareholders of both MDBs why the World Bank and the regional bank should adopt the project lending configuration they propose.

This study has also concluded that in addition to harmonized evaluation systems and country assistance strategies, there is a need for quality assurance in the collective efforts of the MDBs and, if possible, between the MDBs and other agencies—both multilateral and bilateral. A client satisfaction unit would serve this purpose by undertaking spot checks in particular areas that are problematic for interagency coordination, such as procurement. As proposed in this study, such a unit would be a unique and additional complement to existing evaluation units, since its mandate would be to examine problems of coordination and consistency among MDBs and possibly other development agencies on behalf of the client countries.

Notes

This chapter is adapted from a North-South Institute report entitled "Multilateral Development Banks: Toward a New Division of Labour?" commissioned by the secretariat of the Development Committee Task Force on Multilateral Development Banks.

1. See Hardy, *The Caribbean Development Bank*, for a description and analysis of one of the more successful subregional banks.

2. Development Committee, "Serving a Changing World."

3. MDBs, *1991–1993 Annual Reports*.

4. These include Namibia, Seychelles, Equatorial Guinea, Cape Verde, Djibouti, São Tomé and Principe, Comoros, and Swaziland.

5. A high degree of cooperation already exists between the two MDBs and other donors on integration issues, as with the Cross-Border Initiative (CBI), which involves the countries of eastern and southern Africa and the Indian Ocean countries. Until the mid-1990s, however, there was more talk than action (by the MDBs and others) on regional integration in Africa.

6. English and Mule, *The African Development Bank*, p. 182. This could exacerbate the arrears problem, but that would not be the intent. Such

cross-conditionality is already employed between the World Bank and the IMF with great effect. What is suggested here is broadening the cross-conditionality to include other international financial institutions such as the ADB.

7. A striking finding was the almost total lack of input by the ADB into the World Bank's most recent overview paper on development in sub-Saharan Africa.

8. Figures are from Kapur and Webb, "The Evolution of the Multilateral Development Banks," Table 7, p. 242.

9. A harmonized system of evaluation would make it easier to compare the evaluations of the two MDBs in these and other sectors.

10. World Bank, *The East Asian Miracle.*

11. The AsDB's operational efficiency relative to the other MDBs has been noted for some time. An early source was U.S. Department of the Treasury, *United States Participation in the Multilateral Development Banks in the 1980s.*

12. This statement is based on interviews with staff at both MDBs, which would be useful to corroborate with views from their borrowers.

13. EBRD, *1994 Annual Report;* World Bank, *1994 Annual Report.*

14. So does the Asian Development Bank to the Central Asian republics.

15. The EBRD is also the custodian of the Nuclear Safety Account, which will fund the conversion or decommissioning of nuclear reactors built by the Soviet Union.

16. The clearest example of a formal division of labor is the cooperation agreement between the European Bank for Reconstruction and Development and the Asian Development Bank in the Central Asian republics. This agreement specified lead roles for the EBRD (in the private sector and financial development) and AsDB (in the social sectors) but also allows joint participation in the other MDBs' lead sectors through cofinancing.

17. An excellent example of the benefits of competition is provided by the move toward greater selectivity in the currency composition of hard-window loans. This plan was initiated by the AsDB and the EBRD, which were the first to offer clients the choice of single-currency loans rather than only multiple-currency loans based on the pool of MDBs' borrowed currencies—the common practice at the beginning of the 1990s. These two MDBs responded to their clients' concerns about being forced to take loans disbursed in several currencies—some of which appreciated substantially by the time of repayment—and their expressed needs for more control over their debt obligations. Their initiative led the World Bank and other MDBs to follow suit by offering single-currency loans and a broader range of financial products. Another example of the benefit of competition is the financing of a low-tension electricity network in Tunisia by the ADB after the World Bank had refused funding.

18. Only the World Bank has adopted such policies, which result in middle-income countries becoming ineligible for IDA credits and upper-middle-income countries becoming ineligible for IBRD loans. The World Bank's graduation policy is reversible, however; many countries whose economic situations have deteriorated have regained eligibility for the soft or hard window.

19. A distinction should be made between "direct operations overheads"—that is, the cost of preparing and delivering lending operations—and "nonlending services" such as research, which provide public goods.

20. In such instances, the proposed client satisfaction unit discussed later would play a particularly useful role.

21. The IMF does not yet have an evaluation unit, although in recent years its Executive Board has considered establishing one.

22. An increasing number of major bilateral donors also have their own country assistance strategies.

23. See Culpeper, "Multilateral Development Banks," p. 70.

24. The Development Committee Task Force on the Multilateral Development Banks, for which this chapter was originally a background study, can also be regarded as a donor-driven exercise. Certainly, this was the reaction of many of the individuals I interviewed.

25. The Inspection Panels instituted at the World Bank and the IDB are possible exceptions to this assertion. The significant difference between the Inspection Panel and the proposed client satisfaction unit, however, is that the former is strictly reactive to complaints raised by individuals in regard to an MDB project, whereas the latter would be proactive in trying to assess the relative strengths and drawbacks of alternative agencies and programs.

26. A comparator is the secretariat of the Development Assistance Committee (DAC) of the OECD in Paris, which undertakes policy coordination and assessment on behalf of OECD donors.

27. Given the considerable influence wielded by donors in the Development Committee (which reflects their majority shareholding at the IMF and the World Bank), this may not be the best location for a client satisfaction unit that works principally on behalf of the developing countries. On the other hand, this location might facilitate the provision of support from the World Bank (and the IMF) and might also help to provide a bridge between donors and borrowers.

28. The G-24 is a developing country coalition that meets regularly during the Interim and Development Committee meetings and the annual meetings of the IMF and the World Bank. If it were to play the role suggested here, the G-24 would have to assess fees from its members and become a more formal organization than it has been until now.

6

KEY CHALLENGES FOR THE MULTILATERAL BANKS: RESOURCE FLOWS AND DEBT

This chapter looks ahead at two key issues facing the MDBs at the end of the 1990s: the interrelated issues of resource requirements and availability as the MDBs shift from a quantity to a quality focus and the issue of multilateral debt. The first of these issues arose during the work of the MDB task force but was set aside; the second did not arise because it was excluded from the task force terms of reference. Two much larger issues are *not* treated here: the MDBs' objective of poverty reduction and their relationship with the private sector. These are addressed in Chapter 7.

Resources

The era of rapid growth of the resource base of the multilateral banks is probably drawing to a close. This prognosis is based on an analysis of both the supply side—that is, the developed country donor shareholders who provide most of the resources for the concessional windows and whose support is key to approving capital increases for the nonconcessional windows—and the demand side, in the sense of the capacity of borrowers to use MDB resources effectively (rather than the need of borrowers for resources, which is undoubtedly very large). On the supply side, three factors seem paramount: first, general fiscal restraint in most donor countries, which tends to favor spending targeted at domestic objectives over foreign aid and bilateral over multilateral aid channels; second, the rise of the international financial markets, to which a small but growing number of developing countries have direct access, thus reducing their need for the MDBs and official sources of capital; and third, aid fatigue among donor country governments. The latter is based, in turn, on increasing evidence of falling success ratios within the aid agencies, as noted by the World Bank's 1992 Portfolio Management Task Force (the Wapenhans Report), and the lack of progress in much of Africa.

A common theme that emerged from the portfolio reviews and was reiterated in the MDB task force report was a criticism of the culture of approval that has transformed the MDBs into money-moving machines rather than agents of long-term sustainable development. A shift from *quantity* lending targets to *high-quality* programming (in the sense of achieving long-term development results) was also recommended by the task force.

Implementing the shift from quantity to quality objectives[1] should reduce demand for the services of the MDBs in the near term. Identifying high-quality projects before they enter the pipeline (a recommendation of the Wapenhans Report) implies greater selectivity as to which projects the MDBs are actually prepared to finance. More generally, a culture of quality means greater care would also be devoted to ensuring that each project is properly implemented and has an appreciable long-term development impact. Abundant anecdotal evidence suggests that in the past, a certain number of projects have been accepted principally because they helped to meet lending targets rather than to achieve significant development outcomes. If such projects are eliminated without being replaced by an offsetting number of high-quality projects (with equal resource requirements), the demand for resources provided through the MDBs may fall, at least in the short term.[2] Moreover, given the growing criticism of large-scale, environmentally damaging infrastructure projects funded by the MDBs as their portfolios shift from capital-intensive projects toward the social sectors, the demand for increased lending capacity (and thus for capital increases) could well level off.

The question is, which will fall more, supply or demand? With respect to concessional funding, recent replenishments at both the World Bank (IDA 10) and the Asian Bank (AsDF 5 and AsDF 6[3]) have encountered problems of insufficient commitment, which has led to significant carryover of lending capacity. This suggests that for these two MDBs, demand may be falling even more than supply. In the case of the African Development Fund, supply has definitely not kept up with demand: Negotiations over the Seventh Replenishment were delayed as donors withheld funding until the Bank's credit policy was satisfactorily resolved; consequently, the ADF ran out of resources in 1995.[4] On the other hand, it is evident that even if the supply of concessional resources is falling, demand in Africa is also falling, as recent World Bank (IDA) experience indicates.[5] Finally, the other two MDBs are not major users of concessional funds—the IDB's FSO is relatively small, and the EBRD has none.

Similar trends are evident on the nonconcessional side. With regard to the World Bank, commitments in 1995 were $16.9 billion, slightly lower than in 1993 and only slightly higher than in 1991 (when they were $16.4 billion). In the same period (1991–1995), lending headroom (or unused lending capacity between actual levels and the ceiling imposed by the gearing ratio) increased from $61.7 billion to $75.3 billion.[6] These trends, however, are not uniform among the MDBs. At the African Development Bank, loans peaked at $2.25 billion in 1991 before declining to $1.4 billion in 1994 and $669 million in 1995. At the IDB, nonconcessional loans peaked at $5.5 billion in 1992, fell to $4.7 billion in 1994, but recovered sharply to $6.5 billion in 1995 because of the Eighth Replenishment agreed to that year.[7]

If resource supply were falling in the face of constant or growing demands for concessional assistance, the policy implications would be clear: Donors should be urged to find other ways to provide additional aid despite budget and other constraints. This, in fact, has been the conventional diagnosis and prescription in recent years. If resource supply and demand were both falling more or less in step, however, it is possible—to use an analogy from economics—that the "aid market" is roughly in equilibrium, at least for now. The prescriptive implications of such a balance would be directed more to the use and effectiveness of current aid flows than to the volume of those flows.

Whereas some may regard falling demand as a convenient and shallow pretext for aid donors not to honor their obligations to the developing world, it may reflect instead belated recognition by donors and recipients alike that there are limits to the amounts of aid developing countries can usefully absorb at any time. Part of the fall in absorptive capacity has resulted from economic reform programs over the past decade, which (through fiscal restraint) have reduced the ability and willingness of governments to take on additional projects with recurrent financing requirements. Over this period, the lack of recurrent financing has been a major cause of failed projects, one the shift to quality projects with sustainable development impact and local ownership is meant to correct. In other words, whereas the fall in aid flows can be viewed as a negative development, it is positive to the extent that the lower flows are destined for projects with sustainable development impact.

In the longer term, a large need unquestionably exists for additional external financing through the MDBs and other sources. Translating that need into *usable* financing will be different from in the past, when needs were stated as minimal growth rates that, in turn, generated a given rate of investment. Some of the need for recurrent financing would be met domestically, and the balance from external sources. Such an approach, which was established when international private capital exhibited little interest in developing countries, provided the intellectual foundation and political rationale for the MDBs' quantity lending targets.

In the 1990s, despite intense turbulence in international capital markets as exemplified by the Mexican peso crisis of 1994–1995, private investors returned to the developing countries, and their capital flows are greatly overshadowing official financing. The turnaround in the balance between official and private financing in the space of a decade is dramatic. In the mid-1980s, official financing amounted to almost twice the volume of private flows; in the mid-1990s, private flows were more than two and a half times the volume of official flows (see Table 6.1).

Table 6.1   Net Capital Flows to Developing Countries, 1986–1995 (at constant 1995 prices)

	1986	1991	1993	1995
Private				
Net FDI[a]	13.0	37.0	74.0	90.3
Net portfolio equity	0.8	8.1	49.5	22.0
Bank lending and bonds	15.3	20.1	43.8	54.8
Total private	29.1	65.2	167.3	167.1
Official				
Concessional loans[b]	17.3	17.2	14.1	14.1
Nonconcessional loans[c]	17.7	12.5	11.5	17.3
Grants[d]	20.9	39.8	31.9	32.9
Total official	55.9	69.5	57.5	64.3

Source: Development Committee, "Recent Trends in the Transfer of Resources to Developing Countries." Document DC/96-3, Rev. 1 (Washington, D.C., April 5, 1996).
Notes: a. Foreign direct investment.
b. Predominantly from MDBs.
c. Mainly from MDBs but also includes bilateral export credits.
d. Official development assistance, excluding technical cooperation.

In the future, translating the need for external financing into a quantum of resource flows will be considerably more complex. First, a growing portion of external financing requirements may be met by private capital markets. According to the 1996 World Bank Debt Tables, however, such flows are likely to be concentrated in a dozen or so emerging markets in Asia and Latin America, with large portions of the developing world—particularly in Africa—ignored. Moreover, both in the emerging markets and in other countries, the objectives of private investors will differ more and more from those of official agencies. The former will seek high returns, security, and liquidity. Given the globalization of capital markets and the ease with which international financial transactions can be made, private investors will not necessarily seek long-term commitments and may, in fact, be highly volatile, as they were during the Mexican peso crisis.[8]

In contrast, the MDBs, aid organizations, and other official agencies will be more concerned with long-term development impact and the quality of the investment programs they support in collaboration with the recipient countries. Instead of building their lending programs on the macroeconomic contrivance of a financing gap, these agencies will base programs on project- and sector-level investment requirements that will demonstrably lead to the creation of a sustainable capacity to deliver economic and social benefits, particularly to the poor.

The quantity of financing this plan will require remains to be seen; it may build up over the longer term to a level in excess of the present capacity of the MDBs and other development agencies to deliver. This situation will occur if the recipient countries augment their absorptive and management capacities but still generate a stream of demands for external financing of their sustainable development programs.

One characteristic (indeed, advantage) of the MDBs relative to other development agencies is their growing financing autonomy. The hard-loan windows have a capital base that is relatively permanent and does not require replenishment. Even without further capital increases, assuming the MDBs continue to accumulate some of their net income of approximately $2 billion in 1994 as reserves, their lending capacity will continue to drift upward. Moreover, because their soft-loan windows provide repayable low-interest loans, the reflows on past credits will eventually become an appreciable source of funds.

In the case of the IDA, reflows amounted to almost $500 million in 1995 and were forecast to increase to $1 billion by the year 2000 and to $3.3 billion by 2020.[9] By the time of IDA 10, reflows were providing 16 percent of new commitments[10] and had become the third-largest IDA "donor" after Japan and the United States. In the case of the IDB's Fund for Special Operations, in 1993 reflows had become the principal source of new funds, amounting to $400 million annually out of total lending of $423 million.[11] The soft-loan facilities of the AsDF and the ADF are about thirteen years younger than those of the IDA and the FSO and are just beginning to be appreciable. This inertial effect of funding from both hard and soft windows will somewhat offset possible declines in funding from donor countries.

In summary, a leveling off of resource transfers (or even a decline of net transfers) is to be expected from a shift toward quality programming. To the extent that such a state of affairs enhances the long-term human development impact of the MDBs' efforts, it represents an improvement. In the short to medium term, however, a more restrained lending program may engender other negative consequences related primarily to its impact on the borrowers' balance of payments. As we saw in Chapter 2, net transfers from the MDBs as a group have declined steadily since 1987 with rising principal and interest repayments. By the mid-1990s, net transfers from the MDBs had become decidedly negative. Some experts conclude that such trends can only augur a diminishing influence for the MDBs. Mistry indicates that to maintain positive net transfers, by 1999 the MDBs would have to increase their gross disbursements by around $17 billion over 1992 levels.[12] This would require, on Mistry's estimates, lending commitment levels of at least $100 billion by 1999, compared with just $40 billion in 1993–1994.[13]

Such a leap in commitment and disbursement levels is clearly implausible. But the issue raised by Mistry is important and requires further consideration. First and foremost, is it true that MDBs can exercise influence on borrowers commensurate only with positive resource transfers? Such a proposition is precisely the mind-set that informed the approval culture so rightly criticized in the MDBs' portfolio reviews. The proposition suggests that the MDBs' principal obligation is to maintain positive net transfers, which would require ever growing loan commitments just to offset the increasing flow of principal and interest repayments from accumulated past loans—something that is neither possible nor desirable. The premise of any viable lending arrangement is to ensure eventual and timely repayment. The premise of MDB lending must be to help borrowers to expand their repayment capacity to the point at which net transfers will, in fact, be negative and the MDBs can begin a phased withdrawal, with commitments and gross disbursements eventually diminishing to zero.

Things have not worked out so happily for several of the MDBs' borrowers. For them, the issue is not one of negative net transfers per se but of their ability to service their loans to the MDBs. This issue is considered next.

Multilateral Debt

Multilateral debt is the last frontier of the developing country debt problem that erupted during the 1980s, when it was the subject of several international initiatives and high-level meetings. Broadly speaking, there are three sets of creditors to developing countries: the commercial banks, the official bilateral creditors, and the multilateral creditors, including the IMF. The bilateral creditors initiated debt relief at the Toronto G7 Summit in 1988,[14] which was implemented through the Paris Club and was followed by enhanced relief measures during the next six years (up to the 1994 Naples Summit). The commercial banks (in the London Club) pioneered debt swaps (debt for equity and debt for bonds) through the secondary markets during the 1980s and came together under the more formal relief initiative launched by U.S. Treasury Secretary Nicholas Brady in 1989.

The developing country debt crisis was not of the MDBs' making. Rather, it came about because of an inherent tendency (observable over the past two centuries) in international financial markets to precipitate crises periodically through cycles of overlending and subsequent panic. The MDBs were caught unawares by the depth and tenacity of the crisis of the 1980s. When they intervened, they intended to be part of the solution rather than part of the problem.

Yet, the multilateral creditors' growing share of the debt of developing countries has been evident since the 1980s. Many of the debt workout programs designed to refinance the debt of bilateral and commercial creditors during that decade were supported by adjustment loans from the multilaterals, so it is not surprising that their share of debt rose. In 1980, 10 percent of the stock of debt of the severely indebted low-income countries was owed to multilateral creditors; by 1994, the proportion had increased to 28 percent. The figures for debt servicing of this group of countries over the same period show a more dramatic increase—from 20 percent to 52 percent.[15] The various multilateral creditors' share of this debt has changed significantly, with the share of the regional banks increasing, which has been offset by a decline in the share for the IMF and a stable share of the World Bank (see Table 6.2).

Until 1995 the multilateral creditors, among which the World Bank and the IMF are the most significant, adamantly refused to accept the possibility of any special relief from multilateral obligations for borrowers experiencing debt-servicing difficulties and for whom the multilaterals rank among their most important creditors. On the assumption that MDB lending will stabilize or even decline in the short term, such MDB borrowers will experience even more severe debt-servicing difficulties. Moreover, it is contended here that the MDBs (and the IMF, for that matter) urgently need to develop more flexible and pragmatic policies with respect to their own role in problems of indebtedness if they are to continue to be part of the solution rather than part of the problem.

Table 6.2   Composition of Multilateral Debt Stock by Institution, 1985–1989 and 1994

Institution	1985–1989		1994	
	U.S.$ Billions	Percentage of Total MDB	U.S.$ Billions	Percentage of Total MDB
World Bank	107.6	55.8	174.8	56.5
IBRD	75.3	(39.1)	108.6	(35.1)
IDA	32.2	(16.7)	66.1	(21.4)
Regional banks	28.3	14.7	68.3	22.1
ADB/ADF	4.0	(2.1)	14.9	(4.8)
AsDB	7.9	(4.1)	26.4	(8.5)
IDB	16.4	(8.5)	27.1	(8.8)
IMF	38.6	20.1	42.9	13.9
Others[a]	18.2	9.4	23.2	7.5
Total	192.7	(100.0)	309.2	(100.0)

Source: IMF, Official Financing for Developing Countries, p. 46.
Note: a. Includes the Council of Europe, the European Development Fund, the European Community, the European Investment Bank, and non-European creditors.

The issue of debt owed to the multilateral institutions came to the fore during 1995, when reform of the Bretton Woods institutions was on the agenda of the G7 Summit in Halifax. The UK delegation went to Halifax with proposals to initiate some relief of multilateral debt using the proceeds from the sale of some of the IMF's gold stock, but no agreement was reached and the matter was deferred to the IMF and the World Bank. Shortly thereafter, a leaked and premature trust fund proposal emerged from the World Bank suggesting that donors contribute around $11 billion to a facility over a number of years to provide relief to the debtors that were experiencing the most distress with their external debt. Both the Bank and the IMF distanced themselves from the proposal when it turned out there had been little consultation and no agreement with the IMF.

Subsequently, the Bank and the IMF did work together to produce a policy framework within which to address the multilateral debt problem; this framework was submitted at the spring 1996 meeting of the Development Committee in Washington, D.C. Within the framework, several highly indebted poor countries (HIPCs) were identified on the dual criteria of their debt-to-export ratio (in excess of 200–250 percent) and their debt-service-to-export ratio (in excess of 20–25 percent). This generated a list of twelve "possibly stressed" debtors (falling within the ranges indicated) and eight "unsustainable" debtors (coming in above the ranges). Sixteen of the twenty countries are in sub-Saharan Africa, three are in the Americas, and one is in Asia (see Table 6.3).[16]

Table 6.3   **Highly Indebted Poor Countries: Possibly Stressed and Unsustainable Debtors, 1994**

Country	Total Debt Other Stock	Long-Term Debt Stock	Multilateral	IBRD	IDA	IMF
Possibly stressed						
Bolivia	4,749	4,185	2,275	116	648	264
Cameroon	7,275	6,217	1,620	695	406	44
Côte d'Ivoire	18,452	13,882	3,367	1,691	576	328
Congo	5,275	4,667	697	116	172	20
Ethiopia	5,059	4,816	2,124	4	1,391	72
Guyana	2,038	1,788	608	39	182	179
Madagascar	4,134	3,565	1,597	14	1,021	86
Myanmar	6,502	6,099	1,458	0	818	0
Niger	1,570	1,468	827	0	565	61
Rwanda	954	905	749	0	474	13
Tanzania	7,442	6,244	2,643	114	1,998	212
Uganda	3,473	2,955	2,028	11	1,604	383
Total	66,923	56,791	19,993	2,800	9,855	1,662
Unsustainable						
Mozambique	5,491	5,047	1,054	0	714	212
Sudan	17,710	9,868	2,036	6	1,251	980
Zaire	12,336	9,281	2,326	88	1,294	478
Zambia	6,573	4,872	1,989	201	1,043	805
Burundi	1,126	1,064	881	0	556	56
Guinea-Bissau	816	736	364	0	197	5
Nicaragua	11,019	9,006	1,312	76	254	51
Saõ Tomé and Principe	252	229	166	0	47	1
Total	55,323	40,103	10,128	371	5,356	2,588
Total possibly stressed and unsustainable	122,246	96,894	30,121	3,171	15,211	4,250

Source: World Bank, *World Bank Debt Tables,* 1996.

One-third of the long-term debt of these twenty HIPCs was owed to multilateral organizations, and 64 percent of the multilateral debt was owed to the IMF (3 percent of the total) and the World Bank (15 percent of the total). These data understate the relative burden of multilateral debt, however. Because multilateral debt cannot be rescheduled, its obligations are "harder" than the simple debt indicators suggest. In contrast, bilateral and commercial bank debt is susceptible to rescheduling; thus, scheduled debt servicing tends to overstate the actual debt burden to these two classes of creditors. In some cases, however—Bolivia, Uganda, Rwanda, and Burundi—in 1994 multilateral debt accounted for more than half of total debt.[17]

The proposal advanced at the spring 1996 meetings entails debt relief for the HIPCs on a broad front that involves Paris Club creditors, other creditors (e.g., Russian, Arab, and commercial creditors), and the multilateral institutions as a last resort. This framework ensures that the problems of the most acutely debt-distressed countries are addressed within the context of both their overall economic circumstances and their overall debt situation, including their liabilities to different groups of creditors. Although such a holistic approach has merit, more could be done by the MDBs than is suggested in the World Bank–IMF framework.

In the past, multilateral creditors (including the IMF) have rejected suggestions that they should also contemplate debt or debt-service reduction, as did the bilateral and commercial bank creditors before them.[18] First, there is a moral-hazard argument: Granting such relief will encourage others to seek similar treatment or to treat their multilateral obligations as less than firm. Since the multilateral creditors are lenders of last resort, they take the position that providing such relief would severely undermine discipline not only among their own borrowers but also in the international financial markets.

Second, this policy would also undermine multilateral creditors' own solvency, since unlike other organizations, they would not have other creditors to bail them out. The IMF is particularly constrained, since it essentially works as a revolving fund. The World Bank has argued that debt relief would undermine its creditworthiness, since its triple A credit rating is based largely on the unblemished record of repayment by its borrowers. A downgrading would increase the cost of borrowing for the Bank and, ultimately, for all its borrowers. Hence, debt relief would benefit a few countries and penalize all other borrowers, most of which meet their obligations.

Since this book is about the MDBs, this is not the place to address debt owed to the IMF, although the same principle advanced here to alleviate debt owed to the MDBs can also be applied to the IMF and other multilateral creditors. That principle is simply that reduction of debt and debt service is an expedient that is both feasible and desirable in the case of the MDBs, as it has been in the case of the bilateral and commercial bank creditors.

Let us examine each of the arguments leveled by the MDBs against relief. First, is there a moral hazard in providing relief to selected debtors? No more so than has existed with the Paris Club and the commercial bank creditors. In those cases, relief has been provided on an exceptional basis and under stringent conditions. Similarly, with MDB debt relief, eligibility has been restricted only to the poorest countries that meet stringent criteria regarding the burdensomeness of their debt. Moreover, as with Paris and London Club measures, debtor countries have to maintain a track record of economic performance to retain eligibility. These kinds of terms and conditions are unlikely to permit or encourage large numbers of debtors to seek debt relief or to undermine debtor discipline in other ways.

Nonconcessional Debt

What about the impact of debt relief on the financial solvency of the MDBs? This question must be addressed separately for the hard- and soft-lending windows. With regard to the hard windows, the MDBs' conservative (by commercial banking standards) loan assets-to-equity (or gearing) ratio of 1:1 is designed to reassure bondholders that their bonds are backed dollar for dollar by shareholders' capital and not by the loans. In theory, this financial structure protects bondholders from widespread default, or nonperformance (i.e., less than full or timely debt servicing) by MDB borrowers. In practice, however, the structure is an artifice: The conservative gearing ratio is an elegant fiction on which the MDBs have built considerable financial leverage.

First, only a small portion (less than 10 percent, except in the case of the relatively newer EBRD) of shareholders' equity capital is actually paid in; the rest is subject to call. Thus, widespread nonperformance of loans would necessitate a call on capital, thereby triggering potentially large payments. In 1994, for example, the total amount of equity subject to call was $256 billion.[19] In creating and joining multilateral banks, it is unlikely that shareholder governments expected that a call on capital would ever arise. Instead, they have regarded their callable capital as a guarantee, or collateral, on which the MDBs could secure their borrowings from the bond markets.

Moreover, the quality of shareholder callable capital is not uniform, since it is payable in domestic currency, whereas bonds are denominated in hard currencies such as the U.S. dollar, German deutsche marks, or Japanese yen. Hence, the callable capital of a severely indebted low-income country cannot be considered by bondholders to be equal to that of an OECD shareholder. Accordingly, the notion of usable capital arose during the debt-distressed 1980s. Such a concept has no official status but is used informally by rating agencies and financial analysts in assessing the bonds and other borrowing instruments of the MDBs for investors. Usable capital, in this view, refers to the subscribed capital of OECD (developed country) shareholders plus that of some Arab oil-exporting countries and newly industrialized economies—in other words, countries that can redeem their liabilities in usable currency.[20] Whereas such shareholders are in a distinct majority in the World Bank, the AsDB, and the EBRD, other shareholders (whose capital is nonusable) represent a large minority in these banks and constitute a majority in the IDB and the ADB.

All of this suggests that the MDBs are somewhat less solvent than they appear on their balance sheets and that their aversion to debt relief may be justified. This is so, however, only if debt-servicing problems require debt relief on a *large* scale. The MDBs' balance sheets look better if debt-servicing problems among MDB borrowers are exceptional and are confined to smaller borrowers—which appears to be the case, at least in the mid-1990s. First, all of the MDBs have accumulated reserves and retained earnings to protect themselves against unforeseen losses. In 1994, these amounted to $25.4 billion (World Bank, $14.5 billion; ADB, $1.2 billion; AsDB, $4.9 billion; IDB, $4.8 billion). Second, since the mid-1980s some MDBs have set aside loan-loss reserves or provisions; in 1994, these amounted to $4.2 billion (World Bank, $3.3 billion; ADB, $0.21 billion; IDB, $0.71 billion).[21]

There have been precedents for debt relief on the MDBs' hard loans. In 1988, under the special program of assistance (SPA) for Africa, the World Bank established a facility called the Fifth Dimension[22] to meet the IBRD debt-service payments of IDA borrowers no longer eligible for IBRD loans. In 1995 this facility absorbed $246 million, financed by reflows to the IDA. The Fifth Dimension, however, only recognized the debt-servicing problem and found other ways to meet the payments from resources that would normally be contributed to the general IDA pool for relending to borrowers.

The problem with this approach is the *opportunity cost* of the resources used for debt relief. Around $246 million that could have been used for new IDA development lending (which is allocated only to the poorest countries) was, in effect, siphoned off to repay past IBRD loans. The same criticism can be leveled at proposals to use funds from bilateral donors to meet payments due on past MDB loans, assuming that those funds would have otherwise been allocated to poor recipients.

The alternative would be to follow the example of the commercial banks when they face bad debts, which is to charge doubtful loans against accumulated loan-loss reserves—in effect, removing the loans from the balance sheet. This is not the same as debt forgiveness, since the debtor is still legally liable,[23] although the expedient of total forgiveness should be kept open in extenuating circumstances. The policy *would* restore to the MDB balance sheet an unblemished loan performance without the contrivance of other benefactors stepping in to pay the debt. The MDB could then settle with the debtor on a schedule of much lower repayments that would be manageable and would probably incur a certain amount of forgiveness of the original debt. With respect to the IBRD loans of the World Bank, it should be possible to absorb some of the losses through charges against general reserves and loan-loss provisions, which by 1995 had risen to $15.5 billion and $3.7 billion, respectively.[24]

Admittedly, such a measure would still carry an opportunity cost, but that cost would be borne by all the shareholders rather than by the poorest countries in particular. Since reserves are built up through the repayment of loans by borrowing shareholders, some middle-income borrowing members may feel they are bailing out the poorer countries.

The question still remains, Would such measures represent a financial shock of undue proportions to the MDBs? If the overall magnitude of the bad debts is confined to the twenty highly indebted poor countries listed in Table 6.3, half of the $30 billion multilateral debt was owed to IDA (see discussion later) and $3.2 billion to the IBRD. A significant part of the remainder was owed to the African Development Bank (around 10 percent) and the African Development Fund (12 percent), with 12 percent held by the IMF and 10 percent by other multilateral institutions.[25]

The African Development Bank is a more difficult case, in part because it has faced a situation of rapidly accumulating arrears by a growing number of its borrowers. By mid-1994, seventeen borrowers were in nonaccrual status—that is, they were in arrears by six months or more. Arrears were heavily concentrated in Zaire (which is on the HIPC list) and Liberia, which together accounted for 65 percent of $761 million owed to the ADB.[26] The African Bank's general and loan-loss reserves are considerably smaller than those of the World Bank even relative to its own requirements—its accumulated provisions of $208 million constituted only 27 percent of arrears in 1995.[27]

The ADB has proposed several mechanisms to help delinquent borrowers, including refinancing through bilateral donors and commercial banks. A Fifth Dimension–type arrangement similar to the World Bank facility was discussed during the ADF 7 negotiations, as was the creation of a trust fund to which the loans of chronic delinquents would be transferred.[28] The solution for the ADB's bad loans may require a combination of short- and longer-term measures and the establishment of a broader base of reserves.

An implication of the approach suggested here is that the two most seriously affected MDBs (the World Bank and the African Bank) should move to a more aggressive approach to provisioning that is more anticipatory of problems than simply reactive to nonaccruals in debt servicing. The African Bank's provisioning policy was moderately strengthened in 1994 by increasing loan-loss provisions from 2.5 to 3.0 percent of outstanding loans.[29] This seems likely to be insufficient if the multilateral debt problem is not confined to the twenty HIPCs and spreads to other countries.

Concessional Debt

The most striking aspect of Table 6.3 is the proportion (over half) of HIPC multilateral debt that is owed to the IDA, the World Bank's soft-loan affiliate. Moreover, the amount owed to the IDA is almost five times that owed to the IBRD. Although concessional debt is undoubtedly less burdensome than nonconcessional debt, the principal repayments (which constitute the bulk of debt service) eventually loom large, as the earlier discussion of the increasing volume of concessional reflows suggested.

Concessional debt occupies a fundamentally different place in the financial structure of the MDBs than loans based on ordinary capital resources (as they are called by some of the regional banks). Whereas nonconcessional loans are funded through market borrowings, which represent a large liability, concessional loans are funded through outright donations to the development funds. Accordingly, the soft-fund financial statements do not present a conventional balance sheet of assets and liabilities but rather a statement of "sources and applications of development resources."[30]

This is a crucial distinction, since it means the assets represented by soft-fund credits can be managed much more flexibly than, and without the repercussions in terms of liability management encountered by, hard loans. There are no bondholders or credit rating agencies to become nervous; there are only donors who have expensed their contributions and are increasingly apt to view the performance of fund credits in terms of long-term development impact rather than their full and timely repayment.

In other words, with MDB concessional loans it is much easier to write down amounts owed or, in other words, to convert the outstanding portions of the soft loans to grants. There is no impact on the MDBs' credit rating and no implications that shareholders will need to provide callable capital. Of course, as with any debt-relief measure, there are opportunity costs; in this case, the cost is the reduction in the reflows to the IDA from forgiven credits. Many variations are possible: Payments could be suspended for a number of years until the debtor's debt-servicing capacity improves, or they could be reduced to a small proportion. In either case, the total amount due would be the same, but that amount would be repaid over a longer schedule.

Moreover, in the case of the HIPCs, the group of twenty countries represents a small but significant portion of the IDA borrowers. In 1995, they accounted for 23.3 percent of outstanding IDA credits, so the impact of suspending their repayments could affect almost a quarter of future IDA reflows. It could rightly be argued that the opportunity cost of such debt reduction would be a reduction of future concessional flows to the poor, but that is a rather convoluted way of looking at the problem. The IDA and other concessional lending facilities were meant to benefit poor countries.

The issue of the repayment of principal has been a subject of debate since the inception of the IDA, when many donors and recipients expressed a preference for an all-grant facility. The rationale of reflows, however, has been not to repay a financial obligation (since the funds are made available through grants rather than loans) but to exert a mild form of financial discipline on recipients in the hope that doing so would provide an incentive to invest the proceeds fruitfully. The purpose of repayments has never been to provide additional resources to future IDA borrowers: That has indeed been a growing benefit, but it has occurred on top of the other benefits of the IDA's operations. Much more consistent with the spirit of the IDA is to ensure that its existing resources are used to obtain optimum benefits for current borrowers—a consideration that suggests debt relief in the form of suspension or cancellation of repayment obligations.

Nevertheless, the fact remains that the selective suspension of soft-fund repayments will reduce the resources available to future borrowers from the concessional windows. A greater onus will therefore be put on donors to ensure that future replenishments will, in fact, be fully and properly funded. In a sense, a growing stream of reflows lets donors off the hook and transfers the responsibility for resource mobilization to the poor countries. This is surely a regressive state of affairs—perhaps somewhat less so in the case of borrowers or former borrowers that have obviously benefited from sustainable long-term development and are not beset by debt-servicing difficulties. Reducing service payments of distressed soft-loan debtors may also help to remedy this tendency by shifting the responsibility for resource mobilization back to the countries that are more able to pay.

The September 1996 Debt Deal

A comprehensive debt package was finally agreed upon at the 1996 IMF–World Bank annual meetings in Washington, D.C. The package involved potential concessions from the Paris Club, the World Bank and the IMF, the regional development banks (principally the African Development Bank), and bilateral donors outside the Paris Club. The list of potential beneficiary countries (the twenty highly indebted poor countries) remained the same. But the magnitude of relief contemplated was substantially less—between $5.7 billion and $7.7 billion—than that in the earlier leaked World Bank proposal ($11 billion).

The range was calculated on assumptions about the debtors' economic recovery (their export earnings in particular), with the higher figure of $7.7 billion representing debt-relief costs under the worst-case scenario. At this higher level, relief would be funded by the World Bank ($2 billion); the Paris Club bilateral creditors ($2 billion); the IMF ($1.2 billion); regional development banks, principally the ADB ($2 billion); other bilateral creditors[31] ($400 million); and commercial creditors ($100 million).

In fact, however, only a small portion of these amounts was actually committed at the 1996 annual meetings. The only firm commitment was from the World Bank, which pledged $500 million from its retained earnings and indicated that it would make additions up to a total of $2 billion over several years. The IMF would make its assistance available through credits from its semiconcessional Enhanced Structural Adjustment Facility (ESAF). This facility is to be supported by selling up to 10 percent of the IMF's gold reserves on the open market, investing the proceeds, and using the income to subsidize ESAF credits. But consensus could not be reached at the Washington meetings because of opposition from Germany, Switzerland, and a few other countries. The issue was once again deferred to the IMF's Executive Board, although the Fund's managing director suggested that in the meantime other IMF reserves could be used for this purpose.

Commitments from other creditors will be forthcoming on a case-by-case basis. To be eligible for multilateral debt relief, a debtor country must have a record of three years of sound economic policy performance. At that point the Paris Club will decide whether to increase the country's debt relief from the previous maximum level (the so-called Naples terms, which allow forgiveness of two-thirds of eligible debt stock) to 80 percent.[32] Such relief will be provided over an additional three-year period, assuming continued sound economic policy performance. During the same period, other multilateral, bilateral, and commercial creditors will also determine the extent of additional relief required.

In short, the process of debt relief under the 1996 Washington deal is highly restricted and protracted. Under these rules, a very small number of the HIPC debtors (beginning with Uganda) can complete the envisaged cycle by the year 2000; the majority of the debtors will not realize any relief until well into the first decade of the twenty-first century.

Moreover, the plan displays all of the shortcomings of previous multilateral debt initiatives alluded to in this chapter. These initiatives are oriented more to refinancing outstanding obligations than to actually writing them off. It will not be surprising, therefore, if pressures for more far-reaching and speedier relief (such as that suggested here) again build up within a few years.

Summary

Debt obligations continue to plague a number of developing countries a decade and a half after the crisis initially broke out in 1982. After a certain point, debt servicing seriously encumbers development priorities and capabilities by reducing the fiscal latitude of governments to invest in social programs and infrastructure, reducing net export earnings and the capacity to import, and tying up key decisionmakers in never-ending negotiations with creditors. Better economic performance, in the sense of policies that maintain internal and external balance and therefore reduce the propensity to accumulate unserviceable debt, is clearly a part of any sustainable solution. But this is often not enough—if the debt overhang is too large, investment and growth will be too low to allow the country to emerge from crisis.

Since the late 1980s, it has been recognized that debt and debt-service reduction must complement better economic performance to remedy the problem. Some creditors have taken action (commercial banks and bilateral creditors), although they could do more. The multilateral creditors, meanwhile, have done virtually nothing regarding their own debt (although they have spearheaded some relief efforts for commercial debt) and in some ways have made matters worse by continuing to extend credit to debtors who are in unsustainable positions.

The conclusion reached here is similar to that of others who favor a more radical solution to the problem of multilateral debt (e.g., Eurodad, *World Credit Tables: Creditor-Debtor Relations from Another Perspective*)[33] than that traditionally advanced by the multilateral institutions. A policy that is selective and clear and that begins with the twenty most strongly debt-distressed countries listed in Table 6.3

is unlikely to impair the credit rating of the MDBs. In any case, a large portion of the relief would be directed toward the IDA and the ADF, which do not require credit ratings because they obtain their funds from donors rather than from the capital markets.[34]

Notes

1. Implementation naturally depends on the MDBs, which need to change incentives for their staffs to encourage quality rather than quantity. But it also depends on the behavior of borrowers—for example, if government intermediaries or executing agencies benefit from higher lending volumes, there will still be a demand-side bias that favors quantity over quality.

2. One of Rich's most trenchant criticisms of the World Bank is that there has always been a shortage of "bankable projects" (relative to the Bank's lending capacity), which has resulted in the approval of many loans simply to meet lending targets but that have been unjustified in development terms. Rich, *Mortgaging the Earth.*

3. Kappagoda, *The Asian Development Bank*, pp. 111–113.

4. English and Mule, *The African Development Bank*, pp. 132–135.

5. World Bank lending (through both the IDA and the IBRD, although largely through the IDA) to Africa fell continuously from 1992 (when it stood at $4.0 billion) to 1995 ($2.3 billion), when it was significantly below the annual average for the period 1986–1990 ($3.0 billion). This decline has occurred largely because of the portfolio restructuring that took place in the Africa region in line with recommendations of the 1992 Wapenhans Report, as well as the absence of major lending programs in Nigeria and Zaire as the result of political uncertainties. (World Bank, *1995 Annual Report,* pp. 57–59.) Again, this situation represents an indication of absorptive capacity rather than need.

6. Ibid., p. 12.

7. MDBs, *Annual Report,* various years.

8. IMF 1995a, pp. 5–7.

9. International Development Association, "IDA Financial Management," p. 11.

10. Mistry, *Multilateral Development Banks,* p. 117.

11. Ibid.

12. Ibid., p. 217. The issue of net transfers cannot be considered apart from the heterogeneity of developing country borrowers. The more advanced developing countries (those that have graduated or that are about to graduate from MDB borrowing) are clearly in a better position than the poorer developing countries to accommodate negative net transfers.

13. Ibid., pp. 216–217.

14. Some relief was offered to the poorest countries under retroactive terms adjustment in 1978.

15. Eurodad, *World Credit Tables,* pp. 30–33.

16. The criteria employed to distinguish the countries that are stressed or in unsustainable debt positions may seem unusually stringent. Countries with debt indicators lower than the 200 percent (debt-to-exports) and 20 percent (debt-service-to-exports) levels could also be stressed.

17. World Bank, *World Debt Tables,* p. 37.

18. Mistry, *Multilateral Debt.*

19. Mistry, *Multilateral Development Banks,* p. 259.

20. Ibid., pp. 23–24.

21. Another source of the MDBs' financial strength, and a buffer against risk and insolvency, is the policy of holding a considerable part (from 15 percent in the case of the World Bank to 24 percent in the case of the IDB in 1994) of their portfolios in liquid assets. The MDBs' liquid assets (cash, time deposits, short-term tradable instruments, and so on) amounted to around $42 billion in 1994 (the World Bank, $21.7 billion; the IDB, $7.9 billion; the AsDB, $5.9 billion; the ADB, $2.5 billion; and the EBRD, $4.5 billion). The purpose of holding liquidity is to ensure that the MDBs can always meet their contractual obligations to both their bondholders and their borrowers. As Mistry points out, however, the MDBs derive a considerable portion of their income from their short-term liquid holdings—from 9.2 percent in the case of the World Bank to 27.2 percent in the case of the AsDB. Ibid., chapter 5 and Table 6, p. 136.

22. This facility was the fifth of a series of initiatives developed to support adjustment programs in SPA countries; the other four dimensions were IDA credits, the IMF's Structural Adjustment and Enhanced Structural Adjustment Facilities, bilateral and other multilateral financing, and debt relief by bilateral creditors. The Fifth Dimension was initially supported by grants from the Nordic countries and was subsequently financed through reflows—that is, repayments of IDA credits.

23. Commercial creditors would typically sell bad debts to a collection agency at a deep discount, thus realizing some residual value from the transaction. During the debt crisis, commercial banks sold their loans at deep discounts in a growing secondary market, and purchasers of these loans typically used these claims to engage in debt-equity swaps by acquiring real assets, local currency, or property in the debtor country. As suggested earlier, MDBs could instead simply settle with the debtors to pay off, say, a fifth of the amount owed over twenty-five or even forty years, thus incurring a real loss.

24. World Bank, *1995 Annual Report,* pp. 141, 157. Note that the loan-loss provisions have been set aside for lenders with nonaccrual status—that is, not servicing loans for over six months. These include states of the former Republic of Yugoslavia, Iraq, and Syria, which are not among the HIPC group and would not be considered for relief. Some countries, however—including Zaire and Sudan—are among the HIPCs, and specific provisions have been set aside for them.

25. IMF, *Official Financing for Developing Countries,* p. 47. Percentages used apply to a larger list of forty-one HIPCs, including eight non-African countries and thirteen African countries not on the critical list of twenty debt-distressed HIPCs. The percentages used refer to the share of the regional development bank rather than the ADB/ADF per se, but they are likely to be a close approximation for the ADB/ADF.

26. English and Mule, *The African Development Bank,* p. 125.

27. Ibid., p. 127.

28. Ibid., pp. 128–129. At the time of this writing, sources of funding for this facility had been identified (reflows from past ADF loans, cancellations of ADB loans, and special contributions from donors). What remained to be settled was, first, how much was needed (in other words, how much ADB debt was legitimately in chronic arrears and should be eligible for relief

through this facility); estimates ranged from $480 million to $800 million. Second, how much could be provided from the identified sources? For example, no donor contributions had been lined up specifically for the facility.

29. Ibid., p. 127.

30. To use the IDA example, see World Bank, *1995 Annual Report*, 168–169.

31. Primarily Russia and creditors in the Arab bloc, none of which belongs to the Paris Club.

32. Under Paris Club rules, eligibility applies only to precutoff debt—that is, debt contracted from Paris Club creditors prior to the date at which the debtor first applied to the club for relief. Since for many debtors a significant portion owed to Paris Club creditors is postcutoff debt, relief offered under these rules can be highly limited.

33. I am also sympathetic to employing criteria in addition to economic performance to determine eligibility for debt relief—in particular, the debtor's performance with respect to human rights. This criterion would rule out countries such as Sudan, Zaire, and Myanmar and put into question the eligibility of Rwanda and Burundi.

34. At the time of this writing, discussions were ongoing regarding a solution to the problem of multilateral debt, including debt to the IMF. With regard to the latter, an active proposal recommended sale of a part of the IMF's gold stocks, with the proceeds to be invested in income-yielding securities to fund a replenishment of the IMF's Enhanced Structural Adjustment Facility for the poorest countries. No consensus was reached on this issue or on any other part of the multilateral debt issue even at the Lyon Summit of the G7 (June 1996).

7

Do the Multilateral Banks Have a Future?

As we approach the end of the twentieth century, development is at a crossroads. Much of the thinking and institutional infrastructure created in the postwar decades is being shaken up and in some cases jettisoned. The multilateral development banks are in the middle of this turmoil, and some say they deserve much of the blame for it. There are many reasons for the uncertainty about and cynicism toward the development business. These reasons include the change in the geopolitical equilibrium with the demise of Soviet communism; the obvious success of some developing countries; the blatant failures of other countries; skepticism about public tax-funded ventures, including development and its agencies; and a newfound faith in private markets and civil society.

The Future of Development

At the core of the uncertainty and cynicism, perhaps, is the notion that over the past half century development has become a business in the sense of catering not to the needs of the large mass of humanity it was intended to help but instead to the needs of those involved in planning, delivering, and administering it. The true beneficiaries, in this view, are those able to land lucrative contracts to supply the goods and services as well as the bureaucrats in aid agencies and government ministries responsible for aid programs. Ultimately, it is the elite in developing countries who benefit rather than the deprived or the poor. Furthermore, the dramatic rise of international capital markets has made it possible for some developing countries to borrow directly from those markets, without the intermediation of the MDBs or subsidies from the donor countries.

153

At various times, all of these accusations have contained some truth. The accusations have led to changes in the way we think about development and the way we marshal our resources to achieve it. Simpler notions of economic growth and the development policies built upon those notions have clearly obscured or ignored—and sometimes led to—glaring instances of human deprivation. This, in turn, has led to demands that development agencies must achieve a nexus of sometimes complementary, sometimes conflicting social, economic, environmental, and political goals—insistence that development activity must produce tangible and humanly meaningful results. The recent MDB portfolio reviews, with their common refrain of shifting from a money-moving culture to one of long-term sustainable improvements in the human condition, are obvious manifestations of these concerns and the changes they are bringing about.

Two fundamental truths remain. First, development victory cannot be declared on a global scale. The conditions in which up to a quarter of humanity still lives are deplorable. The desperate poverty of these people makes the whole world a poorer, more environmentally fragile, and less secure place in which to live.[1] Second, it *is* possible to change things for the better—even dramatically—despite the enormity of the task; witness the success of increasing portions of the developing world. And despite the frustrations of a multidimensional approach to development, its advantage is that progress is often evident in some domains if not in others.

To be specific, sufficient evidence exists to demonstrate that dramatic economic and social progress has occurred over the past half century—whether that progress is measured by a leap upward in life expectancy from forty-one to sixty-two years, a doubling of the proportion of the population that has access to clean water (from 35 to 70 percent), an increase in adult literacy from less than half to two-thirds, and an increase in food production and consumption at a rate about 20 percent faster than population growth. Development cooperation has played an important role in achieving specific gains, such as a dramatic drop in child mortality, led by the World Health Organization (WHO) and UNICEF. Also, through immunization programs smallpox has been eliminated and polio has virtually been eliminated. Further, the green revolution received international support for agricultural research and development, extension services, irrigation, and production and marketing.[2]

Thus, development as a concept is not dead, and development cooperation has often been proven effective. Older, restrictive notions of what constitutes progress have been supplanted by aspirations more relevant to the increasingly open, democratic, and participatory world of the late twentieth century. But meanwhile, aid budgets are falling, and much of the UN system is in decay because of a lack of financial and political support. The MDBs have not been immune to these trends, as recent smaller replenishments at the IDA and the ADF make clear. If we accept that many urgent development tasks remain to be undertaken—and some will disagree—the question is, How can this state of affairs be turned around? Obviously, the question concerns much more than the MDBs, but any renewal of the MDBs must be informed by a larger vision of where development goes from here.

This concluding chapter attempts to present such a vision by drawing out some key strands of earlier chapters of this volume and the overall findings of the MDB project. It also provides some practical recommendations on how the MDBs can help to turn the vision into reality.

Toward a Vision for the Twenty-First Century

A great transformation, which began in the early 1970s, has overturned our conception of development from an emphasis on the provision of resource inputs to the assurance of tangible improvements in the human condition (see Chapter 3). A primary index of donor success in the earlier approach was the volume of assistance, measured in money terms or as a percentage of GNP to indicate effort relative to ability. In contrast, the indexes of success that have replaced ODF[3] flows or ODA/GNP ratios measure poverty ratios and other aspects of human welfare and capabilities, such as longevity, infant mortality, and literacy.

This transformation has almost run its course. But it still lacks some crucial elements—first, a greater degree of clarity as to what constitute the main human development objectives and, relatedly a time-bound framework within which to achieve those objectives. Other important pieces are missing from the puzzle. We know many of the necessary conditions for the reduction of poverty, such as more investment in human resources and social services, but these are insufficient: They facilitate but do not guarantee the desired result. There are grounds on which to question the consistency of some economic policies advocated for developing countries and their impact on poverty and human development.

An attempt was made at the World Summit on Social Development held in Copenhagen in March 1995 to clarify the main objectives of development.[4] But for two fundamental reasons, that event fell short of presenting a compelling vision for the future. First, with its emphasis on social services spending, expressed by the 20/20 formula,[5] the approach bore the familiar stamp of the old paradigm with its emphasis on inputs rather than outcomes. Second, although the eradication of poverty was a major focus of the conference, when it came to considering the time frame within which this ambitious target was to be achieved, the decision was left open for each member country to determine for itself.

The recent internal MDB reviews of their lending portfolios and the subsequent Development Committee MDB Task Force also stopped short of providing a compelling vision for the next century. In affirming the need to end the approval culture and instead to strive for quality and results—viewed as long-term sustainable human development—however, these exercises pointed the MDBs in the right direction.

That is not enough. More is required if development policies, programs, and institutions are to recapture the respect they once had and garner the attention they require from the public to achieve their objectives.

An objective without a target date for achievement is no objective at all. The intractability of absolute poverty in many parts of the world as well as an analysis of those parts of the world that have decisively vanquished the worst forms of poverty suggests that sustainable human development takes time. Progress occurs over generations and decades; results are not easy to discern from year to year.

Given what we know about what is possible, however, *it is conceivable to eradicate absolute global poverty over the next half century.* A target date of 2044, a century after Bretton Woods and San Francisco, would provide a compelling vision for both the world community and its leading development institutions.

From Vision to Reality

The desirability of an ambitious, time-bound target to eradicate global poverty may be less at issue than its feasibility. The problem with such long-term targets, of course, is that their realization lies beyond the lifetimes of much of the present generation, although such goals can also inspire younger generations to take up the torch and carry it to its destination. Given the incentive problem—the generation in power will not see the final results, whereas the succeeding generation may see the results but currently lacks the power to act—a pragmatic way forward is needed.

The donor country members of the OECD Development Assistance Committee recently adopted a pragmatic approach to achieving a set of longer-term objectives.[6] What is more, the committee's statement of objectives represents a "vision of progress" whose realization "will have a profound influence in shaping the twenty-first century" that is entirely consistent with the time-bound, specific objectives proposed here. The report proposed a global development partnership between donor and recipient countries to achieve several "ambitious but achievable goals."

- A reduction by one-half in the proportion of people living in extreme poverty by 2015
- A series of goals on social development:
  — universal primary education in all countries by 2015
  — demonstrated progress toward gender equality and the empowerment of women by eliminating gender disparity in primary and secondary education by 2005
  — a reduction by two-thirds in the mortality rates of children under five and a reduction by three-fourths in maternal mortality by 2015
  — access for all individuals of appropriate ages to reproductive health services, as soon as possible and no later than 2015
- The goal of environmental sustainability:
  — implementation of national strategies for sustainable development by 2005 to ensure the reversal of current trends in the loss of environmental resources at both the national and global levels by 2015

The OECD report also emphasized the importance of a series of less quantifiable but also essential factors to achieve these goals, such as the evolution of safe, stable, participatory and just societies through effective, democratic, and accountable governance; the protection of human rights; and respect for the rule of law. The achievement of these goals, and the method of achieving them, was depicted as principally the responsibility and prerogative of the people and governments of the developing countries through approaches that reflect local conditions and locally owned strategies. Where such local effort is forthcoming, the members of the DAC indicated they were prepared to make mutual commitments with development partners that were supported by adequate resources, to improve the coordination of assistance and to achieve coherence between their aid and other policies that have an impact on developing countries.[7]

This statement of intentions from the world's leading donor countries has great significance. The statement compensates for the shortcomings of past approaches to development assistance by articulating a series of time-bound, explicit human development outcomes the donor countries are making commitments to realize. If the incidence of extreme poverty is indeed halved by the year 2015, the prospect of complete eradication by 2045 or thereabouts seems eminently achievable.

From Assistance to Cooperation: A Role for the MDBs

A central characteristic of the DAC proposal is its emphasis on partnership between donors and developing countries. In practical terms, this means moving away from the concept of official development *assistance* and embracing official development *cooperation*. Along with local ownership, partnership, and better coordination among donors, the new era of cooperation is apt to look very different from the era of development assistance.

But partnership requires two parties. If the new era of development cooperation is to become a reality, the developing countries will have to agree. It would be sufficient for developing and developed countries of the world to come together and agree on a broad vision, with clearly stipulated, time-bound targets, and then implement their programs. But given the disappointing track record of recent UN summits, with their propensity to espouse objectives that are subsequently ignored (as in the 1992 Earth Summit in Rio) or to fall short of espousing firm objectives (as in the Copenhagen Summit), one's expectations of taking this high road must be acutely restrained.

Progress toward establishing a central galvanizing vision for the twenty-first century may be more assured by taking a low road and building, for example, on the recent declaration of OECD donors. The result will undoubtedly be more piecemeal than a truly universal, consensual approach, and it is likely the objectives will change along the way, but its chances for success are higher. The commitment of individual developing countries is now required to ensure that the targets established are truly their own and that in each case local capacity is commensurate with achieving and sustaining the targets.

Furthermore, establishing broad targets should not be the prerogative of politicians, officials, or experts. Political liberalization permits, indeed demands, growing public participation in policymaking. Public participation will be essential if targets are to be truly owned by the citizenry. Civil society also must have a role in the establishment of targets and of policies to reach them at the national level.

In this regard, the multilateral development banks could play a central and catalytic role. Poverty reduction is now firmly established as the overarching objective of all the MDBs (except the EBRD[8])—

having been reaffirmed in each of the portfolio reviews and by the Development Committee Task Force. But these exercises also fell short of proclaiming a clear, time-bound target or set of targets for poverty reduction.

There are two mutually consistent options. First, each of the Executive Boards could articulate a set of targets for its own MDB. These targets could adopt, adapt, or build on the OECD DAC targets and be operationalized by management and staff. Second, each MDB could develop specific targets at the country level through dialogue with the borrowing member, again building on the DAC targets. The second option would be a natural way of operationalizing the first, but it could proceed without it.

The MDBs are well placed to participate in the kind of agenda suggested by the DAC donors, along with other multilateral donors and the bilateral agencies. Other multilateral agencies, such as UNICEF and WHO, have specific responsibilities and strengths in social sector development; these areas are relatively new to the MDBs, which continue to retain strengths in the traditional sectors of infrastructure investment. Investment in these traditional sectors will continue to be important, but the contribution of these sectors to economic and social progress is now viewed through a different optic. As pointed out in Chapter 5, country strategies now occupy center stage in the relationships between the MDBs and their borrowing members. Such strategies provide the organizing framework within which the MDBs propose new operations, evaluate ongoing operations and the overall performance of the lending portfolio in the country, and conduct a policy dialogue with the government. Other multilateral and the bilateral donors are also moving toward country strategies.

The problem with these current practices is that they are tailored principally to the needs of the development agency rather than to those of the developing country. They reflect the old paradigm of assistance and resource transfer rather than the new paradigm of cooperation and long-term human progress.

At the same time, the process of formulating country strategies could easily lend itself to the partnership mode of development cooperation by putting the developing country in the driver's seat once and for all. The MDBs could assist the developing countries in making their country strategies the principal vehicle for the articulation, organization, coordination, and attainment of the fundamental long-term development objectives over the next two decades. The MDBs are natural candidates for this role because the developing countries and other representatives of the donor community are members of the MDBs. A decision would be required to determine whether the

World Bank or the corresponding regional bank would take the lead in implementing such a plan.

Where there is a consultative group, an aid consortium, or a roundtable forum that brings together various members of the donor community, there is a natural opportunity to discuss the feasibility and acceptability of the longer-term targets and the means proposed by the country to achieve them, as well as the consistency between the country's development strategy and the cooperation strategies of individual donors. If used in this manner, such fora and other coordination arrangements would be radically transformed from their present limited function as information-sharing exercises into a mechanism in which all parties make policy and resource commitments to agreed-upon, long-term, strategic objectives—such as the reduction by one-half of the proportion of the world's population living in extreme poverty by the year 2015. In the absence of such fora, the principal MDB could organize an analogous meeting or, if the number of principal donors is small, devise alternative mechanisms.

A strong advantage of this approach is that it is a pragmatic response to the quandary of how to bridge the gulf between the *necessary* ingredients of poverty reduction (pro-poor economic growth policies and greater access to social services) and a set of initiatives and institutions *sufficient* to ensure that the poor do indeed benefit and that the incidence of poverty is sustainably reduced. This bridge might require considerable latitude on the part of the external donors over what constitutes acceptable economic or social policies. If donors mean what they say about ownership, they should be prepared to accept a wide variety of developing country policies—some less orthodox than others—as long as they help to bring about the desired long-term development outcomes. If they do not do so, a basis exists for dialogue about alternative policies that might be more effective.

In summary, the country strategy could become the basis for development compacts between donors and developing countries. Consistent with the transformation away from assistance to more genuine partnership modalities, the process could be called "country cooperation strategies"[9] by donors and developing countries alike.

From Resource Transfers to Quality Assurance

Two other recommendations were made in Chapter 5. One was to harmonize the evaluation methodologies and procedures of the MDBs; the other was to create a client satisfaction unit. The Development Committee Task Force endorsed the first proposal; if the MDBs implement it, they might go further and harmonize the criteria, techniques, and practices for measuring results with the evaluation units of other multilateral organizations and the bilateral donors. In so doing, the MDBs would greatly facilitate cooperation among donors and with the developing countries and enhance the capacity to learn from the experience of all development partners.

Country cooperation strategies may help to ensure that long-term human development is the fundamental objective of all international cooperation endeavors. Will this necessarily guarantee a shift toward higher-quality projects and programs and away from the approval culture of resource transfers? It would certainly be a large step forward. One of the shortcomings of the present institutional architecture of development cooperation, however, is that the judges of quality are always the donors and never the recipients. In the world of commerce, ultimately it is only the consumer and not the producer who is the final arbiter of satisfaction—and as a business adage puts it, "the customer is always right."

Ensuring client satisfaction is the other side of quality assurance. A quality assurance unit that is independent of all donors would act as a reality check on the multitude of evaluations, reports, reviews, and the like produced annually by multilateral and bilateral agencies. Such a unit would help to identify and remedy inconsistent policies and practices within the entire system of multilateral and bilateral donors as well as discrepancies between the commitments and actual performance of donors. As the world moves into a cooperation mode and toward development compacts, there is a danger that some donors might make commitments only on a "best efforts" basis. Although a quality assurance unit that acts on behalf of developing countries cannot ultimately compel a recalcitrant donor to comply, it can (as with ombudspersons and auditors-general) help to expose shortcomings in performance and exert moral suasion.

It is suggested that such a unit be accommodated outside the existing MDBs, possibly as part of a reorganized Development Committee (or a G-24 secretariat) or as part of a renewed UN organization.

Challenges to the MDBs: Falling Resource Flows and Debt

Resources

A new era of development cooperation that emphasizes results, the quality of cooperative interventions, and long-term sustainable outcomes can readily become a pretext for those (in treasuries and finance departments, for example) who are removed from the realities of aid and development to accelerate plans to reduce ODA budgets. Such a decision would be an entirely perverse outcome of the current orientation toward development results. Although existing resources can possibly be used more effectively and in ways that produce better results with fewer resources (or that achieve more with less), a continual reduction of the resource envelope for development can only undermine quality and sustainable human development. A regime that favors increasing quality is not equivalent to one that favors reducing resource transfers.

The issue is as relevant for the MDBs as for any other agencies, judging from recent soft-fund replenishments at the IDA and the ADF (see Chapter 6). Moreover, the refusal of certain donors (particularly the United States) to honor existing commitments to past replenishments is seriously undermining the multilateral mechanism.[10]

There are thus two challenges—how to prevent donors' negotiated contributions to the concessional funds from falling and, in the case of particular donors such as the United States, how to ensure that donors meet their previously negotiated commitments on time. One possibility might be to credit donors' soft-window (Fund) contributions by allocating them additional voting rights on the Bank side of the MDBs' operations, which is considered to be the more important part of the corporate entity. Such a proposal could not alter the balance between borrower and nonborrower shareholdings by redistributing votes among the donors. An alternative would be to allow decisions to be made in the soft-window affiliates (the Funds) on the basis of actual contributions (rather than commitments, as is the case at present) to, and therefore on the basis of voting power in, the Funds. Such an arrangement would benefit the generous donors and penalize those that are less generous or that refuse to honor their commitments fully.

Since contributions to the concessional window are generally far more expensive than the cash payments for nonconcessional shares,[11] the former more accurately represent the true extent of individual shareholders' support for the MDB. In the case of the World Bank group, the most glaring discrepancy is that between the United States—which has contributed $21.8 billion to the IDA and in 1995 cast almost 17 percent of the votes in the IBRD—and Japan, which contributed $22.5 billion with IBRD voting power of only 6.24 percent. Other countries that are significantly underrepresented in the IBRD relative to the United States include Germany ($10.7 billion in contributions and 4.82 percent voting power), the Netherlands ($3.46 billion in contributions and 2.37 percent voting power), Sweden ($2.25 billion in contributions and 1.01 percent voting power), and Denmark ($1.2 billion in contributions and 0.70 percent voting power). As Catherine Gwin put it, the United States has pressed successfully for ever-greater burden sharing by other developed country members of the Bank, but it has resisted the power sharing that should accompany their growing financial contributions.[12] This issue needs to be resolved before the next IDA replenishment.

Another dimension of this problem is suggested by the fungibility of resources for development. To the extent that any developing country is able to mobilize resources from a wider array of domestic sources (through local savings and taxation) and foreign sources (through a multiplicity of donors and access to private capital markets), the contribution of donors' scarce ODA is less imperative and should be subject to strict criteria—such as eligibility on the basis of per capita income or other social indicators of relative poverty. In other words, it is critical to become more discriminating in determining potential developing country recipients of ODA (which includes the concessional resources of the MDBs).

Debt

Even if replenishments stop their recent free fall, the net financial transfers of the MDBs are likely to continue to drop because of mounting repayments of past hard and soft loans. With regard to multilateral debt, two MDBs—the World Bank and the African Development Bank—along with the IMF need to adopt urgent measures to bring about debt reduction or debt-service reduction, especially for some highly indebted poor countries. The consequences of debt reduction were explored in Chapter 6 and were shown to be much more contained and far less damaging to the financial integrity at least of the World Bank than the Bank has maintained.

The debt problem has more serious consequences for the African Development Bank. Extraordinary measures need to be undertaken to address the overhang of loans that were made to noncreditworthy borrowers before the credit policy was revised in 1995. Donor members successfully pressed the ADB to revise that policy to remedy the problem at its source. It is now up to the donors to complete the task—as they did with the IBRD overhang in Africa—by establishing mechanisms to fund or refinance the ADB's outstanding and unserviceable loans. Again, the problem is limited to a small number of countries, and most solutions will not undermine the ADB's financial integrity. But solutions will require some resources, which are unlikely to be available from ADF 7 because of the meager size of that replenishment.

Nonetheless, the longer such debts remain unpaid, the greater the stain on the ADB's financial reputation and the more vulnerable its triple A credit rating is likely to be; thus, an early solution is preferred. A solution should be found in the next general capital increase (GCI 5), scheduled for 1997. One possibility would be for the nonregional shareholders to agree to the trust fund mechanism suggested by ADB management in return for parity in voting shares (as suggested by Philip English and Harris Mule in Volume 1 of this series[13]); this would follow the example of the IDB, which agreed to voting parity between borrowers and nonborrowers in the Eighth Replenishment.[14]

The issue of multilateral debt was on the agenda of the 1996 G7 Economic Summit held in Lyon. Because of divisions among the members of the G7—with Germany opposed to certain aspects of the relief initiatives (particularly gold sales by the IMF[15]) and the United States, the UK, and Canada in favor—no agreement emerged. Regarding the MDBs, the issue will not necessarily be settled once and for all. It was suggested in Chapter 6 that the MDBs (the World Bank and the African Bank, at any rate) need to consider a more aggressive provisioning policy with regard to doubtful loans in their nonconcessional operations. (As Chapter 6 also suggested, the remedy with respect to concessional loans is financially more straightforward.) For the poorer countries, the debt crisis is, it is hoped, in its last phase, but it is far from over, and the MDBs need to be better prepared for what lies ahead.

Titans or Behemoths?

At their creation, the multilateral banks were arguably the titans of the emerging postwar world of development. As with their mythical counterparts, they were the precursors of a new order they helped to bring into being, an order that eventually overshadowed them and that may be in the process of deposing them altogether.[16] Over four decades, the economic success of many of the MDBs' borrowing members became the rationale for their own growth. In many ways, the MDBs became the lumbering behemoths caricatured by some of their NGO and right-wing critics.[17] Today, however, it is evident that another, much more powerful race of gods—the international financial markets—rules the world. Could the MDBs, along with the IMF, use their still formidable strengths to help bring about a more humane international order?

The general conclusion of this final study of the MDB project is that the multilateral banks have some unique strengths and advantages that are worth preserving and building upon. The MDBs also have some glaring weaknesses, identified in part by increasingly active and critical NGOs (with the help of occasionally sensational media exposure) and in part by the MDBs themselves in a series of portfolio reviews undertaken in the early 1990s. If these criticisms and portfolio reviews are taken seriously, the behemoth-like characteristics of the banks should fall victim to a series of reforms, including decentralization of operations to the field; greater devolution to regional, subregional, and national agencies and the public in borrowing countries; more transparency to the publics in all member countries; and more participation by beneficiaries and stakeholders in the design, implementation, and maintenance of projects. Although such reforms may reduce the size and sophistication of the headquarters complexes of the MDBs, they may not necessarily call for the complexes to be radically downsized.

Some critics tend to exaggerate the relative size of international organizations and their bureaucracies. As Erskine Childers and Brian Urquhart remarked in their study of the UN system, considering its global scope and responsibilities the United Nations and its funds, programs, and agencies have fewer employees (around 51,500) than the civil service of the U.S. state of Wyoming (population 545,000), the public service of the city of Stockholm (population 672,000), or the combined civil services of the Canadian province of Manitoba (population 1.1 million) and the city of Winnipeg (population 650,000).[18]

The same argument can legitimately be made about the relative size of the MDBs. The issue is thus not the absolute size of these institutions but their ability to use their considerable human and other resources effectively. Although there are reasons to agree with some critics, this study parts ways with both those on the left (of the "fifty years are enough" persuasion) and those on the right who claim the MDBs have run their course and should be wound down.[19]

On the other hand, some critics have been instrumental in helping to bring about needed change and reform. The past failings of the MDBs were a result of the fact that their affairs were overseen by a small, tightly knit community of MDB staff, shareholder representatives, and officials in shareholder capitals who made decisions that involved billions of dollars in resources and who purported to act in the public interest. As the MDBs become more open institutions, positive and constructive criticism from those outside this community, and greater interaction with the citizenry in developing and developed member countries, will be even more necessary to ensure that the MDBs are truly serving the public.

In the past two or three decades, the global economy has become highly integrated and has leaped far ahead of the ability of the global human community to manage it and to ensure that it truly serves human welfare. The world will need the MDBs increasingly in the twenty-first century among the institutions that exercise governance over an increasingly interdependent international community of nations.

Reaffirming the rationale of the MDBs, however, is insufficient to justify their existence in their present form. The fact that the criticisms from opposite ends of the spectrum contradict each other does not imply that the MDBs must therefore be doing things right: Indeed, the MDBs have acknowledged that some of the criticisms have been justified. As Killick noted in his study, *IMF Programmes in Developing Countries: Design and Impact,* such institutions must be effective if they are to continue to be supported or even to survive. The critique leveled by this study is that the MDBs must demonstrate greater effectiveness than they have done until now. Demonstrating effectiveness is admittedly no easy matter, and it has become steadily more complicated with the increasing transformation of development into a multidimensional mandate. In seeking to make the MDBs more effective, this study supports a reform agenda for the MDBs so they can continue to make a vital contribution to international cooperation while adapting their mandates and capabilities within a constantly changing global environment.[20]

Conclusion

In a sense, the real subject of both this study and the companion volumes on the regional development banks has been the underlying debate on development rather than the institutional characteristics and dynamics of the MDBs per se, as interesting as these may be. The banks were created, after all, as *means* to certain desired ends. The question, What are the desirable outcomes of development? is no longer as simple as it used to be and thus does not command the same degree of consensus. But progress is possible on many fronts, even though it may not occur evenly across all fronts and developing countries. Because of the diversity of circumstances and institutions in each country, the priorities and policies with which to achieve fundamental ends are bound to differ. Such diversity is not only unavoidable but should be encouraged if people and governments in developing countries are to feel they are truly in command of their own destiny.

This final volume has argued that it is time the MDBs took a leading role in working with the people and governments of developing countries to galvanize the world community around a vision for the twenty-first century, one based on the ultimate eradication of extreme poverty. In any case, their effectiveness will be judged by their ability to help developing countries to reduce poverty substantially.

As suggested earlier, it is conceivable that fifty more years is enough to attain this visionary goal. If so, some may think the MDBs (along, perhaps, with some other development agencies) must face an inevitable sunset once they have achieved their overarching objective. That is a decision for future generations. My view is that the need for genuine global governance will only intensify as markets broaden their scope and deepen their influence over human affairs.[21] Unimpeded markets are not adept at producing public goods, redressing social inequities such as skewed income distributions, or exercising responsible stewardship over natural resources. Thus, with the crucial proviso that they must continually prove themselves to be effective in meeting their social responsibilities and building confidence among the broader public, the MDBs should—indeed, must—have a central place among global institutions in the twenty-first century.

Notes

1. As the Commission on Global Governance put it, "The number of . . . the truly destitute was . . . 1.3 billion in 1993. . . . 1.5 billion lack access to safe water and 2 billion lack safe sanitation; more than 1 billion are illiterate, including half the rural women. . . .The conditions of this 20 percent of humanity—and of millions of others close to this perilous state—should be a matter of overriding priority." Commission on Global Governance, *Our Global Neighborhood*, p. 139.

2. OECD, *Shaping the 21st Century*, pp. 6–7.

3. Official development finance, which includes official development assistance (ODA) plus nonconcessional finance with a grant element of less than 25 percent, such as the hard loans provided by the MDBs. I am not suggesting that these older indexes are unimportant—they are still valuable as yardsticks of efforts or sacrifices made. To use an automobile analogy, the amount and cost of gasoline consumed will always be important, but more important is the number of miles traveled, and most important of all is arriving at the desired destination.

4. United Nations, *The 20/20 Initiative*.

5. The formula refers to the proportion donors and recipients are

advised to spend on primary schooling, basic health care and nutrition, reproductive health and family planning, and low-cost water supply and sanitation. The application of this formula by the UN agencies that sponsored the conference generated an estimate of $30–40 billion a year as the additional amount required to implement the action program. One-third of this amount was to come from donors, which suggests an increase in ODA of about 25 percent over current levels. Even these figures, however, were guideposts rather than binding commitments. See Van Rooy, *A Partial Promise?* p. 13.

6. OECD, *Shaping the 21st Century.*

7. Ibid., p. 2. Time-bound objectives might run counter to the goal of increasing local ownership and local capacity, so it is crucial that target dates are negotiated rather than imposed by donors on developing countries.

8. Although the incidence of poverty is probably lower in most of the EBRD's client countries, in some (the Central Asian republics) it is comparable to that in developing countries elsewhere. Moreover, as pointed out in Chapter 5, distributional issues are likely to emerge in Eastern and Central Europe as the transition to the market economy inevitably widens income disparities.

9. As mentioned in Chapter 5, the World Bank calls them "country assistance strategies."

10. For example, because of overdue U.S. contributions to IDA 10, a one-year interim fund was established to which donors other than the United States contribute while the United States pays off its arrears. The United States is barred from procurement in the interim fund. A similar arrangement was made in 1984, between IDA 6 and IDA 7, because of overdue U.S. contributions to IDA 6.

11. For example, donors' cumulative contributions to IDA were almost $90 billion in 1995. In contrast, the paid-in portion of the capital subscriptions of *all* shareholders (including borrowers) amounted to $10.9 billion.

12. Gwin, *U.S. Relations with the World Bank, 1945–92,* p. 85.

13. English and Mule, *The African Development Bank,* p. 180.

14. Tussie, *The Inter-American Development Bank.*

15. Japan had also opposed gold sales but changed its position at the Lyon Summit.

16. See epigraph on p. vii.

17. Graham Hancock (*Lords of Poverty*) remains one of the most trenchant among the critics.

18. Childers and Urquhart, *Renewing the United Nations System,* p. 28. The IMF and the World Bank (specialized agencies of the United Nations) are *not* included in the Childers-Urquhart list; neither are the RDBs, which are not UN agencies. In 1995, the World Bank's full-time staff numbered 6,059, and it engaged 1,112 long-term consultants. World Bank, *1995 Annual Report,* p. 127.

19. A similar rejection of the "unholy alliance" of left and right critics is shared by Bird, *IMF Lending to Developing Countries,* and Killick, in their studies of the IMF.

20. At the time of this writing, anecdotal evidence had already appeared of backsliding by some of the MDBs with respect to the major recommendations of the portfolio reviews. In particular, the tendency to adopt targets for annual lending levels may be creeping back, thus flouting the notion that the approval culture has been succeeded by an emphasis on quality program-

ming. Such evidence, if true, indicates the need for all those concerned with the effectiveness of the MDBs to be vigilant about their activities on a regular basis. The situation also underlines the importance of the need for transparency and openness so such tendencies can be readily detected and remedied.

21. See Culpeper, "IFIs."

APPENDIX

Table A1 African Development Bank: Voting Power of Member Countries, December 31, 1995 (percentages)

Regionals

Algeria	4.077	Madagascar	0.777
Angola	1.323	Malawi	0.449
Benin	0.257	Mali	0.231
Botswana	2.408	Mauritania	0.383
Burkina Faso	0.219	Mauritius	0.773
Burundi	0.379	Morocco	3.801
Cameroon	1.037	Mozambique	0.756
Cape Verde	0.142	Namibia	0.425
Central African Republic	0.121	Niger	0.389
Chad	0.203	Nigeria	10.143
Comoros	0.065	Rwanda	0.197
Congo	0.590	São Tomé and Principe	0.141
Côte d'Ivoire	4.101	Senegal	1.050
Djibouti	0.134	Seychelles	0.114
Egypt	5.861	Sierra Leone	0.361
Equatorial Guinea	0.066	Somalia	0.214
Eritrea	0.214	South Africa	0.989
Ethiopia	1.850	Sudan	0.916
Gabon	0.931	Swaziland	0.417
Gambia	0.190	Tanzania	0.977
Ghana	2.293	Togo	0.296
Guinea	0.559	Tunisia	1.627
Guinea Bissau	0.077	Uganda	0.616
Kenya	1.686	Zaire	2.103
Lesotho	0.213	Zambia	1.350
Liberia	0.457	Zimbabwe	2.675
Libya	3.863		

Total 65.486

Table A1 (continues)

Table A1   (continued)

Nonregionals

Argentina	0.292	Japan	4.701
Austria	0.419	Korea	0.419
Belgium	0.584	Kuwait	0.419
Brazil	0.419	Netherlands	0.687
Canada	3.227	Norway	1.022
China	0.988	Portugal	0.231
Denmark	1.022	Saudi Arabia	0.204
Finland	0.454	Spain	0.537
France	3.227	Sweden	1.351
Germany	3.539	Switzerland	1.284
India	0.229	United Kingdom	1.467
Italy	2.095	United States	5.697

Total 34.514

Total: Regionals and Nonregionals 100.000

Source: African Development Bank, *1995 Annual Report.*

Table A2   African Development Fund: Voting Power of State Participants, December 31, 1995 (percentages)

African Development Bank	50.000	Japan	7.381
Argentina	0.012	Korea	0.414
Austria	0.655	Kuwait	0.821
Belgium	0.886	Netherlands	1.349
Brazil	0.649	Norway	1.918
Canada	4.943	Portugal	0.357
China	0.733	Saudi Arabia	1.149
Denmark	1.620	Spain	0.831
Finland	0.704	Sweden	2.532
France	4.320	Switzerland	2.026
Germany	4.779	United Arab Emirates	0.055
India	0.297	United Kingdom	1.991
Italy	2.814	United States	6.764

Total 100.000

Source: African Development Bank, *1995 Annual Report.*

Table A3   Asian Development Bank: Voting Power of Member Countries, December 31, 1995 (percentages)

Regionals

Afghanistan	0.390	Micronesia, Federated States of	0.361
Australia	6.009	Mongolia	0.364
Bangladesh	1.354	Myanmar	0.623
Bhutan	0.360	Nauru, Republic of	0.359
Cambodia	0.381	Nepal	0.429
China, People's Republic of	6.651	New Zealand	1.107
Cook Islands	0.358	Pakistan	2.485
Fiji	0.390	Papua New Guinea	0.403
Hong Kong	0.889	Philippines	1.521
India	6.541	Singapore	0.690
Indonesia	3.017	Solomon Islands	0.360
Japan	15.601	Sri Lanka	0.924
Kazakhstan	0.751	Taipei, China	0.889
Kiribati	0.359	Thailand	1.687
Korea, Republic of	5.278	Tonga	0.359
Kyrgyzstan	0.503	Tuvalu	0.358
Lao People's Democratic Republic	0.364	Uzbekistan	1.015
Malaysia	3.017	Vanuatu	0.360
Maldives	0.361	Vietnam	0.691
Marshall Islands	0.358	Western Samoa	0.359

Total 68.279

Nonregionals

Austria	0.690	Netherlands	1.359
Belgium	0.523	Norway	0.690
Canada	5.467	Spain	0.523
Denmark	0.690	Sweden	0.690
Finland	0.690	Switzerland	0.927
France	2.631	Turkey	0.690
Germany	4.583	United Kingdom	2.352
Italy	1.240	United States	7.979

Total 34.514

Total: Regionals and Nonregionals 100.000

Source: Asian Development Bank, *1995 Annual Report.*

**Table A4   Inter-American Development Bank: Voting Power of Member
Countries, December 31, 1995 (percentages)**

Regionals

Argentina	10.63	Guyana	0.17
Bahamas	0.23	Haiti	0.47
Barbados	0.14	Honduras	0.47
Belize	0.12	Jamaica	0.57
Bolivia	0.93	Mexico	6.83
Brazil	11.58	Nicaragua	0.47
Chile	3.18	Panama	0.47
Colombia	3.18	Paraguay	0.47
Costa Rica	0.47	Peru	1.55
Dominican Republic	0.62	Suriname	0.10
Ecuador	0.62	Trinidad and Tobago	0.47
El Salvador	0.47	Uruguay	1.14
Guatemala	0.57	Venezuela	6.21

Total 52.14

Nonregionals

Austria	0.08	Japan	2.09
Belgium	0.17	Netherlands	0.20
Canada	4.36	Norway	0.11
Croatia	0.03	Portugal	0.04
Denmark	0.11	Slovenia	0.02
Finland	0.10	Spain	1.22
France	1.22	Sweden	0.21
Germany	1.24	Switzerland	0.29
Israel	0.10	United Kingdom	0.98
Italy	1.22	United States	34.08

Total 47.86

Total: Regionals and Nonregionals 100.00

Source: Inter-American Development Bank, *1995 Annual Report.*

Table A5   European Bank for Reconstruction and Development: Voting Power of Members, December 31, 1995 (percentages)

Regionals

Austria	2.28	Luxembourg	0.20
Belgium	2.28	Malta	0.01
Cyprus	0.10	Netherlands	2.51
Denmark	1.21	Norway	1.26
Finland	1.26	Portugal	0.42
France	8.62	Spain	3.44
Germany	8.62	Sweden	2.29
Greece	0.65	Switzerland	2.29
Iceland	0.10	Turkey	1.16
Ireland	0.30	United Kingdom	8.62
Israel	0.65	European Community	3.04
Italy	8.62	European Investment Bank	3.04
Liechtenstein	0.02		

Total 63.00

Countries of Operation

Albania	0.10	Latvia	0.10
Armenia	0.05	Lithuania	0.10
Azerbaijan	0.10	Moldova	1.30
Belarus	0.20	Poland	0.49
Bulgaria	0.80	Romania	4.05
Croatia	0.37	Russian Federation	0.43
Czech Republic	0.86	Slovak Republic	0.21
Estonia	0.10	Tadzhikistan	0.10
Former Yugoslav Republic		Turkmenistan	0.01
of Macedonia	0.07	Ukraine	0.81
Georgia	0.10	Uzbekistan	0.21
Hungary	0.80	Unallocated shares reserved	
Kazakhstan	0.23	for countries previously	
Kyrgyzstan	0.10	forming part of Yugoslavia	0.64

Total 12.34

Nonregionals

Australia	1.01	Mexico	0.30
Canada	3.44	Morocco	0.30
Egypt	0.10	New Zealand	0.10
Japan	8.62	United States	10.12
Korea	0.66		

Total 24.65

Total: All members 100.00

Source: European Bank for Reconstruction and Development, *1995 Annual Report.*

Table A6　World Bank: Voting Power of Member Countries, December 31, 1995
(percentages)

Afghanistan	0.04	Greece	0.08	Pakistan	0.64
Albania	0.07	Grenada	0.05	Panama	0.04
Algeria	0.63	Guatemala	0.09	Papua New Guinea	0.06
Angola	0.19	Guinea	0.06	Paraguay	0.10
Antigua and Barbuda	0.04	Guinea-Bissau	0.04	Peru	0.37
Argentina	1.21	Guyana	0.09	Philippines	0.47
Armenia	0.09	Haiti	0.06	Poland	0.74
Australia	1.45	Honduras	0.04	Portugal	0.38
Austria	0.75	Hungary	0.55	Qatar	0.09
Azerbaijan	0.13	Iceland	0.10	Romania	0.28
Bahamas	0.09	India	2.99	Russia	2.99
Bahrain	0.09	Indonesia	1.01	Rwanda	0.06
Bangladesh	0.34	Iran	1.59	St. Kitts and Nevis	0.03
Barbados	0.08	Iraq	0.20	St. Lucia	0.05
Belarus	0.24	Ireland	0.37	St. Vincent and the	
Belgium	1.94	Israel	0.33	Grenadines	0.04
Belize	0.06	Italy	2.99	São Tomé and	
Benin	0.05	Jamaica	0.19	Principe	0.04
Bhutan	0.05	Japan	6.24	Saudi Arabia	2.99
Bolivia	0.14	Jordan	0.11	Senegal	0.09
Botswana	0.06	Kazakhstan	0.13	Seychelles	0.03
Brazil	1.67	Kenya	0.18	Sierra Leone	0.04
Bulgaria	0.36	Kiribati	0.03	Singapore	0.04
Burkina Faso	0.05	Korea, Republic of	0.64	Slovak Republic	0.23
Burundi	0.04	Kuwait	0.90	Slovenia	0.10
Cambodia	0.03	Kyrgyzstan	0.06	Solomon Islands	0.05
Cameroon	0.07	Lao People's		Somalia	0.05
Canada	2.99	Democratic Republic	0.02	South Africa	0.91
Cape Verde	0.05	Latvia	0.07	Spain	1.59
Central African		Lebanon	0.04	Sri Lanka	0.27
Republic	0.05	Lesotho	0.04	Sudan	0.07
Chad	0.05	Liberia	0.05	Suriname	0.04
Chile	0.48	Libya	0.54	Swaziland	0.05
China	2.99	Lithuania	0.07	Sweden	1.01
Colombia	0.44	Luxembourg	0.13	Switzerland	1.78
Comoro Islands	0.04	Macedonia	0.04	Syrian Arab Republic	0.10
Congo	0.05	Madagascar	0.11	Tadzhikistan	0.09
Costa Rica	0.03	Malawi	0.09	Tanzania	0.06
Côte d'Ivoire	0.18	Malaysia	0.56	Thailand	0.44
Croatia	0.17	Maldives	0.05	Togo	0.06
Cyprus	0.11	Mali	0.06	Tonga	0.03
Czech Republic	0.44	Malta	0.09	Trinidad and Tobago	0.12
Denmark	0.70	Marshall Islands	0.03	Tunisia	0.06
Djibouti	0.04	Mauritania	0.05	Turkey	0.51
Dominica	0.05	Mauritius	0.10	Turkmenistan	0.05
Dominican Republic	0.09	Mexico	1.26	Uganda	0.06
Ecuador	0.20	Micronesia	0.05	Ukraine	0.74
Egypt	0.49	Moldova	0.11	United Arab Emirates	0.17
El Salvador	0.03	Mongolia	0.05	United Kingdom	4.62
Equatorial Guinea	0.04	Morocco	0.35	United States	16.98
Eritrea	0.04	Mozambique	0.08	Uruguay	0.12
Estonia	0.05	Myanmar	0.18	Uzbekistan	0.18
Ethiopia	0.08	Namibia	0.07	Vanuatu	0.06
Fiji	0.08	Nepal	0.08	Venezuela	0.77
Finland	0.58	Netherlands	2.37	Vietnam	0.05
France	4.62	New Zealand	0.50	Western Samoa	0.04
Gabon	0.05	Nicaragua	0.06	Yemen	0.10
Gambia, The	0.04	Niger	0.05	Zaire	0.19
Georgia	0.12	Nigeria	0.86	Zambia	0.12
Germany	4.82	Norway	0.68	Zimbabwe	0.24
Ghana	0.07	Oman	0.12		

Total 100.00

Source: World Bank, *1995 Annual Report.*

BIBLIOGRAPHY

Adams, Patricia. *Odious Debts: Loose Lending, Corruption, and the Third World's Environmental Legacy.* London: Earthscan, 1991.

African Development Bank. *Governance and Development in Africa: Issues and the Role of the African Development Bank and Other Multilateral Organizations.* 1993.

———. *The Quest for Quality: Report of the Task Force on Project Quality for the African Development Bank.* April 1994.

AIDAB (Australian International Development Assistance Board). *Review of the Effectiveness of Australia's Membership of the Multilateral Banks in Achieving Australia's Development Assistance Objectives.* Canberra, 1991.

Anand, Sudhir, and Martin Ravallion. "Human Development in Poor Countries: On the Role of Private Incomes and Public Services." *Journal of Economic Perspectives* 7, no. 1 (Winter 1993): 133–150.

Arndt, H. W. *Economic Development: The History of an Idea.* Chicago: University of Chicago Press, 1987.

Asian Development Bank. *Report of the Task Force on Improving Project Quality.* January 1994.

Aturupane, Harsha, Paul Glewwe, and Paul Isenman. "Poverty, Human Development and Growth: An Emerging Consensus?" *American Economic Review* 84, no. 2 (May 1994): 244–249.

Ayres, Robert L. *Banking on the Poor: The World Bank and World Poverty.* Cambridge, Mass.: MIT Press, 1983.

Bandow, Doug, and Ian Vásquez, eds. *Perpetuating Poverty: The World Bank, the IMF and the Developing World.* Washington, D.C.: Cato Institute, 1994.

Bird, Graham. *IMF Lending to Developing Countries: Issues and Evidence.* London: Overseas Development Institute and Routledge, 1995.

Boutros-Ghali, Boutros. *Commission on Global Governance.* Copenhagen: Nordic UN Project, 1991.

———. *An Agenda for Development 1995.* New York: United Nations, 1995.

Bretton Woods Commission. *Bretton Woods: Looking to the Future.* Washington, D.C.: IBRD, 1994.

Carlsson, Jerker, with Gunnar Köhlin and Anders Ekbom. *The Political Economy of Evaluation: International Aid Agencies and the Effectiveness of Aid.* London: Macmillan, 1994.

Cassen, Robert, and associates. *Does Aid Work? Report to an Intergovernmental Task Force,* 2d ed. Oxford: Clarendon Press, 1994.

Chenery, Hollis, Montek S. Ahluwalia, C. L. G. Bell, John H. Duloy, Richard Jolly. *Redistribution with Growth.* London: Oxford University Press, for the World Bank and the Institute of Development Studies, Sussex, 1974.

Childers, Erskine, with Brian Urquhart. *Renewing the United Nations System.* Uppsala, Sweden: Dag Hammarskjöld Foundation, 1994.

Commission on Global Governance. *Our Global Neighborhood.* New York: Oxford University Press, 1995.

Cornia, G. A., Richard Jolly, and Frances Stewart, eds. *Adjustment with a Human Face.* Oxford: Clarendon Press, 1987.

Counts, Alex. *Give Us Credit.* New York: Times Books, 1996.

Culpeper, Roy. "A Note on the Multilateral Creditors and the Debt Crisis." *World Development* 21, no. 7 (July 1993): 1239–1244.

———. *Canada and the Global Governors.* Ottawa: The North-South Institute, 1994.

———. "Regional Development Banks: Exploiting Their Specificity." In Bretton Woods Commission, *Bretton Woods: Looking to the Future.* Washington, D.C.: IBRD, 1994. Reprinted in *Third World Quarterly* 15, no. 3 (1994): 459–482.

———. "IFIs." In Maureen Molot and Fen Hampson, eds., *Canada Among Nations 1996: Big Enough to Be Heard.* Ottawa: Carleton University Press, 1996.

———. "Multilateral Development Banks: Towards a New Division of Labor." In Jo Marie Griesgraber and Bernhard G. Gunter, eds., *Development: New Paradigms and Principles for the Twenty-First Century.* London and East Haven: Pluto Press, with Center of Concern, 1996.

Culpeper, Roy, and Andrew Clark. *High Stakes and Low Incomes: Canada and the Development Banks.* Ottawa: The North-South Institute, 1994.

Culpeper, Roy, and Caroline Pestieau, eds. *Development and Global Governance.* Ottawa: The North-South Institute and the International Development Research Centre, 1996.

Curran, William. "The European Development Banks." In Bretton Woods Commission, *Bretton Woods: Looking to the Future.* Washington, D.C.: IBRD, 1994.

Danaher, Kevin, ed. *50 Years Is Enough: The Case Against the World Bank and the International Monetary Fund.* Boston: South End Press, 1994.

Dell, S. *The Inter-American Development Bank: A Study in Development Financing.* New York: Praeger, 1972.

Department of International Economic Cooperation, Danish Ministry of Foreign Affairs. *African Development Bank in Kenya and Sudan.* Copenhagen: Ministry of Foreign Affairs, 1991.

———. *Asian Development Bank in Nepal and Thailand.* Copenhagen: Ministry of Foreign Affairs, 1991.

———. *Effectiveness of Multilateral Agencies at Country Level: Case Study of 11 Agencies in Kenya, Nepal, Sudan and Thailand.* Copenhagen: Ministry of Foreign Affairs, 1991.

———. *World Bank in Kenya, Nepal, Sudan and Thailand.* Copenhagen: Ministry of Foreign Affairs, 1991.

Development Committee. *Serving a Changing World: Report of the Task Force on Multilateral Development Banks.* Washington, D.C.: IBRD, March 15, 1996.

———. "Recent Trends in the Transfer of Resources to Developing Countries." Document DC/96-3, Rev. 1. Washington, D.C., April 5, 1996.

———. "Comments of the Multilateral Development Banks on the Report of the Task Force on Multilateral Development Banks and Issues for Discussion." Document DC/96-6, April 12, 1996.

Domar, E. "Capital Expansion, Rate of Growth, and Employment." *Econometrica* 14 (1946): 137–147.

Drèze, Jean, and Amartya Sen. *Hunger and Public Action.* Oxford: Clarendon Press, 1989.

———. *India: Economic Development and Social Opportunity.* Delhi: Oxford University Press, 1995.

Emmerij, Louis. "A Critical Review of the World Bank's Approach to Social-Sector Lending and Poverty Alleviation." In UNCTAD, *International Monetary and Financial Issues for the 1990s.* New York: United Nations, 1995.

English, E. Philip, and Harris Mule. *The African Development Bank. Volume 1, The Multilateral Development Banks.* Boulder, Colo.: Lynne Rienner Publishers and The North-South Institute, 1996.

Eurodad. *World Credit Tables: Creditor-Debtor Relations from Another Perspective.* Brussels: Eurodad, 1995.

European Bank for Reconstruction and Development (EBRD). *Basic Documents of the European Bank for Reconstruction and Development.* N.d.

Ffrench-Davis, Ricardo, and Stephany Griffith-Jones, eds. *Coping with Capital Surges: The Return of Finance to Latin America.* Boulder, Colo.: Lynne Rienner Publishers, 1995.

Fishlow, Albert, with Catherine Gwin, Stephan Haggard, Dani Rodrik, and Robert Wade. *Miracle or Design? Lessons from the East Asian Experience.* Washington, D.C.: Overseas Development Council, 1994.

Gardiner, Robert K. A., and James Pickett, eds. *The African Development Bank 1964–1984: An Experiment in Economic Co-operation and Development.* Abidjan: African Development Bank, 1984.

Gavin, Michael, and Dani Rodrik. "The World Bank in Historical Perspective." *American Economic Review, Papers and Proceedings* 85, no. 2 (May 1995): 329–334.

George, Susan, and Fabrizio Sabelli. *Faith and Credit: The World Bank's Secular Empire.* Boulder, Colo.: Westview Press, 1994.

Griesgraber, Jo Marie, and Bernhard G. Gunter, eds. *Rethinking Bretton Woods.* Volume 1. London and East Haven: Pluto Press, with Center of Concern, 1996.

———. *Promoting Development.* Volume 2. London and East Haven: Pluto Press, with Center of Concern, 1996.

Griffith-Jones, Stephany, with H. W. Singer, Alicia Puyana, and Christopher Stephens. *Assessment of the IDB Lending Programme, 1979–92.* Brighton: Institute of Development Studies Research Report 25, November 1994.

Gwin, Catherine. *U.S. Relations with the World Bank, 1945–92.* Washington, D.C.: Brookings Institution, 1994.

Hancock, Graham. *The Lords of Poverty.* London: Macmillan London Limited, 1990.

Hardy, Chandra. *The Caribbean Development Bank. Volume 3, The Multilateral Development Banks.* Boulder, Colo.: Lynne Rienner Publishers and The North-South Institute, 1995.

Harrod, R.F. "An Essay in Dynamic Theory." *Economic Journal* 49 (1939): 14–33.

———. *The Life of John Maynard Keynes.* Harmondsworth: Penguin, 1972.

Inter-American Development Bank. *Managing for Effective Development: Report of the Task Force on Portfolio Management.* October 1993.

International Development Association. "IDA Financial Management." March 1995.

International Monetary Fund (IMF). *International Capital Markets: Developments, Prospects and Policy Issues*. Washington, D.C.: IMF, August 1995.

————. *Official Financing for Developing Countries*. Washington, D.C.: IMF, December 1995.

Jerlstrom, Bo. *Banking on Africa: An Evaluation of the African Development Bank*. Stockholm: Ministry of Foreign Affairs, 1990.

Kappagoda, Nihal. *The Asian Development Bank. Volume 2, The Multilateral Development Banks*. Boulder, Colo.: Lynne Rienner Publishers and The North-South Institute, 1995.

Kapur, Devesh, and Richard Webb. "The Evolution of the Multilateral Development Banks." In UNCTAD, *International Monetary and Financial Issues for the 1990s*, Volume 4, Special Issue. New York: United Nations, 1994.

Kenen, Peter B., ed. *Managing the World Economy: Fifty Years After Bretton Woods*. Washington, D.C.: Institute for International Economics, 1994.

Killick, Tony. *IMF Programmes in Developing Countries: Design and Impact*. London and New York: Routledge, 1995.

Lewis, John P. *Pro-Poor Aid Conditionality*. Policy Essay No. 8. Washington, D.C.: Overseas Development Council, 1993.

Lewis, John P., Richard Webb, and Devesh Kapur. *The World Bank: Its First 50 Years* (working title). Washington: The Brookings Institution, forthcoming.

Lewis, W. Arthur. *The Theory of Economic Growth*. London: George Allen and Unwin, 1955.

Little, I. M. D., and J. A. Mirrlees. *Project Appraisal and Planning for Developing Countries*. London: Heinemann, 1974.

Mason, Edward S., and Robert E. Asher. *The World Bank Since Bretton Woods*. Washington, D.C.: Brookings Institution, 1973.

Mistry, Percy. *Multilateral Debt: An Emerging Crisis?* The Hague: FONDAD, 1994.

————. *Multilateral Development Banks: An Assessment of the Financial Structures, Policies and Practices*. The Hague: FONDAD, 1995.

Morse, Bradford, and Thomas R. Berger. *Sardar Sarovar: The Report of the Independent Review*. Ottawa: Resource Futures International, 1992.

Mosley, Paul, Jane Harrigan, and John Toye. *Aid and Power: The World Bank and Policy-Based Lending*. London: Routledge, 1991.

Nelson, Paul J. *The World Bank and Non-Governmental Organizations: The Limits of Apolitical Development*. London and New York: Macmillan and St. Martin's, 1995.

Netherlands Minister for Development Co-operation and Minister of Finance. *Policy Document on Multilateral Development Co-operation*. The Hague: Sdu Uitgeverij Plantijnstraat, 1991.

Nordic UN Project. *Perspectives on Multilateral Assistance: A Review by the Nordic UN Project*. Stockholm: Almqvist and Wiksell International, 1990.

————. *The United Nations in Development. Reform Issues in the Economic and Social Fields: A Nordic Perspective. Final Report*. Stockholm: Almqvist and Wiksell International, 1991.

————. *The United Nations: Issues and Options. Five Studies on the Role of the UN in the Economic and Social Fields*. Stockholm: Almqvist and Wiksell International, 1991.

The North-South Institute. "Multilateral Development Banks: Toward a New Division of Labour?" Background Study for the Development Committee Task Force on the Multilateral Development Banks. Ottawa: The North-South Institute, August 1995.

Ohlin, Göran. "The Negative Net Transfers of the World Bank." In UNCTAD, *International Monetary and Financial Issues for the 1990s.* New York: United Nations, 1995.

Oliver, Robert. *International Economic Co-operation and the World Bank.* London: Macmillan, 1975.

Organisation for Economic Co-operation and Development (OECD). *Shaping the 21st Century: The Contribution of Development Co-operation.* Paris: May 1996.

———. *Twenty-Five Years of Development Co-operation: A Review.* Report of the Chairman of the Development Assistance Committee. Paris: OECD, 1985.

Otero, María, and Elisabeth Rhyne, eds. *The New World of Microenterprise Finance: Building Healthy Financial Institutions for the Poor.* West Hartford: Kumarian Press, 1994.

Owen, Henry. "The World Bank: Is 50 Years Enough?" *Foreign Affairs* 73, no. 5 (September-October 1994): 97–108.

Payer, Cheryl. *The World Bank: A Critical Analysis.* New York: Monthly Review Press, 1982.

Please, Stanley. *The Hobbled Giant: Essays on the World Bank.* Boulder, Colo.: Westview Press, 1984.

Reid, George. *Shocks and Strategies: Jamaica and the Caribbean Development Bank.* Ottawa: The North-South Institute, 1995.

Rich, Bruce. *Mortgaging the Earth: The World Bank, Environmental Impoverishment, and the Crisis of Development.* Boston: Beacon Press, 1994.

Richardson, Richard W., and Jonas H. Haralz. *Moving to the Market: The World Bank in Transition.* Policy Essay No. 17. Washington, D.C.: Overseas Development Council, 1995.

Riddell, Roger C. *Foreign Aid Reconsidered.* Baltimore: Johns Hopkins University Press, 1987.

Rodrik, Dani. "Why Is There Multilateral Lending?" presented at the Annual Bank Conference on Development Economics. Washington, D.C., May 1–2, 1995. Published in *Annual Bank Conference on Development Economics.* Washington, D.C.: World Bank, 1996.

Rudengren, Jan. *Middle-Power Clout: Sweden and the Development Banks.* Ottawa: The North-South Institute, 1995.

Sandford, Jonathan. *U.S. Foreign Policy and Multilateral Development Banks.* Boulder, Colo.: Westview Press, 1982.

Sen, Amartya. "Development: Which Way Now?" *Economic Journal* 93, no. 372 (December 1983): 745–762.

———. *Inequality Reexamined.* New York: Russell Sage Foundation, 1992, and Cambridge, Mass.: Harvard University Press, 1992.

Sen, Amartya, with John Muellbauer, Ravi Kanbur, Keith Hart, and Bernard Williams. Edited by Geoffrey Hawthorne. *The Standard of Living.* Cambridge: Cambridge University Press, 1987.

Squire, Lyn, and H. G. van der Tak. *Economic Analysis of Projects.* Baltimore: Johns Hopkins University Press, 1975.

Stern, Nicholas. "The Economics of Development: A Survey." *Economic Journal* 99 (September 1989): 597–685.

Stern, Nicholas, with Francisco Ferreira. *The World Bank as an "Intellectual Actor."* London: London School of Economics and Suntory-Toyota International Centre for Economics and Related Disciplines, November 1993.

Stewart, Frances. *Adjustment and Poverty: Options and Choices.* London: Routledge, 1995.

Tussie, Diana. *The Inter-American Development Bank. Volume 4, The Multilateral Development Banks.* Boulder, Colo.: Lynne Rienner Publishers and The North-South Institute, 1995.

United Nations. *The 20/20 Initiative: Achieving Universal Access to Basic Social Services for Sustainable Human Development.* New York: United Nations, January 1995.

United Nations Conference on Trade and Development (UNCTAD). *International Monetary and Financial Issues for the 1990s. Volumes 4 and 5.* New York: United Nations, 1994, 1995.

United Nations Development Programme (UNDP). *Human Development Report 1990.* New York: Oxford University Press, 1990.

United Nations Industrial Development Organisation (UNIDO). *Guidelines for Project Evaluation.* New York: United Nations, 1972.

United States Department of the Treasury. *United States Participation in the Multilateral Development Banks in the 1980s.* Washington, D.C.: U.S. Government Printing Office, February 1982.

Van Rooy, Alison. *A Partial Promise? Canadian Support to Social Development in the South.* Ottawa: The North-South Institute, 1995.

White, John. *Regional Development Banks: Asian, African and Inter-American Development Banks.* New York: Praeger, 1972.

Williamson, John. *The Political Economy of Policy Reform.* Washington, D.C.: Institute for International Economics, 1994.

Wilson, Dick. *A Bank for Half the World.* Manila: Asian Development Bank, 1987.

Woods, George D. "The Development Decade in the Balance." *Foreign Affairs* 44 (January 1966): 214.

World Bank. *World Development Report 1980.* 1980.

———. *IDA in Retrospect.* New York: Oxford University Press, 1982.

———. *World Development Report 1990.* New York: Oxford University Press, 1990.

———. *Assistance Strategies to Reduce Poverty: A World Bank Policy Paper.* September 1991.

———. *Effective Implementation: Key to Development Impact. Report of the Portfolio Management Task Force* (the Wapenhans Report). September 22, 1992.

———. *Poverty Reduction Handbook and Operational Directive.*

———. *The East Asian Miracle: Economic Growth and Public Policy.* New York: Oxford University Press, 1993.

———. *Getting Results: The World Bank's Agenda for Improving Development Effectiveness.* 1993.

———. *Implementing the World Bank's Strategy to Reduce Poverty: Progress and Challenges.* 1993.

———. *1994, 1995 Annual Report.*

———. *Governance: The World Bank's Experience.* 1994.

———. *Bureaucrats in Business: The Economics and Politics of Government Ownership.* 1995.

————. *World Development Report 1995: Workers in an Integrating World.* New York: Oxford University Press, 1995.

————. *World Bank Debt Tables: External Finance for Developing Countries,* Volume 1, 1996.

Index

African Development Bank (ADB), xiii, 1, 11, 12, 13, 17, 18; antipoverty strategies, 89–90, 93; concessional lending, 53; country strategies, 124–125; debt relief proposals, 145–146; financial health, 53; history, 28; institutional characteristics, 30–31, 63; lending procedures, 36, 63; nonconcessional loans, 108, 109, 110; policy recommendations for, 52–54; policy-based lending, 37, 42; portfolio review of, 62–63; relationship with World Bank, 108–110; resources, 33, 38–40, 135; specialization, 52–53, 109; Task Force on Project Quality, 62–63; voting system, 12, 30

African Development Fund (ADF), 11; debt owed to, 145; financial structure, 33–34; lending strategy, 36; resource depletion, 134; scale of operations, 108

Agricultural lending, 35, 91, 109, 117

Asian Development Bank (AsDB), xiii, 1, 11, 12, 13; antipoverty strategies, 89–90, 92; approval culture in, 61–62; cooperation agreement with European Bank for Reconstruction and Development, 112; country strategies, 124; development objectives, 111; evaluation system, 123; financial structure, 34; institutional characteristics, 17–18, 30, 51; lending strategy, 36, 52; lending volume, 110–111; as model of efficiency, 113; origins, 28; policy recommendations for, 50–52; policy-based lending, 42; portfolio management assessment, 61–62; project orientation of, 51; relations with World Bank, 111–112; resource flows, 38–40; structural adjustment lending, 37; Technical Assistance Special Fund, 112; voting system, 30, 31

Bonds, 7, 8–9, 74, 143

Borrowing member countries: debt, 76; loan guarantees by, 75–76; project ownership, 13, 59, 135, 157

Brady Plan, 41

Brazil, 80

Canada, 33

Capital: callable, 9, 143; as development stimulus, 73; transfer, 73–78; usable, 143–144

Caribbean Development Bank (CDB), xv; comparative advantages, 54–55; infrastructure projects, 54–55; lending volume, 54; policy recommendations for, 54–55

Chenery, Hollis, 85

Child mortality, 154, 157

Colombia, 80

Consultative Group to Assist the Poorest (CGAP), 99

Consultative groups, 126

Country strategies, 59, 61, 62, 64; as basis for development compacts, 159–160, 161; harmonization of, 124–126

Debt, 138–150; concessional,

146–147; crises and problems, 49–50, 87, 139; of highly indebted poor countries (HIPCs), 140–141, 141*tab*, 149; markets, 7; nonconcessional, 143–146; servicing, 40–41, 76, 139, 141, 144, 149

Debt relief: conditionality in, 84; coordination of, 110; debt forgiveness, 19, 144–145; debt rescheduling, 144–145; MDBs' aversion to, 144; opportunity costs of, 144, 145, 147; September 1996 debt package, 147–150

Development: basic human needs approach to, 86–87, 105*n61*; beneficiary participation in, 93–94; cost-benefit analysis, 82, 104*n29*; environmental issues, 37, 84, 118, 157; gains, 154; global partnerships in, 157, 158–161; growth models of, 72, 102*n4*; impact, xvi, 5, 60, 79–84; income per capita measure of, 95–96; indexes of success, 155; inputs emphasis in, 156; and interventionist policies, 95; multidimensional targets of, 84–85; objectives, 14–15, 134, 155–158; outcomes focus, 72, 84; people-centered objectives, 96, 105*n61*; political agenda in, 84; private sector, 5–8, 65–66, 75–76, 116, 117, 118, 136–137; public participation in, 158; and reconstruction, 6, 25–26; shift from quantity to quality, 134, 150*n1*; time framework in, 155, 156–157, 159, 168*n7*; 20/20 formula, 155–156, 167–168*n5*

Development Committee MDB Task Force, 156

Development Finance Companies (DFCs), 58

Economic Commission for Latin America and the Caribbean (ECLAC), 115

Economic growth: and poverty alleviation, 77, 85, 86, 91, 94, 105*n63*

Employment creation, 89, 91, 95, 98

Environmental issues, 37, 84, 118, 157

Equity markets, 7

European Bank for Reconstruction and Development (EBRD), xv, 1, 20*n2*; cooperation agreement with Asian Development Bank, 112; economic transition mandate, 36, 37, 90, 115–116, 117; environmental issues, 37; establishment of, 28–29; financial structure, 34; institutional characteristics, 32; lending strategy, 36–37; mandate, 12–13, 17, 21*n22*, 90, 115–116, 117; political transition objective, 84, 90; poverty issues, 158, 168*n8*; private sector projects, 116, 117, 118; relationship with World Bank, 117–118; resource flows, 38–40; shareholders in, 34–35; as transaction driven, 116

European Investment Bank (EIB), 1, 20*n2*, 45*n14*

Evaluation: project, 47, 59, 60, 63, 126–128, 161. *See also* Portfolio review(s)

Global Environment Facility, 43

Grameen Bank (Bangladesh), 98, 99

Grants, 11, 12, 21*n17*, 146, 147

Gross national product (GNP), 71, 85, 102*n1*

Iglesias, Enrique, 49

India, 81

Infrastructure projects, 15, 58, 81, 83, 84, 100, 101

Integrated sector investment programs, 109, 112

Inter-American Bank, 24, 27

Inter-American Development Bank (IDB), xiii, 1, 12, 28; capital resources, 33; country portfolio assessment, 61; country strategies, 125; debt-reduction programs, 49–50; evaluation system, 123; financial structure, 32; Fund for Special Operations (FSO), 32, 33; hemispheric leadership role, 48–49; institutional characteristics, 30–31; lending capacity, 113–114; loan conditionality, 50; mandate, 16–17; membership in, 33; policy recommendations for,

48–50; policy-based lending, 114; portfolio assessment, 60–61, 115; poverty reduction policy, 88–89, 92–93, 114–115; project lending, 81; relationship with United States, 48–49; relationship with World Bank, 114–115; resource flows, 38–40; social projects, 35–36, 49, 114–115; structural adjustment lending, 37, 42; and trade liberalization, 114; voting system, 12, 30, 31, 33

International Bank for Reconstruction and Development (IBRD). *See* World Bank

International Development Association (IDA), xiv, 76; creation of, 32–33; debt owed to, 145, 146, 147; division of labor with World Bank, 55; economic growth emphasis, 71; funding of, 10–11; mandate and purposes, 27, 72–73; scale of operations, 108

International Finance Corporation (IFC), xiv, 116; competition with European Bank for Reconstruction and Development, 117–118; mandate, 21n22; origins, 26–27; private sector investment, 75–76, 118

International Monetary Fund (IMF), 1, 6, 67; debt owed to, 145, 152n34; debt relief, 139, 140, 142; Enhanced Structural Adjustment Facility (ESAF), 148, 152n34; origins, 24–25; World Bank Development Committee Task Force, 64–67, 107

Investments: foreign, 6–7, 103n10

Keynes, John Maynard, 6, 20n12

Loan(s): agricultural, 35, 91, 109, 117; areas, 4–5; balance-of-payments, 110; capacity of regional banks, 12; comparative sectoral allocation, 37–38; concessional (soft), 8–10, 32–33, 76–77, 85, 134–135, 137; conditionality, 84, 87, 101, 120; and exchange rates appreciation, 76, 103n16; guarantees, 75–76; infrastructure, 15, 58,

81, 83, 84, 100, 101; loan-loss reserves, 144, 145, 151n24; nonconcessional (hard), 8–10, 108, 109, 110, 137; policy-based, 13, 37–38, 41–42, 44, 83, 87, 109; priorities, 12; repayment of principal, 147; structural adjustment, 37–38, 47

Market failure, 73–74, 103n10

Markets, foreign exchange, 6–7

Marshall Plan, 26

McNamara, Robert, 35, 77, 83, 85, 87, 102n1, 104n34

Microenterprise/microcredit, 98–99, 101

Multilateral development banks (MDBs), xiii; administrative overheads, 120, 121; collaboration and coordination among, 108–118, 121–122; comparative advantages, 16–18; competition among, 119, 120; culture of approval in, 59, 61–62, 63–64, 134, 138; current roles of, 66; division of labor, 118–122, 131n16; evaluation systems, 123–124, 126–127; financial intermediation function of, 73–74; financing autonomy of, 137; historical perspective, 71–99; mandates, 1; outcomes focus, 72, 84; specialization, 109, 120–121; systemic principles and structures, 1, 118–123. *See also individual banks*

Multilateral organizations: development contributions of, 159, 161; efficacy of, 2–4

Official development assistance (ODA), 103n18, 136–137, 167n3; recipient determination, 163

Official development finance (ODF), 155, 167n3

Organisation for Economic Co-operation and Development (OECD), 6; Development Assistance Committee, statement of objectives, 156–158

Organization of Eastern Caribbean States (OECS), 55, 68n22

Pakistan, 80–81

Paris Club, 41, 139, 142, 148, 152n32

Performance evaluation, 59, 63

Policy: investment emphasis in, 71, 72; liquidity, 151n21; macroeconomic, 109; market-oriented economic reform, 96–98, 105n63; objectives, 71–72. See also individual banks

Portfolio performance indicators, 115

Portfolio review(s), 47, 58–67, 154, 156; common themes in, 63–64; recommendations, 65–67. See also individual banks

Poverty, 82, 154, 167n1; absolute vs. relative, 85–86, 91, 104n34; impact of adjustment programs on, 87–88

Poverty reduction, 5, 83, 85–102, 155; collaborative, 111; conventional economic approach to, 94–95; as fundamental development objective, 14, 15, 66, 77, 83; programming and projects, 97–99, 114–115; regional bank policies, 88–90; successful, 100; time-bound targets for, 156–157, 159–160

Private sector: financial flows to developing countries, 78; financial intermediaries in, 58; funding, 5–8, 65–66, 116, 117, 118; investments, 6–8, 75–76, 103n15, 118, 136–137

Project(s): cofinancing, 43; as core activity, 56; cost-benefit analysis, 82; evaluation system, 47, 59, 60, 63; impact on development, 80–82; need for improvement in, 13, 57; lending priorities, 35; ownership, 13, 59, 135, 157; quality, 59, 60, 64

Quality: assessment, 61, 63, 126–128, 161; criteria, 19, 60, 62, 64; and falling resource flows, 161–162; project, 59, 60, 64

Redistribution with Growth, 85

Reform, 165; devolution measures, 13, 57–58; fiscal policy, 83–84; of

institution culture, 60–61, 63–64; institution policy, 2–4, 8, 52, 56; sectoral-level, 56–57

Regional development banks (RDBs), xv, 1; historical perspective, 27–29; relationships with World Bank, 41–44

Regional economic integration, 109–110, 130n5, 115

Replenishments, 11, 16–17, 32, 33, 48, 53, 68n17, 76, 92, 108–109, 111, 113, 114, 134, 147, 155

Research collaboration, 110, 111–112, 120

Resource(s), 133–138; allocation, 120; concessional, 27, 32–35, 162–163; financial, 18–19; inputs, as MDBs' focus, 71; mobilization, 11; net flows, 4, 20n6, 136tab, 138, 150n12; private sector vs. official, 136–137; problems with, 162–163; reflows on past credits, 137, 147; supply and demand changes in, 133–135

Social development, 35–36, 91, 92–93, 109, 114–115, 157

Social Dimensions of Adjustment (SDA), 93

Structural adjustment lending, 37–38, 47, 83–84, 95, 96; efficacy of, 92; impact on borrowing countries, 87

Subregional banks, 1, 20n1; institutional character of, 54. See also Caribbean Development Bank

Technical assistance funding, 112

Trade agreements, 114

United Kingdom: capital shares in World Bank, 25; debt relief proposals, 140

United Nations, 20n5, 158; capital flows, 78; Economic Commission for Asia and the Far East (ECAFE), 28; organizations, 67; size of, 154

United States: contributions to IDB, 33; overdue payments of, 10–11, 162, 168n10; relationship with

IDB, 48–49; resistance to power sharing, 163

Wapenhans Report, 47, 124, 134
Woods, George, 77
World Bank, xiv, 1, 20n5; architecture, 25–26, 29–37; Country Assistance Strategy, 124; debt relief policy, 139, 140, 142, 145–146, 148; as direct lender vs. guarantor, 73–75; division of labor with International Development Association, 55; historical perspective, 23–27; infrastructure projects, 81; lending to Asia, 110–111; lending capacity, 113, 116; lending priorities, 18, 35; loan guarantees, 74–75; nonconcessional loans, 108; objectives, 6, 18, 72–74; policy shifts, 18, 60; political culture, 29; portfolio management assessment, 47, 58–60; poverty reduction policy, 85–88, 90–92, 96; private sector competition, 8; program of targeted interventions (PTI) classification, 92, 98; project performance, 80; relations with African Development Bank, 108–110; relations with Asian Development Bank, 111–112; relations with European Bank for Reconstruction and Development, 116–118; relations with Inter-American Development Bank, 114–115; relations with regional development banks, 41–44; resource flows, 38–40, 135; social projects, 18, 35; structural adjustment lending, 37; voting powers in, 25. *See also* International Bank for Reconstruction and Development (IDA); International Development Association (IBRD); International Finance Corporation (IFC)
World Development Report (WDR), 86, 90, 94, 96

ABOUT THE BOOK AND AUTHOR

The multilateral development banks are powerful forces in the international community, providing loans of more than $250 billion to developing countries over the last half-century. The best-known of these, the World Bank, has been studied extensively, but the "regional development banks" are little understood, even within their own geographic regions.

This book synthesizes the insights of four "regional" books, summarizing key points and also examining the multilateral banks (including the World Bank and the recently created European Bank for Reconstruction and Development) as a genre of development agencies. Among the difficult questions Culpeper addresses are: How effectively do the multilateral banks assist the world's 1 billion desperately poor? What has been their role in the evolving debt crisis? In an era of diminishing aid budgets and rising private-sector flows to developing countries, do these institutions even have a future?

Roy Culpeper has been president of The North-South Institute in Ottawa, Canada, since 1995. Before joining the Institute in 1986, he was for three years adviser to the Canadian executive director of the World Bank. He coordinated and directed the Institute's series of studies of the regional banks and previously published *High Stakes and Low Incomes: Canada and the Development Banks.* He is also senior editor of *Global Development Fifty Years after Bretton Woods* (London: Macmillan, 1997).